Challenges and Opportunities in the Artificial Intelligence Era

Carolina Machado · Joao Paulo Davim
Editors

Challenges and Opportunities in the Artificial Intelligence Era

Springer

Editors
Carolina Machado
Department of Management
School of Economics, Management
and Political Science
University of Minho
Braga, Portugal

Joao Paulo Davim
Department of Mechanical Engineering
University of Aveiro
Aveiro, Portugal

ISBN 978-3-031-85271-8 ISBN 978-3-031-85272-5 (eBook)
https://doi.org/10.1007/978-3-031-85272-5

This Springer imprint is published by the registered company Springer Nature Switzerland AG
The registered company address is: Gewerbestrasse 11, 6330 Cham, Switzerland

Preface

Artificial intelligence (AI) has emerged as a transformative force in business, triggering a revolution in business innovation. By integrating advanced algorithms, machine learning, and data analytics, organizations have unlocked unprecedented potential for optimizing processes, making smarter decisions, and creating innovative products and services. In essence, AI provides a paradigmatic shift in the way how businesses operate, enabling efficient automation of routine tasks and freeing up human resources for more strategic and creative activities. This not only increases operational efficiency but also creates an environment ripe for innovation as teams can focus on solving complex challenges and exploring new opportunities. One of the sectors most impacted by AI is data analysis. The ability of artificial intelligence to process large volumes of information in real time enables more accurate predictive analysis, identification of patterns and trends, and valuable insights to guide strategic decisions. This not only drives operational effectiveness but also serves as a foundation for developing innovative strategies. In creating products and services, artificial intelligence stands out by enabling large-scale personalization. With algorithms that understand and anticipate customer preferences, companies can offer tailored experiences, building deeper, longer-lasting relationships. AI also fuels product innovation by analyzing market data and identifying gaps that can be filled with unique, disruptive solutions. Furthermore, AI plays a crucial role in automating decision-making processes. Intelligent systems can analyze complex information, evaluate scenarios, and suggest options, providing business leaders with a comprehensive and informed view of their strategic choices. This ability to make informed decisions in real time is critical to staying competitive in a dynamic and constantly evolving business environment. However, it is important to highlight that the successful implementation of artificial intelligence requires a balanced approach, considering ethical, privacy, and security issues. Transparency and accountability in the development and use of algorithms are fundamental to ensuring that AI is a positive force in business innovation, contributing to organizations' sustainable and ethical advancement. In short, artificial intelligence is redefining the parameters of business innovation. By powering automation, advanced data analytics, personalization, and informed decision-making, AI not only increases operational efficiency but also drives the creation of innovative solutions. The challenge now is to integrate these technologies ethically and responsibly, ensuring that innovation drives sustainable progress and benefits society as a whole.

Aware of this reality, this book entitled *Challenges and Opportunities in the Artificial Intelligence Era* aims to offer several significant contributions, both to academic knowledge and business practice. In particular, some of the main contributions include, among others, an in-depth understanding of the practical applications of artificial intelligence in business, highlighting success stories and challenges faced; highlighting specific innovation opportunities that artificial intelligence offers to companies in different sectors, from process optimization to the development of innovative products; address ethical issues related to the use of AI in business and propose guidelines for ethical and socially responsible implementation; identify the challenges faced by companies when adopting AI technologies and suggest solutions to overcome these obstacles; analyze the impact of AI on employment and necessary skills, proposing strategies for adapting the workforce to changes induced by automation; in short, present future perspectives on the role of AI in business innovation, considering emerging trends and the potential for technology evolution.

These and other issues are just a few of the challenges and changes organizations face in the context of great technological evolution, such as the one we are currently experiencing with AI.

Aimed at everyone interested in better understanding the challenges and opportunities of the artificial intelligence era, this book, organized in eleven chapters, starts by focusing "Dave's Decision: What Would You Do?", highlighting then the "Language and Culture: Imperative Strategic Assets for Organizations in the AI Era". It follows an approach to "Roadmap for Aligning AI in Production Systems to the Organizational Culture", presenting the next chapter, "Artificial Intelligence (AI), Labor Relations and Human Resource Management". The "Harmony in the Workplace: Human-Robot Collaboration and Tuning Employees' Perceptions Through HRM Practices" is also a target of analysis, following a discussion about "AI in Finance: Applications and Challenges". Highlighting the next chapter, "AI Revolutionizing Marketing: Applications and Other Considerations", the book continues with "From Theory to Practice: How Generative Artificial Intelligence is Revolutionizing Digital Marketing", followed by "Artificial Intelligence (AI) in Marketing and Firm Competitiveness". The book ends with an approach to "AI-Driven Integrated Marketing Communications (IMC): Exploring the Role of AI in Planning, Executing, and Evaluating IMC" and finally "Unlocking Potential: How the Digital Age is Shaping Tomorrow's Human Resource Management".

Highlighting all these demands and changes, *Challenges and Opportunities in the Artificial Intelligence Era* looks to be a critical tool that will allow managers, engineers, researchers, academics, and all those that belong to the different types of organizations to more effectively lead and manage artificial intelligence potential, to face the new challenges most effectively. This book is designed to increase the knowledge and effectiveness of all those involved in these areas, whether in the profit or non-profit sectors or the public or private sectors.

Challenges and Opportunities in the Artificial Intelligence Era can be used by various potential stakeholders, including academics/researchers, managers, engineers, practitioners, and other professionals in the different areas of business, management, and engineering. A very special target audience consists of students from various undergraduate/graduate levels (undergraduate, master, and doctoral/Ph.Ds.) from the areas of management and industrial engineering, for which the book proposed here will constitute relevant support capable of providing a focused and current view about the key challenges, trends, implications, strategies, and ways of overcoming, that dynamic and competitive organizations are facing today and increasingly in the near future.

Contributing to the advancement of knowledge in the field of AI and business while providing valuable guidance for organizations looking to explore and effectively integrate artificial intelligence into their innovation strategies, the diversity of subjects discussed in this book reflects the knowledge and know-how of different experts from the most diverse areas of management/business and industrial engineering.

The editors acknowledge their gratitude to Springer for this opportunity and their professional support. Finally, we would like to thank all chapter authors for their interest and availability to work on this project.

Braga, Portugal — Carolina Machado
Aveiro, Portugal — Joao Paulo Davim

Contents

Editors and Contributors

About the Editors

Carolina Machado received her Ph.D. degree in Management Sciences (Organizational and Policies Management area/Human Resources Management) from the University of Minho in 1999, Master degree in Management (Strategic Human Resource Management) from Technical University of Lisbon in 1994, and Degree in Business Administration from University of Minho in 1989. Teaching in Human Resources Management subjects since 1989 at University of Minho, she is since 2004 Associate Professor (with Habilitation since 2022), with experience and research interest areas in the field of Human Resource Management, International Human Resource Management, Human Resource Management in SMEs, Training and Development, Emotional Intelligence, Management Change, Knowledge Management and Management/HRM in the Digital Age/Business Analytics, Sustainability and Higher Education Sustainability. She is Head of the Human Resources Management Work Group at the School of Economics, Management and Political Science at University of Minho, Coordinator of Advanced Training Courses at the Interdisciplinary Centre of Social Sciences, Member of the Interdisciplinary Centre of Social Sciences (CICS.NOVA.UMinho), University of Minho, as well as Chief Editor of the International Journal of Applied Management Sciences and Engineering (IJAMSE), Guest Editor of journals, Books' Editor and Book Series Editor, as well as Reviewer in different international prestigious journals. In addition, she has also published both as Editor/Co-Editor and as Author/Co-Author several books, book chapters, and articles in journals and conferences.

e-mail: carolina@eeg.uminho.pt

Joao Paulo Davim is Full Professor at the University of Aveiro, Portugal. He is also distinguished as Honorary Professor in several universities/colleges/institutes in China, India and Spain. He received his Ph.D. in Mechanical Engineering, M.Sc.

in Mechanical Engineering (materials and manufacturing processes) and Mechanical Engineering degree (5 years), from the University of Porto (FEUP), the Aggregate title (Full Habilitation) from the University of Coimbra and the D.Sc. (Higher Doctorate) from London Metropolitan University. He is Fellow (FIET) of IET-London and Eur Ing by Engineers Europe FEANI-Brussels. He is also Specialist Engineer by the Portuguese Order of Engineers with an MBA and Specialist Titles in Industrial Management as well as in Metrology. He has more than 35 years of teaching and research experience in Manufacturing, Materials, Mechanical and Industrial Engineering, with special emphasis in Machining, Tribology & Surface Engineering. He has also interested in Design, Management, Sustainability, Industry 5.0, Engineering Education and Higher Education for Sustainability. He has guided large numbers of postdoc, Ph.D. and master's students as well as has coordinated and participated in several financed research projects. He has received several scientific awards and honors. He has worked as Evaluator of projects for ERC-European Research Council and other international research agencies as well as Examiner of Ph.D. thesis for many universities in different countries. He is Editor in Chief of several international journals, Book Series Editor and Scientific Advisory for many conferences. He has been listed in World's Top 2% Scientists by Stanford University study.

e-mail: pdavim@ua.pt

Contributors

Filomena Almeida Instituto Universitário de Lisboa (ISCTE-IUL) and Business Research Unit (BRU-IUL), Lisbon, Portugal

Catarina da Silva Nogueira School of Economics, Management and Political Science, University of Minho, Braga, Portugal

Jairo Simião Dornelas NEPSI/MGP/PROPAD/DCA, Universidade Federal de Pernambuco (UFPE), Recife, Brazil

Diana Dragomir Technical University of Cluj-Napoca, Cluj-Napoca, Romania

Mihai Dragomir Technical University of Cluj-Napoca, Cluj-Napoca, Romania

Florin Sabin Foltean Faculty of Economics and Business Administration, West University of Timişoara, Timişoara, Romania

Mine Afacan Fındıklı Department of Business, Istinye University, İstanbul, Turkey;
UBI Business School, Brussels, Belgium

Diana Ilea Technical University of Cluj-Napoca, Cluj-Napoca, Romania

Ana Junça-Silva Instituto Universitário de Lisboa (ISCTE-IUL) and Business Research Unit (BRU-IUL), Lisbon, Portugal

Cristiana Cerqueira Leal Centre for Research in Economics and Management (NIPE) and Management Department, School of Economics, Management and Political Science, University of Minho, Braga, Portugal

Sara L. Lopes Instituto Universitário de Lisboa (ISCTE-IUL) and Business Research Unit (BRU-IUL), Lisbon, Portugal

Ricardo Lourenço-Silva Instituto Universitário de Lisboa (ISCTE-IUL) and ESPP, Lisbon, Portugal

Carolina Feliciana Machado School of Economics, Management and Political Science, University of Minho, Braga, Portugal;
Interdisciplinary Centre of Social Sciences (CICS.NOVA.UMinho), University of Minho, Braga, Portugal

Xabier Martínez-Rolán University of Vigo, Pontevedra, Spain

Flor Morton Department of Management, Universidad de Monterrey, San Pedro Garza García, Mexico

Benilde Oliveira Management Department, School of Economics, Management and Political Science, University of Minho, Braga, Portugal

Emilio Arnau Pineda School of Humanities and Education, Tecnológico de Monterrey, Monterrey, Mexico

Teresa Piñeiro-Otero Universidade da Coruña, A Coruña, Spain

Florin Popişter Technical University of Cluj-Napoca, Cluj-Napoca, Romania

Denisa Szabo Technical University of Cluj-Napoca, Cluj-Napoca, Romania

Teresa Treviño-Benavides Department of Management, Universidad de Monterrey, San Pedro Garza García, Mexico

Laura Zapata-Cantú Department of Management and Leadership, School of Business, Tecnológico de Monterrey, Monterrey, Mexico

Dave's Decision: What Would You Do?

Jairo Simião Dornelas

Abstract The text attempts to reflect on the use of artificial intelligence, while avoiding the temptation to idolize it, showing it as a recent, necessary, definitive and evolving technology. It mentions its constituent elements, namely machine learning and neural networks. It also presents modern examples of the use of technology, highlighting the evolved social and operational relationship and warning of the dangers of believing that it is a panacea for all modern social problems. The conclusion reached is that, like Dave, the character who is an accessory to the plot, artificial intelligence persists in wondering people, but human talent still makes it succumb.

Keywords Artificial intelligence · Promises and perils of use artificial intelligence · Market tendences to artificial intelligence · Reflections on artificial intelligence trajectory

1 Introduction

Touted as the technology that will domines the technological field over the next few years, artificial intelligence (AI) is attracting attention across all social classes, both due to its massive diffusion and the facilities it creates in terms of facilitating routine activities.

In fact, everything, or almost everything, that is currently being planned for the use of information and communication technology (ICT) on the social front, derives from some use of AI or routines associated with it. We will discuss this further in a specific section.

But what is artificial intelligence all about? The apparently eccentric premonition attributed to the fantastic and still unattainable HAL 9000,[1] initially treated

[1] HAL 9000—central cybernetic character in Stanley Kubrick's masterpiece entitled "2001: A Space Odyssey".

J. S. Dornelas (✉)
NEPSI/MGP/PROPAD/DCA, Universidade Federal de Pernambuco (UFPE), Recife, Brazil
e-mail: jerh57@gmail.com

C. Machado and J. P. Davim (eds.), *Challenges and Opportunities in the Artificial Intelligence Era*, https://doi.org/10.1007/978-3-031-85272-5_1

as fanciful, actually prophesied what would initially be an intelligent automaton, programmed with excellence for control activities, today easily packaged and based on best practices in integrated systems, distinguished as enterprise resource planning (ERP), as reported by Griffin et al. (2024), highlighted the possibility of reusing knowledge to train its databases, the principle of the current wave of use of generative AI (Limongi 2024), but foresaw the failure of feelings treatment worked on from contexts and heuristic association of situations (Trainum et al. 2023), something not yet completely addressed by computer science and its associated ICT branches.

It also remains to be considered if that machines will retaliate someday. Some time ago, ACCA (2015) stated that the major problem for the dissemination of AI was conceptual and resided in the fundamental difficulty of having clarity about the construct of intelligence, given that if there was an AI it was because there would be, in academic and social consensus, a consistent notion of natural intelligence that is exclusive to creatures that exist in the animal and plant kingdoms. However, Gardner (1983) already discussed the existence of degrees of intelligence and different acceptances of them.

Returning to the prophetic Hal 9000, it is worth noting that if the heuristic of reading lips from a distance is a feasible task according to Bevilacqua et al. (2023) and being able to execute queries associated with identified terms or categories, sounds banal in any proposition related to data technology (Van der Aalst 2016), interpreting indications as threats and deducing actions as countermeasures, accumulating intentions of retaliation and feelings against users, fortunately still only inhabits the fictional universe.

2 Some Technical Concepts

Artificial intelligence is the main concept that guides concerns about machine learning and its architectural subsets (Cavalcanti et al. 2024).

Following highlights concepts about machine learning and explores its links with automation and artificial intelligence.

2.1 Machine Learning

Machine learning—and its components of deep learning and neural networks—is an umbrella term that refers to a wide range of algorithms that perform intelligent predictions based on a set of data, configuring itself as a subset of artificial intelligence (AI). It focuses on teaching computers to learn from data and improve with experience—rather than being explicitly programmed to do so (El Naqa and Murphy 2015). In fact, machine learning applications improve with use and become more efficient if the process gains greater access to a large data repository such as big data.

For Gomes et al. (2022), nowadays, applications linked to the field of machine learning potentially learn around us, capture data from various facets of our activities and their algorithms explore this data by establishing relationships that allow learning and increasing their intelligence, without needing any additional programming. In fact, Medvedeva et al. (2020) argue that with the continued refinement of software, the level of semantic understanding and information extraction has come very close to the human level of concatenation of ideas and textual production.

Schematically, machine learning is based on several algorithmic techniques, and the great task of qualifying these algorithms is the so-called training, meaning putting the machine to learn. This training can be achieved through four learning strategies (Lurdermir 2021):

- Supervised—when the machine is taught to obtain desired values, that is, from given inputs it must arrive at given outputs. The desired answers are configured as correct answers, and the machine learns to recommend options that are identical or close to those labeled as the answer, through comparisons and similarities. The Waze app is one of the apps in this group;
- Semi-supervised—becomes viable when large amounts of raw and unstructured data are present, since it consists of expanding the set of so-called labeled data to increase sets of unlabeled data, in order to increase the speed and accuracy of learning, using correlative properties that can be applied to unlabeled data. The analysis of a time series is a case of this type;
- Unsupervised—in this type, the machine is not given the answer key. The machine studies the input data—which is unlabeled and unstructured—and begins to identify patterns and correlations, using all relevant and accessible data. A typical use of this type is facial recognition applications;
- Reinforcement—this type does not include a response key, but instead inputs a set of allowed actions, rules, and potential end states. In this way, the system learns from your experience and with gained reward. Applications of reinforcement learning include computer game development and high-stakes stock trading.

Using either training modality, the most well-known concepts associated with machine learning are neural networks and deep learning.

Neural networks are now well-established, but their first concepts were proposed in the 1960s, and rediscovered decades later (Lecun et al. 2015) and experienced an explosion in the 2000s because of big data (Haykin 2001). In general terms, neural networks seek to adapt to biological constitution, structuring themselves as a network of nodes organized in interconnected layers, where data is multiplied by a series of different weights between each node, until a final layer gives the regression or classification response that is sought. These nodes are called artificial neurons (Haykin 2001). The critical factor in a neural network is formation in search of the appropriate weight for each node in the chain (Chaudhari et al. 2024).

Deep learning emphasizes the use of neural networks, providing hidden layers that help to capture complex and abstract patterns through intensive use of data (Lecun et al. 2015), generating dynamic results, thanks to the ability to parallelize simultaneous tasks. From this perspective, it is possible to increase the learning and representation capacity at multiple levels of abstraction and versatility and also increase the power of precision (Kelan 2024). Training for this type of arrangement requires massive parallel processing and the secret is the adjustment of weights between artificial neurons.

The increase in computational capacity means that machine learning applications are increasingly incorporated into everyday life, including those listed in Table 1 (Nichols et al. 2019; Boot 2022).

Despite all these potentialities, Vigen (2015) warns of the potential flaws, challenges, and adjustments that can be made in the use of machine learning, precisely because the basis for building correct reasoning is a large set of data that can bring misleading insights or biases that can generate spurious correlations, which can quickly propagate throughout the neural network, compromising its results.

Table 1 Machine learning from a procedural and business perspective

Activity	Description
Natural language processing	Especially in speech recognition, which has been widely used by browsers and personal assistants
Diagnosis and screening through images	Diseases are identified much more quickly and efficiently by comparing images with large databases. Exams are scheduled by digitally interpreting requests
Dynamic marketing	With the intention of generating leads and guiding them through the sales funnel. Modern consumers generate a huge amount of varied data—from chat transcripts to image uploads, and deep learning helps marketing understand this data and provide real-time engagement
Fraud detection	The standardization of information and data allows the identification of fraudsters and their scam profiles, so that when assimilated by algorithms they enable preventive action
Sentiment analysis	Use of machine learning in markets such as advertising to identify what users feel when viewing content on access, making it possible to detect what is right in an awareness strategy
Recommender systems	Seek to capture the tastes of each user according to their searches, purchases and clicks, indicating the ideal products for each one. Recommendation systems have applications in many retail and shopping platforms, but are definitely standing out with music and video streaming services
Computer vision	Use to identify objects and scenarios in real time, processing all the information seen in an intelligent and fast way, being useful for urban mobility in health, for exams in tomography, MRIs, etc.; and in the military sector, in anti-missile systems, for example
Failure prediction Predictive maintenance	Anticipating failures in various equipment, with virtual tests and also based on user experiences, including IoT devices, providing visibility and efficiency throughout the business
Virtual protection	Advances in software such as spam filtering and network intrusions

Source Compilation from Nichols et al. (2019) and Boot (2022)

An additional challenge comes from machine learning models in which the algorithm and its output are so complex that they cannot be explained or understood by humans. This is the so-called black box model and puts companies at risk when they find themselves unable to determine how and why an algorithm reached a specific conclusion or decision (Lacity and Willcocks 2016).

Fortunately, as the complexity of data sets and machine learning algorithms increases, so do the tools and resources available to manage risks (Lacity and Willcocks 2016). Best-in-class companies are working to eliminate errors and biases by establishing robust and up-to-date AI governance guidelines and best practice protocols (Lurdermir 2021).

2.2 *Robotic Process Automation*

Organizations are striving to improve the efficiency of their operations by redesigning and managing their business processes to remain competitive, and this has led to the use of a specific area of automation: the Robotic Process Automation (RPA).

In essence, RPA is a technology that comprises software agents called bots that mimic the manual path taken by a human, through a variety of computer applications to solve a problem, by performing certain typically rules-based, well-structured, and repetitive tasks in a business process (Lacity et al. 2015).

Although more targeted at industry, RPA has proven itself suitable for inclusion in fields such as banking and insurance (Cavalcanti et al. 2024) and to some extent allows us to think about well done and deep use of artificial intelligence, but does not require new APIs or software services to replace current practices, since it installs software robots that perform the modeled activities (Lacity and Willcocks 2016); causing a kind of isomorphism (Boulton 2017).

This approach makes RPA different from more invasive automation solutions (Penttinen et al. 2018) and points to the use of ready-to-use low-code platforms (Van der Aalst 2016).

RPA projects generally involve low costs and are usually not managed by the IT department, but by the business departments that are directly affected by process automation (Davenport and Kirby 2016).

In short, RPA can be defined as a technology for lightweight and rapidly deployable automation of tasks and processes using software robots (Geyr 2015). Thus, RPA as a lightweight ICT, which only accesses the presentation layer, is characterized as an intelligent application that has the disadvantage of being a one-off solution, which simply aims to automate a process (Van der Aalst 2016).

To achieve automation today, RPA relies primarily on clearly defined tasks consisting of simple if-then-else statements or business rules (Anagnoste 2018), which, despite being trivial, are anchored, why not, in artificial intelligence methods and are being explored, so that the next task can be determined automatically from the data (Suri et al. 2017) or to reach a cognitive decision-making that make a replace the current rule sets and process models. This implies that one can distinguish between symbolic RPA, which relies on handcrafted process models and rules, and intelligent RPA, which uses AI technology to enable human-like cognitive abilities for selected tasks (Fernandes et al. 2022).

3 Uses of Artificial Intelligence Based on Machine Learning

Since the recent explosion in the IA use of everyday tasks via online and standardized computing, which has led to increased use of many robotic routines, there has been a massive increment in references to the use of artificial intelligence, imbued with citations to machine learning, deep learning and neural networks, as the evolutionary trajectory to humanity, and the greatest icon of this outburst, there is no doubt, is the ChatGpt® (Santaella 2023).

However, when it comes to referring to this application and, by extension, to AI itself, people only marvel at its excellence and precision of use and are enchanted by the artifact, overlooking the pitfalls of ChatGPT. According to Santaella (2023), the ambiguity generated by our understanding of the application's conversational capacity and its plethora, since it can make statistical associations between billions of words and phrases with syntactic coherence, offering consistent and sophisticated responses, leads us to forget that the system only portrays the statistical occurrence of words that humans use in their ideas.

Hence the calm Boucher's observation (2020, p. 11) when reflecting that "it is dangerous to believe that AI really understands something when, in fact, it is just very good at behaving as if it did". Thus, in its unbridled use, what has already gained so much social notoriety occurs: the massive production of fake news (Sarlet and Molinaro 2020), raising debate on ethical issues, highlighting the misuse of personal data.

In the organizational sphere, concerns are also being raised about the possibility of excessive standardization of activities, restricting creativity and personal initiatives in the execution of tasks, which ultimately leads to concerns about business strategy and employee employment (Harari 2024). It is no wonder that, although there are inferences regarding the possibility of artificial intelligence surpassing human action capacity, the idea that, as a technique, AI can increase social inequalities, rather than mitigate them, is exacerbated (UNESCO 2022).

Nevertheless, considering the market hype, we are seeing the launch in Japan of GPT-Next, an optimized artificial intelligence that eliminates the need for large data centers and promises to move towards the innovative direction of autonomous AI runs according Open-AI.[2]

But while there are more sophisticated uses such as the one planned for GPT-Next, there is also room for less recommended, perhaps unacceptable, uses, such as the case reported on the infosecurity website, of a young American who became a pop star using AI. He created bots to listen to his songs, which were also created

[2] Go to the site https://next-gpt.github.io/.

by AI, and these bots, with it actions, transform the fake produced music in truly champions on streaming platforms such as Spotify®, Amazon® and Apple Music®. The criminal practice was discovered, but there is nothing to prevent aforementioned platforms from being affected by new maneuvers that are not well tolerated.

3.1 Artificial Intelligence in Areas and Practices

As mentioned, the wave associated with artificial intelligence is practically spreading across almost all dimensions of human expertise, whether through advanced research, provocative incursions, or the dominance of the few and powerful players in the segment.

Harari (2024), in his study on the evolution of technology uses in today's society, shows us that the explosion of AI was a predictable feature, given the advance in capacity and mobility made possible by networks (speed) and the ease of access to data of different types (variety) and in different places (volume), which would be adding value to various organizational and social actions, as long as the veracity of the data is ensured. This is where the big data cycle emerges (Davenport and Kirby 2016) and brings immense learning possibilities to the neural networks and intelligent algorithms discussed in Sect. 2.1.

In this line, it is estimated that the use of AI has excellent contributions to introduce up in sensitive areas, with possibilities of assisting people who have visual, motor and even emotional difficulties (Vaswani et al. 2017). For example, people who have difficulties can use applications and artifacts such as those developed by the company OrCam MyEye.[3] Its flagship product is an assistive device with AI software that, coupled with glasses, makes content of various types accessible, representing an accessibility relief for the disabled and geeks.

Another area in which AI artifacts are extremely attractive is around interior design, especially with the coupling to virtual reality (Silva 2024). This author speculates that there are visible advantages in incorporating machine learning, especially for image processing, overcoming outdated color catalogs, as well as devising architectural varieties such as the design of buildings adaptable to changing climate conditions.

However, a prime area in which AI, and more specifically robotics, with walking and talking creatures, has been making a mark in society is human assistance (Jecker 2021). In fact, two pieces of evidence are worth mentioning here:

- The Japanese robot Papero, which initially operated during the COVID-19 pandemic in Fujieda city and was designed to minimize social isolation and was expanded to bring joy to people when real people cannot do this; that is, programmed to recognize contexts and interact with informational or ceded aspects. Papero is able to converse naturally with people, especially the elderly. In

[3] Visit to enterprise site https://www.orcam.com/en-us/low-vision.

the city itself, the implementation of the robot is planned to interact with people who are lonely in hospitals, nursing homes and other places (Santana 2024);

- Along the same lines, at the "We Robot"[4] technology event that took place in California in 2024, whose biggest highlight was TESLA's autonomous cyber taxi (Feng et al. 2021), the humanoid robot Optimus was also presented, which revealed in the demonstration all its capacity for oral, textual and visual interaction, which, according to its sponsor, billionaire Elon Musk, is a link in the trajectory of transforming the machine more intelligent than man in 20 years.

Alongside of pictorial elements such as those listed above, there is evidence of disruptions in terms as: authorship, creativity, and autonomy; caused by Generative AI (Chen et al. 2024). In the meantime, systems that operate based on neural network models, that is, use multimodal learning to connect the semantics between texts and images, appear to be competitors for professionals in the areas of visual production (cinema, fashion) and architecture and communication advertising.

Such features cause oscillation between admiration and astonishment regarding the creative content of these maneuvers, as cited for specific cases around music or visual arts (Kaufman 2019). In these fields, questions related to authorship, ownership and originality and textual references arise as dilemmas to be faced.

But the most electrifying item that was found in this search for opportunities to machine learning use (inclusive deep learning and neural networks) was the possibility of the biological computer. In fact, Lin et al. (2024) managed to build a computer using DNA technology, ushering in an era that could see the emergence of molecular biology using the same principles and achieving the same results as traditional silicon-based technologies.

According to these authors, this technology, which is still experimental, promises to be capable of executing all typical computational actions in a programmable manner using a nanoscale fiber network, which will exponentially increase storage capacity in terms of compactness, providing an increase in processing power.

This once again leads us to resort to science fiction imagery, as in the beginning, now pointing out the film Minority Report.[5]

3.2 *Warnings About Excessive Use*

Geffrey Hinton, considered by many to be one of the fathers of modern artificial intelligence, gave an interview in May 2023,[6] in which he stated that it is necessary to curb our expectations regarding the unbridled use of AI. First, he understands that

---

[4] See https://acontecendoaqui.com.br/inovacao/we-robot-sedia-lancamento-de-nova-linha-de-robos-humanoides/.

[5] Steven Spielberg's 2002 film, in which super gifted human beings (precogs) are in a kind of liquid sap with conductive properties, connected to each other and could access intelligent computers, to, through premonition, use anticipatory intelligence for the criminal area.

[6] Douglas Heaven's live interview with Hinton at EmTech Digital in May 2023.

only large companies appear to be profiting from the gains, that is, there is a risk establishing a domination of single-minded thinking that has always proven to be harmful to the advancement of society. Recognizing this, this luminary proposes an ethical debate on the consequences that the unbridled use of AI routines can bring to human tasks and their execution. Thus, it is necessary to keep in mind that several activities still require—and will require—human intervention, especially those that demand creativity and innovation.

Critical Thinking is certainly one of them activities and pointed out elements in future relationships is not necessarily defined on the present or on a repetitive profile as the famous generative AI does.

Thus, moral dilemmas arise when facing the fine line between what is natural and artificial intelligence (of artifacts), and this confrontation is apparently a pointless struggle. And, in fact, the social implications and consequences of the use of AI for humans are issues that require regulation, as suggested by several guidance documents (UNESCO 2022).

Despite this legitimate concern, the AI industry is betting on the concept of alignment (Robot Framework 2024), which, when implemented, with its differentiated system of weights for training neural networks, will generate more performance in services, replacing, for example, IVRs, themselves a type of AI, and their highly rationalized scripts (Silver et al. 2017).

Areas such as health and law should benefit on a large scale, if there is a commitment to the responsible use of data (Hagendorff 2020).

Along these lines, a very interesting weekly newspaper[7] raises the possibility that these regulations could meet good practices for confronting the massification of AI, the so-called "laws" of good cooperation with artifacts and with the growing proposals for the penetration of artificial intelligence into everyday activities. The statements of these laws, clearly reflected in the three laws of robotics, stated in the 1950s in an idea by the author Isaac Asimov, state that:

- The Law of Beneficence—the well-being and benefit of humanity will be prioritized, ensuring that AI actions promote positive results and minimize harm;
- The Law of Autonomy and Consent—there will be respect for human autonomy and the right to informed consent, ensuring that individuals control how their data is used and how AI decisions impact their lives;
- The Justice and Equity Act—algorithmic treatment derived from AI will follow principles of justice, avoiding prejudice and ensuring equal treatment for all individuals and groups.

Therefore, concerns and a search for control are perceived to prevent technology from being used for the purpose of marginalization, invasion of privacy and discrimination, which becomes a big challenge, since there are and perhaps will always be few holders of this technological domain, as one of the gurus of knowledge production in AI has already warned.

[7] Available at: https://www.linkedin.com/newsletters/thoughts-on-ai-weekly-6887834658919202816/. Acesso em 01/11/2024.

These risks are also present when contemplating the use of generative AI artifacts in public service (Filgueiras 2023), including the potential risk of exposing information that should remain confidential. Thus, governments and social entities call for an effort to raise awareness among managers that the use of artificial intelligence in the public sector must always be associated with an assessment of the social and personal risks of the technology (Filgueiras 2024).

Thus, even if the absurd prediction attributed to Elon Musk in 2020, that "artificial intelligence within five years would surpass human intelligence on its way to becoming an "immortal dictator" over humanity", did not happen, and there are real counterpoints that this will never happen (Filgueiras et al. 2023).

In this sense, Landgrebe and Smith (2022) admit that no matter how refined it is now or in the future, it still offers a framework far from anything resembling the capacity of humans. Furthermore, those authors argue that any incremental progress that is occurring in the field of AI research will not bring it closer, in practical terms, to the possibility of the human brain functioning fully. They then reinforce that claims to the contrary only serve to inflate the potential of AI and distort public understanding of the nature, possibilities, and limits of the technology.

Finally, still in the view of the pair of researchers, "the idea of AI emulating and going beyond the general intelligence of humans rests on fundamental mathematical impossibilities that are analogous, in physics, to the impossibility of building a perpetual moving machine" (Landgrebe and Smith 2022, p. 87). And they add that "in certain confined scenarios, completely determined by rules, machine learning can be used to create algorithms that surpass humans", says the duo of writers, "but this does not mean that they can "discover" the rules that govern any activity that occurs in an open environment, which is what the human brain achieves every day."

This is what is discussed quite frequently in Whatsapp® groups, as shown in the excerpt from our conversation, whose reproduction was permitted as show the Annex I:

- [15:14, 09/11/2024] Jairo Dornelas: Relax... while machines only know how to do what we know how to do better than us and need to be programmed for this, we are in the running and with higher odds. HAL 9000 is still a work of fiction;
- [15:18, 09/11/2024] Álvaro Pinheiro: And according to many neuroscientists, it is something very unlikely to be achieved (AGI), since the cognitive algorithmic functions are what are understood and mapped, all non-cognitive functions are unknown to neuroscience, so you cannot mathematically model something that you do not know.

Expanding our reflection, we will now address one of the first areas that suffered the impact of ChatGPT® and similar ones: knowledge production.

3.3 *Artificial Intelligence in Knowledge Production and in Education*

According to UNESCO (2022), AI technologies present great opportunities for scientific knowledge and practice, if researchers are aware of the benefits, limits and risks of their use.

But how can texts originating from a technology such as ChatGpt® be incorporated into an academic paper?

Santaella (2023) states that it is lawful for AI systems to support scientific activities, performing tasks ranging from digitizing databases of articles to making text corrections and improving writing. With this same guideline, Santos et al. (2024) point out that these systems can and should be allies of knowledge, as long as there is adequate regulation, which encompasses ethical and copyright issues.

Nevertheless, challenges, limitations, permissiveness, and excesses persist in the incorporation of this technology into learning and the how to do of work in these segments. Such concerns involve skills training, competency development, teaching and pedagogical models, assessments, and feedback, which, according to Santaella (2023), are still very embryonic.

Therefore, there are impacts that stress the possibility of the end of critical thinking (Lo 2023), reflected, for example, the initial ban in 2020, on its use as it was done at the University of Michigan, but also those more malleable ones such as in King (2023) who projects the use of the artifact in an environment of ubiquitous content production. Thus, according to the author, it is necessary to rethink traditional pedagogical practices and incorporate ChatGPT® (and other AI systems) into everyday school and academic life.

The fact is that there are diverse opportunities, and many companies offering directions for uses that range from support in bureaucratic activities, preparation of lesson plans, and bibliographic design (Cabitza et al. 2017). More incisively, Santaella (2023, p. 87) points out that the important thing is to break the pedagogical inertia by understanding that a "broader change in the role of the teacher is necessary, since information, previously exclusive to classrooms, is now everywhere: first online, then in chatbots".

Filgueiras et al. (2023), in their own words, note, however, that more authentic attention should be paid to the problems of southern countries, where the reality of education is that of overworked teachers, precarious schools, without basic resources and with a low level of connectivity. Such a condition can delay the arrival of AI to the less favored, increasing the social gap, the distance of access to the opportunities offered by technologies, thus indicating the need to establish social governance in relation to the creation of public policies to guarantee equity and social justice in education. Returning to the issue of knowledge production in the epilogue, we come across an artifact like the AI Scientist®, designed to be a type of technology that acts like a researcher, conducting studies autonomously. Such a device would automate the entire research life cycle, from generating new ideas for work to viewing and presenting the findings in a complete scientific manuscript. The company that owns the rights to use the software exposes the conceptual process of execution on its website and in an open format.

There, it shows how the platform selects ideas from databases and labels them with a degree of novelty. It then codes search algorithms itself and, upon reaching a certain degree of consensus, writes the text and passes it on to an intelligent machine configured with the required quality standard. The result is equivalent to a peer-reviewed paper with an acceptance standard, capable of being published in a qualified and impactful publication.

A conceptual illustration of The AI Scientist, including the detailed definition of each of the steps involved in the process, it is available on the company's website.[8] This entire script shows that teaching activities and scientific knowledge production tend to be experiencing a new boom in their activities and we cannot remain indifferent to this boom.

4 Conclusion

Santaella (2023) in his thought-provoking work warns that AI systems can display something very similar to the way human thought, understanding and creativity operate. However, they lack the ability to deal with dissonance, the human task of abstracting, being subjective, irrational, and yet having an outlet for all variants, even the unthinkable ones, something that the phenomenal machine learning algorithms, even in their multi-layer neural deep learning, are still in their infancy.

Returning to discuss the types of human intelligence (Gardner 1983), and anchoring in those, we perhaps could talk about this one new type, an artificial intelligence as a reserve to be activated, by access to an intelligent, non-corporeal machine, which performs raw or even deductive reasoning, but which only prepares for the selection of the human being. This concept It also ratifies in passing the idea of antithesis devised by Kaufman (2019): the illogical, abstract, and sensitive human vis-à-vis the logical, objective and even self-programmed computer.

Thus, for Santaella (2023), there is room and opportunity for coexistence of both types understanding the possibility of other capacities and intelligences different from the human, but without supremacy or banishment. Thus, that one author recognizes that AI leads humans to do well, things that they would not do so well without the help of machines: good things (helping with a medical diagnosis); unscrupulous things (generating and spreading fake news).

Another point, as highlighted by Filgueiras (2024), lies in the regulation to restrict access and indiscriminate manipulation of data, the structuring of government to deal with public data, the valuation of ethics as a model for the development of current and new AI. Figuratively, these are Bucci's (2023) red flags that flutter over the digital universe, where few large companies capitalize and project a priced and manufactured ignorance.

---

[8] https://sakana.ai/ai-scientist/.

As a final word, it is worth mentioning the observation about reasoning, the greatest strength of human cognition. Kaufman (2022) states that human reasoning is seen as the guide from which our logic and reflection are born. Is that so? If we do not consistently know what natural intelligence is and the gift of reasoning is attributed to it as a panacea, and we are subject to fallacies, confusing decisions, experiential, life-like and sentimental mismatches, how dare we say that a machine, certainly intelligent, thinks logically as if it were the perfect heir to something that we do not have full control over?

Thus, fortunately it seems ironic to expect AI to reason better than humans: it would be an unspecified paradox.

In the film mentioned at the beginning, we refer to HAL 9000, an AI that is not even 25% implemented today, and its question: "What are you doing, Dave?".

Dave's action was illogical and risky, but it was the only possible way to deal with a vengeful AI determined to be the center, to have power and control of the situation. Dave somehow won and subdued the AI. We have hope.

Annex I

Excerpt from our conversation in the Artificial Intelligence Whatsapp® group with request and authorization to quote excerpts from the exchange of messages.

[15:13, 10/11/2024] Jairo: My dear, good afternoon.

[15:13, 10/11/2024] Jairo: I received an invitation for a book chapter and I ask for your authorization to quote this forum.

[15:29, 10/11/2024] Álvaro Pinheiro: Good afternoon, Professor. You're always welcome to make calls and posts in the group.

[15:30, 10/11/2024] Álvaro Pinheiro: Quotes, …

[15:33, 10/11/2024] Jairo: ok. I'll make references to the forum and the group!!

[15:33, 10/11/2024] Jairo: Thank you.

[15:34, 10/11/2024] Álvaro Pinheiro: Thank you.

References

ACCA Global (2015) The robots are coming? Implications for financial shared services

Anagnoste S (2018) Setting up a robotic process automation center of excellence. Manag Dyn Knowl Econ 6(2):307–322

Bevilacqua R et al (2023) Social robotics to support older people with dementia: a study protocol with Paro seal robot in an Italian Alzheimer's day center. Front Public Health 11:21

Boot W (2022) Technology design and implementation to promote equity, inclusion, and diversity. Innov Aging 6(1):252

Boucher P (2020) Artificial intelligence: how does it work, why does it matter, and what can we do about it? Bruxelas, European Union. Disponível em: https://www.europarl.europa.eu/thinktank/en/document/EPRS_STU(2020)641547. Acesso em: 16 out 2024

Boulton C (2017) What is RPA? a revolution in business process automation computerworld Hong Kong
Bucci E (2023) Incerteza: um ensaio - como pensamos a ideia que nos desorienta (e orienta o mundo digital). Autêntica, São Paulo
Cabitza F, Rasoini R, Gensini GF (2017) Unintended consequences of machine learning in medicine. JAMA. https://doi.org/10.1001/jama.2017.7797
Cavalcanti GDC, Mendes-da-Silva W, Dos Santos Felipe IJ (2024) Recent advances in applications of machine learning in reward crowdfunding success forecasting. Neural Comput Applic 36:16485–16501. https://doi.org/10.1007/s00521-024-09886-6
Chaudhari S, Aggarwal P, Murahari V (2024) RLHF deciphered: a critical analysis of reinforcement learning from human feedback for LLMs. Disponível em: http://arxiv.org/abs/2404.08555
Chen Z, Chen C, Yang G, He X, Chi X, Zeng Z, Chen X (2024) Research integrity in the era of artificial intelligence: challenges and responses. Medicine 103(27):e38811–e38811. https://doi.org/10.1097/md.0000000000038811
Davenport TH, Kirby J (2016) Just how smart are smart machines? MIT Sloan Manag Rev 57(3):21–25
El Naqa I, Murphy MJ (2015) What is machine learning? In: El Naqa I, Li R, Murphy M (eds) Machine learning in radiation oncology. Springer, Cham. https://doi.org/10.1007/978-3-319-18305-3_1
Feng S et al (2021) Intelligent driving intelligence test for autonomous vehicles with naturalistic and adversarial environment. Nat Commun 12:748
Fernandes DFA, Silva AMR, Paiva ACR (2022) Cybersecurity test automation: experiences with robot framework and OWASP ZAP technologies. Dissertação de Mestrado, Instituto Superior Técnico, Universidade de Lisboa
Filgueiras F (2023) Inteligência artificial e riscos existenciais para a humanidade – A armadilha do desenvolvimento Interesse Nacional. Disponível em: https://interessenacional.com.br/portal/fernando-filgueiras-inteligencia-artificial-e-riscos-existenciais-para-a-humanidade-a-armadilha-do-desenvolvimento/. Acesso em 02/11/2024
Filgueiras F (2024) Artificial intelligence and education governance. Journals.sagepub.com 19(3). https://doi.org/10.1177/17461979231160674
Filgueiras F, Medonça R, Almeida V (2023) Governing artificial intelligence through a sociotechnical lens. IEEE Internet Comput 27(5):49–52. https://doi.org/10.1109/MIC.2023.3310110
Gardner H (1983) Frames of mind: a theory of multiple intelligences. Basic Books, New York
Geyr J (2015) Adopting robotic process automation requires initiative from workforce and leadership alike. Ind Mainten Plant Oper
Gomes P et al (2022) Artificial intelligence-based methods for business processes: a systematic literature review. Appl Sci 12(5):2314
Griffin G, Wennerström E, Foka A (2024) AI and Swedish heritage organizations: challenges and opportunities. AI Soc 39(5):2359–2372
Hagendorff T (2020) The ethics of ai ethics: an evaluation of guidelines. Minds Mach 30:99–120. https://doi.org/10.1007/s11023-020-09517-8
Harari YN (2024) Nexus: a brief history of information networks from the stone age to AI. Fern Press, New York. ISBN 978-1911717089
Haykin S (2001) Redes neurais: princípios e práticas, 2ª. Bookman, Porto Alegre
Jecker NS (2021) You've got a friend in me: sociable robots for older adults in an age of global pandemics. Ethics Inf Technol 23(S1):35–43
Kaufman D (2019) Dá pra fazer arte com inteligência artificial? Época Negócios. https://epocanegocios.globo.com/colunas/IAgora/noticia/2019/08/da-pra-fazer-arte-com-inteligencia-artificial.html. Acesso em 07 mar. 2024
Kaufman D (2022) Desmistificando a inteligência artificial. Autêntica, São Paulo
Kelan EK (2024) Algorithmic inclusion: shaping the predictive algorithms of artificial intelligence in hiring. Hum Resour Manag J 34(3):694–707

King MR (2023) The future of AI in medicine: a perspective from a chatbot. Ann Biomed Eng 51(2):291–295. https://doi.org/10.1007/s10439-022-03121-w
Lacity M, Willcocks L (2016) Robotic process automation at Telefonica O2 MIS Quart. Exec 15(1):21–35
Lacity M, Willcocks L, Yan A (2015) Are the robots really coming? Service automation survey findings. Pulse Mag 17:14–21
Landgrebe J, Smith B (2022) Why machines will never rule the world artificial: intelligence without fear, 1a ed. Routledge. ISBN 9781032309934
Lecun Y et al (2015) Deep learning. Nature 521:436–444
Limongi R (2024) The use of artificial intelligence in scientific research with integrity and ethics. Futur Stud Res J Trends Strat 16(1), e845. Disponível em: https://www.revistafuture.org/FSRJ/article/view/845
Lin KN, Volkel K, Cao C (2024) A primordial DNA store and compute engine. Nat Nanotechnol. https://doi.org/10.1038/s41565-024-01771-6
Lo C (2023) What is the impact of ChatGPT on education? A rapid review of the literature. Educ Sci 13:410. https://doi.org/10.3390/educsci13040410
Lurdermir TB (2021) Inteligência artificial e aprendizado de máquina: estado atual e tendências. Estudos avançados 35(101). https://doi.org/10.1590/s0103-4014.2021.35101.007
Medvedeva M, Vols M, Wieling M (2020) Using machine learning to predict decisions of the European Court of Human Rights. Artif Intell Law 28:237–266
Nichols JA, Chan B, Matthew AB (2019) Machine learning: applications of artificial intelligence to imaging and diagnosis. Biophys Rev 11(1):111–118. https://doi.org/10.1007/s12551-018-0449-9
Penttinen E, Kasslin H, Asatiani A (2018) How to choose between robotic process automation and back-end system automation? In: Twenty-sixth european conference on information systems (ECIS2018)
Robot Framework (2024) Robot framework user guide. Disponível em: https://robotframework.org/robotframework/latest/RobotFrameworkUserGuide.html. Acesso em: 27 ago. 2024
Sarlet GBS, Molinaro CA (2020) Questões tecnológicas, éticas e normativas da proteção de dados pessoais na área da saúde em um contexto de big data. Revista Brasileira de Direitos Fundamentais & Justiça 13(41), 183–212. Disponível em: http://dfj.emnuvens.com.br/dfj/article/view/811
Santaella L (2023) Há como deter a invasão do ChatGPT? São Paulo: Estação das Letras e Cores. 124 p
Santana RP (2024) I: um agente inteligente para auxiliar idosos. CIN Press Release. https://cin-ufpe-agentes-inteligentes.pubpub.org/pub/paperoi/release/1
Santos AAL, Ramos ASM, Andrade APV (2024) A Ética no Uso do *ChatGPT* na Pesquisa Acadêmica: um estudo qualitativo com estudantes de mestrado e doutorado em Administração. Anais do XIII SBTI Maceió
Silva AL (2024) Dueto criativo: especulando arquitetura via arte e computação. Convergências: Revista de Investigação e Ensino das Artes XVII(33), 143–152. https://doi.org/10.53681/c1514225187514391s.33.214. ISSN 1646-9054
Silver D et al (2017) Mastering the game of go without human knowledge. Nature 550(7676):354–359. https://doi.org/10.1038/nature24270
Suri VK, Marianne E, Van Hillegersberg J (2017) Software bots—the next frontier for shared services and functional excellence. In: Global sourcing of digital services: micro and macro perspectives
Trainum K et al (2023) Robots in assisted living facilities: scoping review. JMIR Aging 6:e42652
UNESCO (2022) Recommendation on the ethics of artificial intelligence. https://unesdoc.unesco.org/ark:/48223/pf0000381137. Acesso em 16 abr. 2024
Van der Aalst W (2016) Data science in action. Springer, Berlin, Heidelberg

Vaswani A, Shazeer N, Parmar N, Uszkoreit J, Jones L, Gomez AN, Kaiser L, Polosukhin I (2017) Attention is all you need. Adv Neural Inf Process Syst 30
Vigen T (2015) Spurious correlations. Hachette Books, New York

Language and Culture: Imperative Strategic Assets for Organizations in the AI Era

Laura Zapata-Cantú and Emilio Arnau Pineda

Abstract With its remarkable potential to take on traditional 'human' tasks in organizations, AI has depersonalized critical situations in our professional lives. However, this also raises an intriguing question: Can AI contribute to one of the most critical processes for a firm's long-term survival and competitive advantage: innovation? AI should be "less artificial" and more human, conceptualizing the role of these new technologies in social relations. This shift is not just a possibility but an urgent need. The present chapter argues for the importance of organizations in this AI era restoring their "human dimension" to humans with a sense of urgency, freeing them from routines, and amplifying creativity and socialization. It asserts that even if technologies replaced employees' routinized tasks, they would not diminish the importance of communication and language but amplify them, which is crucial for knowledge sharing and innovation. This chapter also underlines the potential of AI to enhance human creativity and socialization, thereby contributing to a more optimistic view of the future of work.

Keywords Language · Culture · Imperative strategic assets · Organizations · AI

1 Introduction

Today, with the help of AI, we can quickly draft a variety of documents, from welcome speeches to resignation letters. However, the personal or organizational values that used to be embedded in these activities, reflecting our identity, have become less relevant. We have depersonalized critical situations in our professional lives. However, can we afford to do the same for strategic activities? With AI's potential to take on traditional 'human' tasks in organizations, we must consider whether AI can

L. Zapata-Cantú (✉)
Department of Management and Leadership, School of Business, Tecnológico de Monterrey, Monterrey, Mexico
e-mail: laura.zapata@tec.mx

E. A. Pineda
School of Humanities and Education, Tecnológico de Monterrey, Monterrey, Mexico

C. Machado and J. P. Davim (eds.), *Challenges and Opportunities in the Artificial Intelligence Era*, https://doi.org/10.1007/978-3-031-85272-5_2

play a role in one of the most critical processes for a firm's long-term survival and competitive advantage: innovation.

Over the years, literature has consistently highlighted the utmost importance of knowledge sharing and innovation. Companies that can respond swiftly and flexibly to product innovation and effectively coordinate and redistribute their competencies are the winners in the global market (Teece et al. 1997). The knowledge management (KM) literature has made significant efforts to promote this relevance, identifying where knowledge is, how to create it, and how to share it. It has been established that tacit knowledge is not just a critical strategic asset for innovation but an urgent one that we must recognize and utilize.

Furthermore, information technology (IT) advancements are widely seen as catalysts for organizational change programs in the knowledge management (KM) literature. However, it is essential to remember that people-centered activities such as socialization are crucial for knowledge-sharing (Nonaka and Takeuchi 1995)—one of the critical questions concerns whether technologies empower or disempower workers. Artificial intelligence (AI), "a broad collection of computer-assisted systems for task performance" (Von Krogh 2018: 405), is a technology that is becoming increasingly pervasive in companies. AI, with its potential to empower workers, provides two types of results: "decision results," when an algorithmic conclusion is based on the data collected, and "solution results," which consider alternative actions for solving a problem based on both conjectural explanations and data mining (Von Krogh 2018). This potential of AI to empower workers is a promising aspect of the future of work and a positive development in the AI era.

So, AI, per se, represents one of the biggest challenges of the forthcoming decades. Specifically, the debates on AI are concerned with the ability of robots/superintelligence to develop consciousness, coupled with a deliberate ability to strategize and take actions intentionally. Given certain constraints in information processing, the central premise is that AI can deliver higher quality, greater efficiency, and better outcomes than human experts (Haefner et al. 2021).

In other words, AI should become an extension and amplifier of human potential and consciousness. There are plenty of examples: applications of nanorobotics in medicine and personalized medicine, use in routine or hazardous jobs and operations, making sense of large-scale datasets of memories, and aid in disaster zones, among others. Possibilities are infinite, indeed (Del Giudice et al. 2023).

As AI and KM are inexorably bound up with the natures of knowledge and learning, recent advances in AI can provide new foundations for transforming KM in organizations (Sanzogni et al. 2017). There are two complementary techno-organizational orientations in this space: (1) KM, which is directly concerned with managing knowledge in organizations, and (2) AI, seen as a branch of computing, which is primarily focused on developing systems that can mimic human knowledge and learning activities.

According to this framework, KM in organizations helps deliver products and services by creating, storing, retrieving, sharing, and applying knowledge. These processes are essential for an organization to learn, reflect, and develop core competencies to sustain its competitive edge in the knowledge-based economy (Jarrahi et al. 2023). In AI, the loss of knowledge sharing among practitioners can limit both the feedback required for algorithms and the optimal data needed to train models (Toscani 2023).

AI should be "less artificial" and more human, conceptualizing the role of those new technologies in social relations. In this regard, the present chapter claims the relevance that organizations in this IA era restore to humans their "human dimension," freeing them from routines and amplifying creativity and socialization. It declares that even if technologies replaced employees' routinized tasks, they would enhance organizational practices and values with high human involvement, such as communication and language, which are crucial for knowledge sharing and innovation (Del Giudice et al. 2023).

In this regard, the present chapter aims to contribute to the current literature on knowledge sharing and artificial intelligence for organizational innovation, understanding that the human side of organizations is embedded in organizational culture and language so that it cannot be ignored in implementing new technologies at work, becoming strategic assets.

The chapter is structured as follows: Sect. 2 reviews the literature on knowledge sharing with particular emphasis on tacit knowledge, socialization, and human interaction to innovate. Section 3 exposes a review of the literature on knowledge sharing and artificial intelligence, in which explicit knowledge based on automatization plays a crucial role in putting aside human intervention. Section 4 shows a conceptual model and discusses the literature review. Section 5 exposes conclusions, implications, limitations, and further research lines.

2 Knowledge Sharing for Continuous Innovation

The world today looks remarkably different from the last two decades, during which technology provoked a radical change, invading the workplace at a speed that would have been unimaginable. In this regard, organizations require more efficient individual knowledge-sharing, interaction, communication, and problem-solving processes to innovate, co-create, and survive.

Knowledge sharing is the most widely studied process in the literature at KM. It has been analyzed from different perspectives: as a strategic process that gives the organization the ability to assimilate new knowledge to foster innovation or to achieve operational efficiency and as a communication process where media tools are critical to effectively sharing knowledge from one agent (source) to another (receiver).

Additionally, knowledge sharing involves a complex social process in which organizational interactions depend on people's closeness, communication frequency, and access to the comprehensive communication mechanisms necessary for transferring critical information and experiencing a group's solidarity (Zapata-Cantu 2021).

In this regard, the adoption of AI could detriment the way of working as a "collective" in knowledge sharing because it involves a process that encompasses their emotions and their cognitions in a non-codifiable format, without the need for further description, calculation, or explanation (Huang 2018). Face-to-face interactions are instrumental in building and maintaining effective social innovation networks, generating the trust, respect, and commitment necessary for continuing interaction and knowledge sharing, even in globally dispersed organizations.

The real question is how firms can maintain the knowledge-sharing process when technology is becoming the protagonism, moving so fast, for example, in adopting AI, and there is an inextricable need to innovate. For this process, the qualities of the spatial dimension, such as relationships between spaces, mixed-used space, scale, and the relationship between the building's interior and the exterior, are all fundamental (Zapata-Cantu 2021). Despite this perspective on AI processes, there is agreement in the literature about how innovation depends on knowledge sharing (Castaneda and Cuellar 2020), specifically the transfer of tacit knowledge embedded in people.

Sanders and Wood (2019) argue that adopting AIs is not a "plug-and-play model" but involves ethical aspects that maintain the human side of an organization. The relevance of the "human" dimension in strategic human capital is in terms of the "rediscovering of humans." Organizations need to emphasize the relevance of implementing socialization tactics within a company to improve the human resources environment (Del Giudice et al. 2023), even more so in this artificial and highly technological world.

2.1 Tacit and Explicit Knowledge for Innovation

KM for organizations embodies a vital dimension of personalization, focusing on individual workers and their "personal inquiry" (Gorman and Pauleen 2016). For that reason, conceptualizations of knowledge often recognize the centrality of each worker in defining the concept of knowledge. For example, Davenport (1998, p. 5) defines knowledge as "a fluid mix of framed experience, values, contextual information, and expert insight that provides a framework for evaluating and incorporating new experiences and information" (Jarrahi et al. 2023).

Knowledge can be divided into explicit and tacit forms. Explicit knowledge is easily articulated, impersonal, and formal, frequently taking the form of documents. In turn, tacit knowledge focuses on practical intelligence, mental models, know-how, beliefs, intuition, skills, and insights. It is rooted in an individual's experience and values and is essential to strategic planning performance.

It could be said that innovation based on AI responds effectively when knowledge is subject to clear rules or "highly structured domains," such as playing chess games against an AI opponent or diagnosing pathologies based on images. However, it is limited in understanding context and is ineffective given contextual changes and nuances (Hadjimichael and Tsoukas 2019). Furthermore, tacit knowledge sharing positively contributes to innovation capability associated with knowledge quality (Ganguly et al. 2019).

Moreover, decision-making speed can compound biases, which are affected by emotions given the "quantities of data, multiple types of data, and data that are often subject to interpretation" (Huang 2018, p. 1822). Such human biases can affect classification algorithms that rely on human-generated input data, including ingenuity and domain knowledge, to make decisions (Shrestha et al. 2021); thus, the prediction algorithms generated may exacerbate errors unless accurate planning considers employee knowledge sharing. However, algorithm-assisted induction can still occur, amplifying sampling errors or flaws that go undetected when measuring the data (Shrestha et al. 2021).

Nevertheless, organizations must promote repeated social interactions and physical proximity to maximize tacit knowledge transfer. Social interactions enable the spread of job-related information, encourage the spontaneous generation of solutions and ideas, strengthen social ties between colleagues, improve the quality of communication, and develop shared goals. Physical proximity co-produces relational proximity, which promotes learning and mutual understanding. Although physical proximity is not a sufficient or necessary precondition for knowledge sharing, relational forms of proximity may facilitate actors' communication roles as sources and receivers.

2.2 *Organizational Factors: Culture and Language*

Personal relationships between workers, most likely forged through face-to-face interactions and a solid respect for one another's professional capabilities, are required to share tacit knowledge. Nowadays, with technological advances, organizational culture and the way organizations communicate and interact are critical.

Organizational culture is a key to innovation success. Firms renowned for their ability to create and commercialize new technologies frequently emphasize their unique cultures. Salient examples are Apple, 3 M, and Google. Apple offers its staff the opportunity to work for a bigger whole and create new groundbreaking technologies. Also, 3 M highlights that it is a fundamentally science-based company, while Google celebrates its employees' individuality and freedom.

Organizational culture is defined as a design of fundamental presumptions created by the labor community to develop an integrative system dealing with external factors and coordinating internal relationships within an organization. Organizational culture is a "complex set of values, beliefs, assumptions, and symbols that define how a firm conducts its business" (Barney 1986). Another study characterizes organizational culture as a shared cognitive system that guides organization members' perceptions, thoughts, and language (Hofstede 2015).

Both processes, knowledge sharing and innovation, require counting on an organizational culture that motivates the organization's members to seek new ways of doing things, where timetable flexibility and interaction among its members facilitate this search. At the same time, this organizational culture should be open; that is, it encourages employees to share their knowledge and facilitates communication among firm members as a source of internal knowledge creation.

Language is the base of all cultural structures and the main channel for communication activities within any institution. At the beginning of the twentieth century, literary theory was born out of a need for an objective and scientific study of literature (Bradford 1994). Roman Jakobson was one of the leading members of Moscow's Linguistic Circle, where he founded some of the most essential ideas for structural linguistics and communication theory. In Jakobson's communication circuit, language is the medium by which people share messages, and it is only complete when the recipient of the message has responded positively to the addresser (Jakobson 1960). The importance of an active communication cycle resides in the fact that language can shape relationships inside an organization, where skills and expertise is passed down within the institution.

Language has whatever significance it has because of its relation to cognition: "Languages—said Gottfried Wilhelm Leibniz—are the best mirror of the human mind." Without language, none of the higher cognitive functions (memory, judgment, reasoning) would be possible. Even a solitary individual, independently of his or her communicative needs, needs language. Such a language may be public or private, and it may be conceived either as constitutive of cognitive processes or as an indispensable tool for them. Be this as it may, language has an internal rather than external connection with thought (Dascal 1992).

Our social selves are shaped by the language we use. What shapes our language, therefore, impacts our conceptual worlds. AI's fast adoption and training of generative AI through human interaction with the algorithm amplifies the trajectory. Thus, AI can rewire our linguistics and conceptualizations of our experiences (Berthon et al. 2024). Communication is the basic process through which people form perceptions of others, build and maintain social relationships, and achieve cooperative outcomes. Nevertheless, there is a lack of in-person public speaking opportunities since language is used first and foremost to organize thoughts and communicate (Chomsky and Noam 2002), adding high use of social media and digital channels to communicate conveniently. Generative AI that draws from Large Language Models (LLMs) is poised to change how we communicate (Hohenstein et al. 2023).

Culture and language became critical for innovation based on tacit knowledge sharing, preserving organizational values and rules in strategic initiatives.

3 Knowledge Sharing and Artificial Intelligence

One of the critical challenges of knowledge sharing is overcoming silos to connect disparate people with the practices and knowledge that they need. AI approaches can redress this by discovering and strengthening weak ties, thus facilitating community-based learning.

In this context, the most fundamental use of AI for knowledge sharing pertains to its contribution toward collaborative intelligence, something not attainable by traditional database systems. AI can help animate creative thinking, create a shared memory among various team members, and facilitate feedback and peer review.

These intelligent features are increasingly embedded into enterprise or personal communication systems such as Slack or Yammer, providing more than just a communication channel for connecting workers (Jarrahi et al. 2023).

Furthermore, by collaborating with humanoids, employees may augment their potential and expand their knowledge. Companies' capacity to integrate different actors' knowledge sets and engage in joint explorative and exploitative activities is assuming an increasingly strategic role. The interaction humans-humanoids combines the potential of both knowledge and intellectual capital creation.

In this regard, AI's future should help people recoup their humanity using an individual approach. The individuality approach exalts human capital as the main component of intellectual capital because humans can generate innovations. This also reinforces Keynes' thoughts on developing creativity outside of a job placement.

General knowledge sharing appears crucial to AI output because information-processing and decision-making authority can be delegated across roles and units to mitigate humans' limited capacity for processing information—or worse still, their susceptibility to consciously ignore information-related problems (Von Krogh 2018). Therefore, knowledge sharing also has a personality angle. Combining tacit and explicit knowledge, human interaction is instrumental in translating top management's grand concepts into concepts for service systems (Nonaka and Takeuchi 1995).

3.1 *Tacit and Explicit Knowledge for Automation*

AI practitioners' mutual human–machine involvement in AI project implementation requires a tacit knowledge-sharing approach and is understood as an indicator of AI production. Tacit knowledge is personal insofar as the tacit integration of focal and subsidiary awareness makes knowledge possible. Therefore, tacit knowledge can only be transferred and acquired through social interactions (Hadjimichael and Tsoukas 2019).

Although some AI practitioners have tried to support tacit knowledge-sharing, especially at the executive level, most have become isolated and have focused solely on explicit knowledge at an individual level. However, using this knowledge is more connected to operational issues and is, therefore, less likely to have significance. Tacit knowledge is critical to performance, especially in enabling spontaneous performance and, in turn, allowing agents to respond to situations with minimal time and effort (Hadjimichael and Tsoukas 2019).

However, the two separate behavioral frames, cognitive and emotional, should be considered: the cognitive framing of decisions may affect the emotional experience just as emotional experiences affect cognitive decision-making (Kahneman and Tversky 2000). This blurring of the lines between purely cognitive and emotional behaviors reinforces the moderating role of tacit knowledge sharing for overcoming AI failure.

Therefore, in Toscani's (2023) study, AI practitioners characterized by a collective view and guided by a high exchange level of tacit knowledge will score higher in innovation and create more "significance" for AI production than those exhibiting a moderate exchange level of tacit knowledge. This stresses the importance of focusing on management techniques that foster human interactions within a collective tacit knowledge-sharing approach (Nonaka and Takeuchi 1995).

However, tacit knowledge sharing will constitute a challenge for AI practitioners who are not extroverted enough to share their own experiences, and organizations are not sufficiently open to allow it. People will need training and support from an organizational culture that promotes implicit knowledge exchange.

3.2 Organizational Factors: People

Shortly, the workforce will need to think and behave in a linked manner and have a skill set of means to connect, cooperate, and communicate within a company, not only from the employees' perspective but also from a leadership perspective to innovate, create, deal with the structural changes (Foerster-Metz et al. 2018). Due to technological advancement in cloud computing, advanced algorithms and artificial intelligence are interconnected and significantly impact how people behave within and outside organizations (Scuotto et al. 2023).

More than ever, organizations must develop new skills to adapt to evolving digital technologies, which is essential in fostering innovation (Mariani et al. 2023). Human-centered decision-making still exists, such as sensing opportunities in the environment, anticipating changes, and enhancing an organization's innovation ability, but AI can enhance these human capabilities. For instance, AI impacts innovation management by complementing human decision-making by increasing rationality with data and creativity with specific methodologies (Pietronudo et al. 2022).

Previous studies on AI technology in organizations have focused on its technical advantages. However, more scholars have found that using technology alone is not enough to benefit enterprises from innovation directly. Technology can only bring value when it forms irreplaceable and imitable organizational capabilities.

Scholars are concerned that firms should pay attention to cultivating appropriate human skills in the organization when adopting AI technology (Mariani et al. 2023). Cultivating the corresponding managerial skills is essential. Because managerial AI skills are more comprehensive than technical AI skills and more familiar with the organization's business, simply introducing AI technology provides valuable insights for organizations seeking to optimize human AI skills.

While the debate about having a human person instead of an AI chatbot continues, several companies have started implementing chatbots into their user experiences with amplified technological and pedagogical effects (Berthon et al. 2024). Automatization of processes allows people to focus on strategic and innovative tasks. In this regard, training becomes essential to coexisting human decision-making and humanoids' autonomic processes.

4 Discussion: Conceptual Model

Artificial Intelligence impacts innovation management by complementing human decision-making through increasing rationality and creativity (Mariani et al. 2023). Considering AI's potential to take on traditional 'human' tasks in organizations, organizations may ask whether a role for AI can be used in pursuing one of the most critical processes affecting a firm's long-term survival and competitive advantage, such as innovation (Haefner et al. 2021). Even with its magnificence to be more efficient, the idea that firms could and should use AI and machine learning for innovation may seem almost exaggerated. After all, innovation has traditionally been seen as a domain for humans, given their 'unique' ability to be innovative (Haefner et al. 2021).

Some scholars have realized that the role of human skills in the innovation process cannot be ignored (Gupta et al. 2020; Mikalef and Krogstie 2020; Patrick et al. 2020). Even when AI can provide instrumental assistance beyond the scope of humans and potentially be applied in innovation settings, the knowledge of AI technology and human skills is still limited. To address this research gap, we developed a conceptual model that exposes the tacit knowledge embedded in people as critical for innovation (Fig. 1). On the other hand, explicit knowledge extrinsic to technology allows the effectiveness of AI at work. We propose that there are organizational elements such as culture and language that will promote innovation based on AI and become strategic assets (Barney 1986).

Human-organized innovation management is crucial in companies' ability to reinvent themselves through exploratory initiatives. Despite AI's potential downsides compared to humans, firms may incorporate AI into their innovation processes for several compelling reasons. These reasons include the increasingly volatile and competitive global markets, rival technologies, and rapidly changing political landscapes that innovation managers face (Haefner et al. 2021).

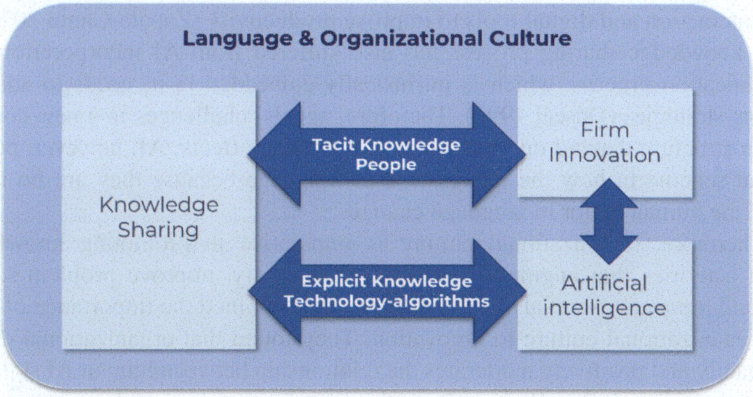

Fig. 1 Language and culture as the missing link between knowledge sharing and AI. *Source* Authors' elaboration

The use of AI and machine learning for creativity and innovation differs significantly from the established areas where AI has replaced traditional management (Haefner et al. 2021). For instance, according to Gallup's study of nearly 19,000 US individuals, among employees who frequently use AI, four in 10 use it to carry out "routine tasks," three in 10 use it to "learn new things," and one-quarter use it to "identify problems." Only 11% use AI to collaborate with coworkers (Brecheisen 2024).

Our chapter proposes that innovation management research enriches by revealing the critical role of human skills and organizational elements, such as language and culture, in enabling AI-based innovation. Leaders may be keen to promote a culture of agility, collaboration, and innovation, actively fostering trust and ensuring that leaders and collaborators navigate the AI landscape together (Brecheisen 2024).

The innovative capability could be affected by AI (Odugbesan et al. 2023) due to the intrinsic lack of contextual sensitivity within AI, in which algorithms still involve many trade-offs and can only support human judgment rather than being "magic bullets" that replace it. Some studies analyze the thinking partnership between AI practitioners and AI-powered machines as well as the subsequent impact of human learning and decisions on AI, finding that "gut feeling" is also an essential criterion and driver of decision-making—even though the gut feeling is impulsive, emotional, unconscious, prone to error, and therefore inherently biased.

KM becomes crucial for organizations to provide repositories with explicit knowledge to reinforce AI and identify key people to promote innovation and support knowledge sharing in a highly technological environment. However, human interaction remains critical to strategic initiatives. For instance, the evolution of the knowledge-sharing process based on technology has suffered from a lack of social face-to-face interaction and a high use or exposure to digital tools. Knowledge sharing becomes relevant through socialization and physical proximity. Socialization brings collaboration and a combination of knowledge in different people, spaces, and times, provoking creativity and innovation. However, organizations must seek the best option in digital environments to balance physical and virtual spaces built on human social interaction and digital tools to improve productivity (Zapata-Cantu 2021).

The knowledge-sharing process has also suffered from AI incorporation. The communication process, which is intrinsically embedded in it, needs to adapt its language strategies (Dascal 1992). Therefore, agents' challenges in a new communication structure depend on their needs and relative effects. AI, however, poses a different scheme in how the addresser uses language because they are no longer people; the human factor in language changes.

Furthermore, organizational culture is imperative in promoting knowledge-sharing activities that augment personnel productivity, improve problem-solving skills, and innovate. An et al. (2024) empirically examined the importance of traditional organizational culture to innovation. They found that organizational culture significantly and positively moderates the relationship between human AI skills and organizational innovation. By improving the digital atmosphere of the organizational environment, organizational culture can strengthen the impact of human AI skills on organizational innovation.

Organizational culture motivates collaborators to share and create knowledge. Knowledge creation occurs because companies are social organizations specializing in creating and transforming knowledge (Nonaka and Takeuchi 1995), given the assumption that knowledge cannot exist without human subjectivities and the context surrounding humans. Knowledge creation is precious because it tends to be unique, specifically with a sizeable tacit component, which makes it more difficult for competitors to imitate and gives the organization a strategic advantage (Zapata-Cantu et al. 2009).

5 Conclusions, Limitations, and Further Research Lines

Technological advances will come, and some will become obsolete or useless in the short term. To be sustainable, organizations must reinforce their culture, language, and people training to preserve their innovation process. They are embedded in their routines and will be the differentiators for firms in a changing environment. These elements have been built over years, even generations, giving them singularity and uniqueness and a pillar for competitive advantage.

Technology, with its disruptive forces, compels organizations to adapt and evolve. For instance, machine learning algorithms like the one used for ChatGPT are inherently designed to learn from user data. This feedback loop of user training the technology and technology training the user can amplify the technology's intended or unintended consequences on people and society (Berthon et al. 2024). AI systems will likely percolate throughout the KM foundation of organizations. However, it is crucial to remember that knowledge production and management are inherently human-centered (Jarrahi et al. 2023).

In this context, organizations face the challenge of navigating technological changes while preserving their unique essence. This balance is where knowledge management and innovation processes, such as organizational contextual elements like language and culture, become critical. In the 1990s, the knowledge-based economy banner promoted the relevance of tacit knowledge as a critical strategic asset. This postulation assumes that people-centered activities such as socialization are crucial to transferring and creating knowledge.

Theoretical implications. More than ever, knowledge-sharing studies must incorporate culture and language as strategic assets to innovate and survive. Organizational culture became critical in motivating people to find new ways of doing things, where flexibility in performance, interaction, and socialization among collaborators facilitate this search. This culture should be open; that is to say, from management, the employees should be encouraged to share their knowledge, and communication among firm members should be facilitated, even when the lack of time to share knowledge represents the principal restriction/limitation to achieve this objective.

Language in the study of tacit knowledge sharing will reinforce the idea of organizational values and perceptions that give firms their uniqueness. Language is the primary channel for communication activities within any institution and is the medium by which people share messages. It is only complete when the recipient has responded positively to the emitter. In this regard, tacit knowledge embedded in messages can be a source of sustainable competitive advantage if it is based on two important properties: (1) That it be based on accumulated experience more than on the task, which implies that it has a significant quantity of tacit knowledge, which makes it difficult to transfer it from one firm to another and imitate it by its competitors, and (2) That it not only revolve around individuals but rather in the form in which these individuals interact amongst themselves (Nonaka and Takeuchi 1995), highly implicit values, perception and language.

Another aspect to consider is how the parallelism of the communication process has supported knowledge-sharing studies, which are facilitated by socialization and human interaction. Communication is the basic process through which people form perceptions of others, build and maintain social relationships, and achieve cooperative outcomes. Effective internal knowledge sharing is possible due to the commitment of the emitter and receiver and the lack of ambiguity in tacit knowledge; in this process, common language and organizational culture play a critical role (Zapata-Cantu et al. 2009).

Generative AI that draws from large language models (LLMs) is poised to change how we communicate fundamentally. AI applications like ChatGPT are increasingly used to produce any language, from text messages and social media posts to computer programs and speeches (Hohenstein et al. 2023). However, technology alone does not facilitate knowledge transfer; employees should be convinced and motivated to create and transfer knowledge face-to-face or use technology-based conduits (Zapata-Cantu 2021).

Practical implications. Recent breakthroughs in deep learning have dramatically improved algorithms' capacity to simulate human capabilities such as "seeing" (image recognition), "hearing" (voice recognition, natural language processing), and "deciding" (analytical processing).AI tools draw from various approaches to simulate human intelligence, including supervised machine learning (ML), neural networks, and deep learning (Jarrahi et al. 2023).

Therefore, innovation based on internal knowledge creation must be reinforced and consistent with certain aspects, such as teamwork, to support knowledge socialization and sharing. In this regard, human resource management must identify more adequate mechanisms at the workplace and suggest ways to provoke social interaction and balance physical and virtual proximities.

Implementing socialization tactics within a company to improve the human resources environment (Del Giudice et al. 2023) is even more relevant in this artificial and highly technological world. For instance, firms that invest in cultivating socialization and creativity among their workforce have better organizational performance, which is heightened when this creativity is a precursor to digital skills (de Vasconcellos et al. 2021). Furthermore, more creative organizations that build digital skills may minimize the negative impacts of time since the firm's inception and any employee-number constraint, making them more dynamic, agile, and adaptive to the digital and technological environment (de Vasconcellos et al. 2021).

On the other hand, leaders must align their teams and the company's culture, understanding what AI adoption currently looks like within their organization. If leaders remain skeptical about AI, employees may forge ahead without guidance. Organizations must bridge this perception gap as quickly as possible, actively fostering trust and ensuring that leaders and employees navigate the AI landscape together (Brecheisen 2024).

Limitations. National culture impacts the way organizations conduct themselves. It can be argued that national culture is an essential determinant of firm performance without countering corporate culture (Fukuyama 1995). In collectivist cultures such as Mexico, frequently described as a low-trust society (Hofstede et al. 2010), the reluctance to share information is expected. However, at the same time, employee social ties are critical enablers that contribute to the organization's well-being.

Employee social ties might be a critical enabler of behaviors that seek to contribute to the organization's well-being. A national business culture—that is, the "premises and belief about work"—and management style—a 'particular approach to management"—are deeply rooted in Mexican society (Ramirez and Zapata-Cantu 2023). In this regard, national culture matters when tacit knowledge sharing is under study.

At least in Mexico, maintaining innovation indicators is required to potentialize socialization, interaction, and creativity, mainly in physical space. Mexican organizations must design and implement a specific innovative culture and activities to avoid decreasing innovation indicators. Organizations should promote communication channels to share new ideas and assign time and space to seek new ways of doing things to explore new processes and activities (Zapata-Cantu 2021).

Future research lines. Moreover, the research process must be adapted as new conditions and variations emerge and are discovered. Examples might include exploring the tacit knowledge challenge of amplifying human potential with the help of AI technologies (Del Giudice et al. 2023). The proposed conceptual model needs to be tested across a broader range of situations considering geography, cultural context, and size and type of organization.

References

An M, Lin J, Luo XR (2024) The impact of human AI skills on organizational innovation: the moderating role of digital organizational culture. J Bus Res 182:114786

Barney JB (1986) Organizational culture: can it be a source of sustained competitive advantage? Acad Manag Rev 11(3):656–665

Berthon P, Yalcin T, Pehlivan E, Rabinovich T (2024) Trajectories of AI technologies: insights for managers. Bus Horiz 65(5):461–470

Bradford R (1994) Roman Jakobson: Life, language, art. Routledge

Brecheisen, J. (2024). What Companies Don't Know About How Workers Use AI, *Harvard Business,* May

Castaneda DI, Cuellar S (2020) Knowledge sharing and innovation: a systematic review. Knowl Process Manag 27(3):159–173

Chomsky N, Noam C (2002) On nature and language. Cambridge University Press, Cambridge

Dascal M (1992) Why does language matter to artificial intelligence? Mind Mach 2:145–174

Davenport TH (1998) Working knowledge: how organizations manage what they know. Harvard Business School, NewYork
Del Giudice M, Scuotto V, Orlando B, Mustilli M (2023) Toward the human–centered approach. A revised model of individual acceptance of AI. Hum Resour Manage Rev 33(1):100856
de Vasconcellos SL, da Silva Freitas JC, Junges FM (2021) Digital capabilities: bridging the gap between creativity and performance. In: The Palgrave handbook of corporate sustainability in the digital era. Palgrave Macmillan, Cham, pp 411–427
Foerster-Metz US, Marquardt K, Golowko N, Kompalla A, Hell C (2018) Digital transformation and its implications on organizational behavior. J EU Res Bus 3:1–14
Fukuyama F (1995) Trust: the social virtues and the creation of prosperity. Free Press Paperback
Ganguly A, Talukdar A, Chatterjee D (2019) Evaluating the role of social capital, tacit knowledge sharing, knowledge quality and reciprocity in determining innovation capability of an organization. J Knowl Manag 23(6):1105–1135
Gorman GE, Pauleen DJ (2016) The nature and value of personal knowledge management. In: Personal knowledge management. Routledge, pp 1–16
Gupta S, Kumar V, Karam E (2020) New-age technologies-driven social innovation: What, how, where, and why? Ind Mark Manage 89:499–516
Hadjimichael D, Tsoukas H (2019) Toward a better understanding of tacit knowledge in organizations: taking stock and moving forward. Acad Manag Ann 13(2):672–703
Haefner N, Wincent J, Parida V, Gassmann O (2021) Artificial intelligence and innovation management: a review, framework, and research agenda. Technol Forecast Soc Change 162
Hofstede GJ (2015) Culture's causes: the next challenge. Cross Cult Manage 22:545–569
Hofstede G, Hofstede GJ, Minkov M (2010) Cultures and organizations: software of the mind. McGraw-Hill, New York. NY
Hohenstein J, Kizilcec RF, DiFranzo D, Aghajari Z, Mieczkowski H, Levy K, Jung MF (2023) Artificial intelligence in communication impacts language and social relationships. Sci Rep 13(1):5487
Huang L (2018) The role of investor gut feel in managing complexity and extreme risk. Acad Manag J 61(5):1821–1847
Jakobson R (1960) Closing statements: linguistics and poetics. In: Sebeok T (Ed) Style in language. MIT Press, pp 350–377
Jarrahi MH, Askay D, Eshraghi A, Smith P (2023) Artificial intelligence and knowledge management: a partnership between human and AI. Bus Horiz 66(1):87–99
Kahneman D, Tversky A (2000) Choices, values, and frames. Cambridge University Press, Cambridge
Mariani MM, Machado I, Magrelli V, Dwivedi YK (2023) Artificial intelligence in innovation research: a systematic review, conceptual framework, and future research directions. Technovation 122:102623
Mikalef P, Krogstie J (2020) Examining the interplay between big data analytics and contextual factors in driving process innovation capabilities. Eur J Inf Syst 29(3):260–287
Nonaka I, Takeuchi H (1995) The knowledge creating company. Oxford University Press, Oxford
Odugbesan JA, Aghazadeh S, Al Qaralleh RE, Sogeke OS (2023) Green talent management and employees' innovative work behavior: the roles of artificial intelligence and transformational leadership. J Knowl Manag 27(3):696–716
Patrick M, John K, Paul P (2020) Exploring the relationship between big data analytics capability and competitive performance: the mediating roles of dynamic and operational capabilities. Inf Manage 57(2)
Pietronudo MC, Croidieu G, Schiavone F (2022) A solution looking for problems? A systematic literature review of the rationalizing influence of artificial intelligence on decision-making in innovation management. Technol Forecast Soc Chang 182:121828
Ramirez J, Zapata-Cantu L (2023) HRM experiences from a Danish firm in Mexico: "Changing" Mexican Culture. In: Castro-Christiansen L, Biron M, Farndale E, Kuvaas B (eds) The Global human resource management casebook. Taylor and Francis, London, UK, pp 318–327

Sanders NR, Wood JD (2019) The Humachine: Humankind, machines, and the future of Enterprise. Routledge

Sanzogni L, Guzman G, Busch P (2017) Artificial intelligence and knowledge management: questioning the tacit dimension. Prometheus 35(1):37–56

Scuotto V, Tzanidis T, Usai A, Quaglia R (2023) The digital humanism era triggered by individual creativity. J Bus Res 158:113709

Shrestha YR, He VF, Puranam PV, Krogh G (2021) Algorithm supported induction for building theory: how can we use prediction models to theorize? Organ Sci 32(3):856–880

Teece DJ, Pisano G, Shuen A (1997) Dynamic capabilities and strategic management. Strateg Manag J 18(7):509–533

Toscani G (2023) The effects of the COVID-19 pandemic for artificial intelligence practitioners: the decrease in tacit knowledge sharing. J Knowl Manag 27(7):1871–1888. https://doi.org/10.1108/JKM-07-2022-0574

Von Krogh G (2018) Artificial intelligence in organizations: new opportunities for phenomenon-based theorizing. Acad Manage Discoveries 4(4):404–409

Zapata-Cantu L, Rialp J, Rialp A (2009) Generation and transfer of knowledge in IT-related SMEs. J Knowl Manag 13(5):243–256

Zapata-Cantu L (2021) The evolution of knowledge transfer in Mexico from physical to virtual spaces. In: International HRM and development in emerging market multinationals. Routledge, pp 173–191

Roadmap for Aligning AI in Production Systems to the Organizational Culture

Mihai Dragomir, Florin Popişter, Diana Dragomir, Diana Ilea, and Denisa Szabo

Abstract The present work approaches the topic of aligning AI systems to the culture of a production organization for use within the manufacturing system. As AI has a very high potential to transform manufacturing, companies must make sure that the way in which it is used conforms to the values and principles they knowingly and tacitly employ. The methodology utilized starts from a literature review and is centered around working with a group of experts to define an integration vision and based on this, a possible generic road map for companies. The knowledge and experience of specialists is distilled through back casting (backward forecasting) of specific characteristics of AI technologies, tailored to the needs of the production sector, the definition of three possible implementation scenarios for adoption within companies and risk assessments attached to these scenarios. By employing such an approach, a production firm can choose beforehand the application path that is best suited to its needs and, thus, will have a higher probability of success.

Keywords AI alignment · Organizational culture · Production systems

1 Introduction

Artificial intelligence is probably the most popular technology to sweep the world at the moment with far reaching implications for most aspects of life, society and economy. As companies are rushing to implement various solutions based on AI (many of them just LLM and generative images/videos) to keep up with the competition, there is still little concern over the consequences of this transformation, with the exception of the fear of job and worker replacement. However, as the hype will soon be gone and settled into a more realistic outlook, it is time to think of AI in terms of practical implications and one of the possible ways to achieve this is by integrating the AI tools alongside humans at various levels of company management

M. Dragomir (✉) · F. Popişter · D. Dragomir · D. Ilea · D. Szabo
Technical University of Cluj-Napoca, Cluj-Napoca, Romania
e-mail: mihai.dragomir@muri.utcluj.ro

C. Machado and J. P. Davim (eds.), *Challenges and Opportunities in the Artificial Intelligence Era*, https://doi.org/10.1007/978-3-031-85272-5_3

and processes. For this to be successful, the two sides must find proper ways to cooperate and "align" in terms of values, principles and sanctioned means of action.

As humans working in a company, under a structured framework of vision-mission-principles, develop over time the so called "organizational culture", the current work seeks to understand how AI can become an active and integral part of this culture and how it can, in its turn, influence its development along the businesses' life cycle. Furthermore, the practical aspects of creating the proper framework conditions and procedures for effective alignment are also discussed and studied. In order to do this, the chapter makes use of a conceptual approach rooted in modern management, as well as in the technical intricacies of relying on automated self-reliant solutions.

The goals of this research are related to proposing a roadmap that both implementing companies and AI developers can follow to bring their expectations and expertise closer to the other's point of view, for fostering improved AI adoption and generating an enhanced stakeholder experience that will ultimately translate into better performances in terms of product delivery, customer engagement, environmental footprint and social netting reinforcement. Starting from the current state of the art and factoring in the experience of a group of experts, the authors apply a number of research and development tools and instruments to define the role and tasks of culturally aligned AI within a generic organization. Since most of the work is performed in terms of future predictions, there is considerable uncertainty about the prescriptions and recommendations comprised in this chapter. However, the proposals made are based on a logically derived demarche that takes into consideration the needs and limitations of both firms and people, on one side, and AI and its responsibility and accountability, on the other side. It is to be expected that implementing these provisions will serve in the future to create better and more agile companies, where AI and humans co-exist and enhance each other's work and contributions.

2 Methodology

The research methodology used is built around the premise that AI systems to be employed by companies need to be tailored to the dynamic corporate culture of the business, which is influenced by its leadership, its staff, its stakeholders and the social and economic constraints in which it operates (Fig. 1). The focus is on production SMEs which operate one or a handful of units in similar socio-demographic conditions.

The first step is dedicated to performing a literature review on the published results regarding similar initiatives to deploy and align AI systems in companies and manufacturing firms. The second step involved the creation of a group of experts with experience in both domains: AI applications and production management. This group was comprised of 7 people with considerable expertise in the area of merging these two trends in the past few years in various domains of the manufacturing industry (e.g., automotive, machinery, consumer goods, etc.). In the third step, the experts have

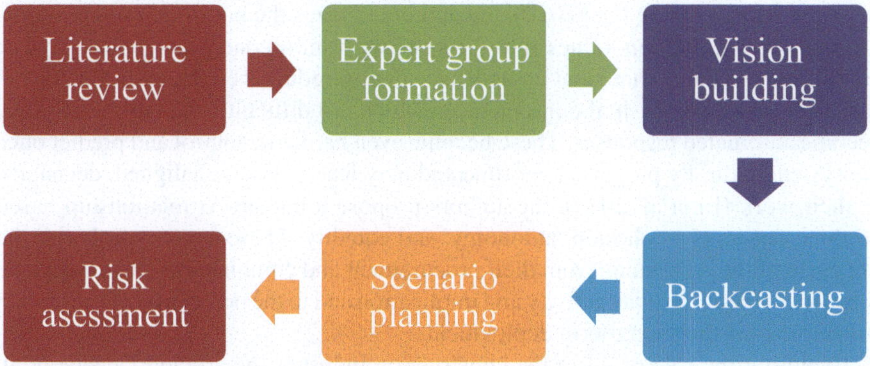

Fig. 1 Research methodology for road mapping AI alignment

been asked to co-create a common vision for AI alignment to company culture in manufacturing, which was achieved through 4 successive iteration of brainstorming, affinity determination and (re)formulating.

Starting with the fourth step, the specific road-mapping techniques are being applied in succession to achieve the desired end work scheme. Backcasting has been applied to connect the current situation identified in literature and in the experts' own companies with the desired vision, by revealing the most important directions of intervention. Based on these, a number of three alternative scenarios have been defined including key activities, main stakeholders and critical advantages and drawbacks specific to each of them. Finally, the final step, that definitizes that work is dedicated to risk assessment specific to each scenario, including possible mitigation measures.

3 Literature Review

The literature review for this paper has been concentrated upon the past 5 years of publications, relating either to AI applications within the realm of corporate culture, or the ethical implications of AI alignment.

The ethical perspective upon researching emergent AI behavior and incorporation in to the work practices is defined by Brendel et al. (2021) as incorporating three axes: decision making, ethical concerns and micro/macro environmental aspects. In the framework proposed by Rajaram and Tinguely (2024) for using generative AI solutions in SME, the role of company values and culture, as well as the need for cooperation, are considered among the deciding factors in ensuring the success of such initiatives. The authors Chowdhury et al. (2022) reinforce the idea that business results can be improved by a collaborative relationship of human workers and AI system, when the later are based on transparency, trust and explainability.

In the paper (van de Poel 2020), the author analyzes the possibilities and pitfalls of incorporating human values into AI systems from a conceptual point of view, highlighting the fact that such an endeavor can introduce new risks to the AI and can also produce undesired consequences which are difficult to monitor once they become automated responses. These become even harder to control and predict once the system naturally progress over time and may lead to poor, unaligned, decisions. In their work (Li et al. 2023), the authors propose a human-AI relationship based on three concepts—cohesion, autonomy, and equality. These aspects deal with the life cycle of the AI system, from their procurement and combination into a workable solution, to their everyday activity and implication and to the perception of the human collective over their long-term deployment.

Exploring the role of AI in the construction industry, the article (Tjebane et al. 2022) analyzes 17 supporting factors for achieving a successful integration company wide, with the organizational culture being at the forefront of these demarches. The authors include here two characteristics that are of interest within the current study too, namely the "work culture" and the "attitude to innovation", that can shape the human-AI relationship. The study (Isensee et al. 2021) find that AI tools can be a valuable support to managers and decision-makers to ensure the company performs in line with the corporate culture, especially concerning sustainability and environmental guidelines, as they become incorporated both in the technology and the human side of an organization.

The authors Guler and Kirshner (2024) illustrate the impact and usefulness of combined large language model—machine learning approaches in data and text rich environments, in this case in literature review. Similar models can be applied using the documented part of the organizational culture, e.g., meeting minutes, emails, presentations, etc. One of the possible uses is well documented in Abulibdeh et al. (2024), which investigates the use of ChatGPT for sustainable development education, a topic of interest in most manufacturing companies which must ensure their personnel is ready for environmental challenges. Similarly, Ray (2023) focuses on ChatGPT and similar systems and proposes a complex evaluation framework that approaches the applicability and coherence of the system provided answers. The author highlights the importance of user feedback and its continuous integration for future system development.

AI, especially big data analytics, proves to be a useful tool in activities which are based on ethical considerations, such as humanitarian relief, where profit, productivity or scrap-rate are not the main focus, according to a study by Dubey et al. (2022). In this context, it is conceivable that moral drivers and conditioners of activities can be considered compatible with the use of AI systems in any organization. Moreover, in Loufek et al. (2024), the authors discuss the organizational mechanisms needed to integrate and align AI to medical and ethical considerations in a highly regulated environment, such as the delivery of medical services.

4 Results and Discussion

The collaboration with the expert group took place over a period of 1 month and comprised three different meetings: the first one dedicated to them presenting their companies and expertise, a second one comprising a free form brainstorming session and a third, critical one, in which the initial ideas have been analyzed from the point of view of suitability and adequacy to the sectoral conditions and the perceive traits of the generic organizational culture in the field of production engineering. The result is a vision for AI development that serves manufacturing companies and correctly aligned with the needs and characteristics of most firms in the area (Fig. 2), structured on 3 layers of interest with specific features assigned to each.

In the following step (Fig. 3), the same expert group, this time with the assistance of the authors has performed a process of backcasting, trying to identify the most important contributions that AI tools which are most popular and promising at the moment can have towards achieving the stated vision. These categories include large language models (like OpenAI ChatGPT, Google Gemini and Microsoft Copilot), generative AI art tools (like OpenAI DALL-E, Google Imagen and Microsoft Designer's Image Creator), AI intelligence suites (like Microsoft Power BI and Google Data Studio) and AI perception instruments (usually specific tools developed based on OpenCV, TensorFlow or Microsoft Azure). For each of them, the most important characteristics needed to contribute to AI alignment along the project path have been retained.

Next, the group of experts was guided by the research team to define three possible scenarios in which a manufacturing company, active in the production sector, could follow the formulated vision, while incorporating the desire AI systems and tools mentioned. For each of the scenarios, the road map states the objective or outcome defined by the experts as a materialization of the vision, a list of key activities, a list of the main stakeholders needed to be involved in the scenario implementation,

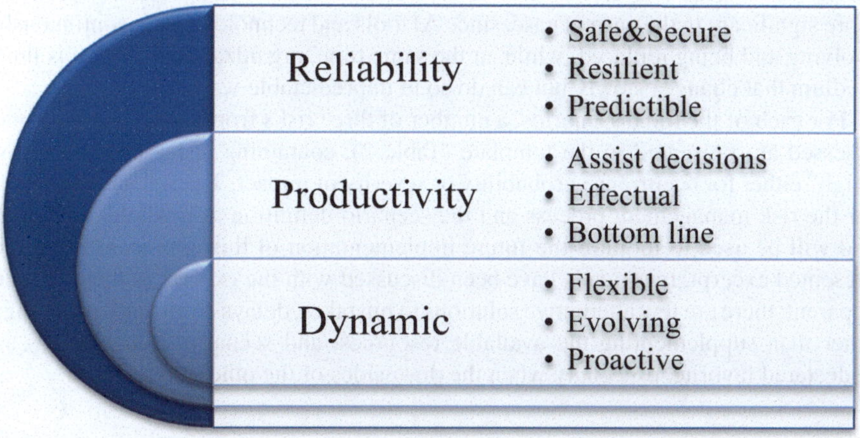

Fig. 2 Vision generated by experts for AI alignment

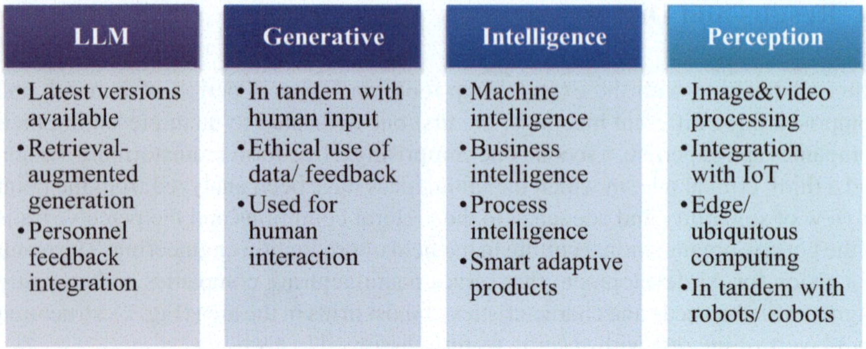

Fig. 3 Backasting AI categories and characteristics

as well as an analysis of the advantages and drawbacks that can be detected. The scenarios cover the "store type solution" that relies on off-the shelf bought tools and is fast and potentially cheap (but not very effective), the "get help" scenario that is based on subcontracting which makes it very fast and potentially expensive (with a varying degree of success), and the "my way" scenario which seeks to develop in-house capabilities at moderate costs, but will take long and will be potentially the most effective in AI alignment to the organizational culture. The pathways are not mutually exclusive, but commitment to one of them in the early phase will make it difficult to switch directions along the way. Moreover, since they actually describe design, development and implementation projects, these routes must be carefully administered through proper budgets, schedules and personnel assignments, which can be complex in their own ways (Table 1).

When deploying any of the scenarios within a production company, it is important to carry out a thorough process of risk assessment, to prevent the appearance of factors and events that can disturb the achievement of the set goals. This is even more significant in the current case, since AI tools and technologies are continuously evolving and being replaced, while, at the same time, organizational culture is fluid medium that changes slowly but can do so in unpredictable ways.

For each of the three scenarios, a number of three risks from those identified and assessed are presented in the template (Table 2), containing at least one score of "high" either for occurrence probability or severity of impact. The full analysis, both for the risk management process and the scenario definition as a whole, are larger and will be used to monitor the future implementation of this approach. From the presented excerpt, two trends have been discussed with the experts as they became apparent: there are few alternative solutions to mistakes, delays or misunderstandings other than supplementing the available resources, and scenario 2 emerged as an undeclared favorite, especially when the downsides of the other too are clear.

Table 1 Scenarios for AI deployment

	Scenario 1 "store type"	Scenario 2 "get help"	Scenario 3 "my way"
Objective	Use off-the shelf AI solutions	Employ/subcontract to specialized companies	Develop in-house expertise for AI customization
Key activities	Identification and testing of tools Trial-and-error runs Assembly of solutions	Contracting experts for design Contracting specialized companies for development Delivery and commissioning	Selection and upskilling of personnel Elaborating policy, project and budgeting Developing and implementing sequentially or in parallel
Main stake-holders	Company Customers Authorities	Company Customers Authorities Subcontractors Facilitators	Company Customers Authorities Training providers Research partners
Advantages	Fast implementation and minimal costs	Very fast implementation, high to very high costs	Slow implementation, average costs
Drawbacks	Alignment to organizational culture will be minimal	Alignment to organizational culture dependent on the understanding of the providers	Full alignment and compliance to organizational culture

Table 2 Risk assessment examples

	Scenario 1 "store type"	Scenario 2 "get help"	Scenario 3 "my way"
Risk	No suitable tool(s) found	Project too complex	Project taking too long
Occurrence	*High*	*Average*	*High*
Severity	*Very high*	*High*	*High*
Mitigation	(Partial) go to scenario 2	Find more exp. provider	(Partial) go to scenario 2
Risk	Insufficient tech support	Misunderstand culture	Personnel churning
Occurrence	*High*	*Average*	*High*
Severity	*Average*	*Very high*	*Average*
Mitigation	Allocate more time/res	Allocate more time/res	Strong docum. requir
Risk	Assembly mismatching	Limited expandability	Final result not mature
Occurrence	*High*	*Average*	*Average*
Severity	*Very high*	*High*	*Very high*
Mitigation	Find alternative tools	Restart project anew	Allocate more time/res

5 Conclusions

In conclusion, the work necessary to align AI systems and corporate culture in manufacturing companies is both a difficult and prolonged one, and a rewarding experience that might significantly contribute to the success and competitiveness of the firms. The planning exercise undertaken in this chapter connects the most important points in defining this approach and arrives at a recommendation in the form of a roadmap of transformations and activities, structured on three alternatives depending on the targeted goal (production efficiency and bottom line, organizational agility and resilience or enhanced accountability and strengthened organizational culture). The implementation of these scenarios is highly dependent on context in which each company operates but following a predetermined path has the potential to shorten the time and diminish the effort necessary to arrive at a successful conclusion of the project. Following the proposed roadmap can lead to more robust and ethically based systems that contribute in a seamless manner to a successful company existence both in relation with its own employees and its interaction with the customers, the external stakeholders and the markets as a whole.

The future work to be accomplished in this direction by the authors includes the realization of a practical test within one of the companies that participated in the study and achieving the adaptation of general AI support systems in the area of Business intelligence and Quality 4.0/5.0 to the values exhibited within the company culture in relation to the customers and the markets. In this way, the limitations of the generic approach will become visible and will be removed, at least regarding some of the business functions.

References

Abulibdeh A, Zaidan E, Abulibdeh R (2024) Navigating the confluence of artificial intelligence and education for sustainable development in the era of industry 4.0: challenges, opportunities, and ethical dimensions. J Clean Prod 437:140527. https://doi.org/10.1016/j.jclepro.2023.140527

Brendel AB, Mirbabaie M, Lembcke T-B, Hofeditz L (2021) Ethical management of artificial intelligence. Sustainability 13:1974. https://doi.org/10.3390/su13041974

Chowdhury S, Budhwar P, Dey PK, Joel-Edga S, Abadie A (2022) AI-employee collaboration and business performance: Integrating knowledge-based view, socio-technical systems and organisational socialisation framework. J Bus Res 144:31–49. https://doi.org/10.1016/j.jbusres.2022.01.069

Dubey R, Bryde DJ, Dwivedi YK, Graham G, Foropon C (2022) Impact of artificial intelligence-driven big data analytics culture on agility and resilience in humanitarian supply chain: a practice-based view. Int J Prod Econ 250:108618. https://doi.org/10.1016/j.ijpe.2022.108618

Guler N, Kirshner SN (2024) A literature review of artificial intelligence research in business and management using machine learning and ChatGPT. Data Inf Manage 8:100076. https://doi.org/10.1016/j.dim.2024.100076

Isensee C, Griese K-M, Teuteberg F (2021) Sustainable artificial intelligence: a corporate culture perspective. Nachhaltigkeits Management Forum 29:217–230. https://doi.org/10.1007/s00550-021-00524-6

Li X, Rong K, Shi X (2023) Situating artificial intelligence in organization: a human-machine relationship perspective. J Digital Econ 2:330–335. https://doi.org/10.1016/j.jdec.2024.01.001

Loufek B, Vidal D, McClintock DS, Lifson M, Williamson E, Overgaard S, Pardi DS (2024) Embedding internal accountability into healthcare institutions for safe, effective, and ethical implementation of artificial intelligence into medical practice: a mayo clinic case study. Mayo Clinic Proc Dig Health. https://doi.org/10.1016/j.mcpdig.2024.08.008

Rajaram K, Tinguely PN (2024) Generative artificial intelligence in small and medium enterprises: navigating its promises and challenges. Bus Horiz 67:629–648. https://doi.org/10.1016/j.bushor.2024.05.008

Ray PP (2023) Benchmarking, ethical alignment, and evaluation framework for conversational AI: advancing responsible development of ChatGPT. BenchCouncil Trans Benchmarks, Stan Evaluations 3:100136. https://doi.org/10.1016/j.tbench.2023.100136

Tjebane MM, Musonda I, Okoro C (2022) Organisational factors of artificial intelligence adoption in the south african construction industry. Front Built Environ 8, 823998. https://doi.org/10.3389/fbuil.2022.823998

van de Poel I (2020) Embedding values in artificial intelligence (AI) systems. Mind Mach 30:385–409. https://doi.org/10.1007/s11023-020-09537-4

Artificial Intelligence (AI), Labor Relations and Human Resource Management

Filomena Almeida, Ana Junça-Silva, Sara L. Lopes, and Ricardo Lourenço-Silva

Abstract This chapter explores the evolution of human resource management (HRM), highlighting the shift from an administrative function to a strategic role driven by technology, culminating in algorithmic management. Algorithmic management, which uses algorithms and artificial intelligence (AI) for workforce-related decisions, offers advantages such as increased efficiency and data-driven decisions, but also presents significant challenges, including lack of transparency and dehumanization. The chapter addresses the ethical and legal issues associated with this practice, including algorithmic biases, privacy concerns, job security, and the impact on workplace relationships. Ultimately, algorithmic management has the potential to positively transform labor relations, provided it is implemented responsibly, with attention to equity, transparency, and respect for workers' rights.

Keywords AI · Algorithmic management · Human resource management · Artificial intelligence · Labor relations

1 Introduction

"Success in creating AI would be the biggest event in human history. Unfortunately, it might also be the last, unless we learn how to avoid the risks." Stephen Hawking.

Artificial intelligence (AI) has seen significant growth in recent years, yet there is still much to learn about its implications. Opinions on the use of AI in business settings are divided. Some argue in favor of AI, highlighting its potential benefits, while others express concerns about its impact. Calo (2015) warned that AI, particularly through machine learning, could displace millions of jobs, leading to a substantial increase in

F. Almeida (✉) · A. Junça-Silva · S. L. Lopes
Instituto Universitário de Lisboa (ISCTE-IUL) and Business Research Unit (BRU-IUL), Lisbon, Portugal
e-mail: filomena.almeida@iscte-iul.pt

R. Lourenço-Silva
Instituto Universitário de Lisboa (ISCTE-IUL) and ESPP, Lisbon, Portugal

C. Machado and J. P. Davim (eds.), *Challenges and Opportunities in the Artificial Intelligence Era*, https://doi.org/10.1007/978-3-031-85272-5_4

unemployment. Additionally, the adoption of AI without clear and transparent policies might shift the balance of power unfavorably for employees (Tong et al. 2021), fostering negative perceptions and resistance towards AI. Potential issues include workplace surveillance that could erode trust and create uncertainty (Junça-Silva and Caetano 2024), negatively impacting employee morale and motivation (Cheatham et al. 2019; Chamorro-Premuzic et al. 2018), and ultimately harming performance levels (Carpenter 2019; Teich 2020). These challenges necessitate changes in business and managerial policies, including overhauling infrastructure and procedures, ensuring transparent policymaking, and updating laws and regulations regarding AI in the workplace.

Conversely, other researchers and practitioners advocate for AI in business. Burgess (2017) suggested that AI enhances employee tasks by providing immediate and precise access to necessary knowledge and information, helping employees execute their duties more swiftly and reducing the time spent gathering and analyzing data. AI can also assist employees in navigating challenging scenarios by presenting alternative solutions (Jarrahi 2018), contributing to more reliable decision-making inputs, and improving performance and efficiency (Bader and Kaiser 2019).

This chapter aims to evaluate the usefulness of AI for employees and organizations by summarizing the main advantages and disadvantages and exploring how human resource management can enhance its application.

2 The Evolution of Human Resource Management

The major changes in the history of the organization of work are the result of human discoveries and inventions that directly affect ways of working: from the stone to the wheel, from the steam engine to oil and electricity and from the first computers to artificial intelligence. What marks our time is the speed of technological change, which makes the transition from "old jobs" to "new jobs" more complex and drastic.

The use of the expression "people management" has its origins on the nineteenth century, however, it was only at the beginning of the twentieth century that it became more functional and important for companies. It emerged on the need to control the workforce, and where human resources were viewed as a crucial component of an organization's ability to compete. People Management departments began to take on greater responsibility in the 1960s. Although they were still in charge of administrative matters, they also began to include, for the first time, the tasks of developing selection procedures, training programs, and reward systems. It also placed more of an emphasis on performance evaluation and workforce planning for the future. In the 1980s, because of several factors such as globalization and rapid technological advancements, companies required strategic planning, which is the act of anticipating future changes and aligning the organization's many components to maximize organizational performance and efficiency. Human Resource Management started to be recognized as an essential instrument for companies to attain their strategic goals. The twenty-first century has brought the establishment of Industry 4.0, side by side with the emergence of automation, AI and robotics. Organizations are now using algorithms to hire, train, and fire employees (Park et al. 2022).

There is no doubt that technology has helped to extend our lives, improve healthcare provision, make many forms of work more productive and less repetitive, enable us to communicate more quickly and cross geographical boundaries with an ease that in the past was totally unknown (and, unthinkable). AI develops its product based on computation through algorithms and mathematical models that are based on data and information from the past. In other words, the machine needs to understand the past and relate it in order to produce some kind of knowledge.

3 Algorithmic Management and AI: A Brave New World in Labor Relations?

Algorithmic management can be defined as the autonomous data-driven decision-making process in workforce management through the use of self-learning algorithms and artificial intelligence (Lee 2018). Thus, since AI's introduction into the workplace, algorithmic management has had a significant impact on labor relations, and it will undoubtedly have a significant impact on labor's future. Due to its disruptive capacity, algorithmic management has been taking the attention of managers and academics. The question that arises is whether algorithmic management will supplement or replace traditional managerial approaches.

Algorithmic management is changing workplace dynamics and connections among employees, supervisors, and algorithms (Jarrahi et al. 2021). Although algorithm-supported decisions are responsible to create new and previously non-available opportunities to work environments (Kinowska and Sienkiewicz 2023) there are some disadvantages that are worth to be mentioned and will be explored in the upcoming sections of this chapter.

Since the algorithm is capable of making decisions or giving answers based on artificial intelligence from a set of data supplied to it, a question is introduced into the system, to which, naturally, an answer is required, and the system will try to respond. However, before the algorithm is ready to help, it is taught/trained through a set of data provided to it, which will teach it how to answer the question. So, as a first and very important note, the nature of the data provided to the algorithm is crucial, as this will determine the quality of the answers. This means that an algorithm can fail and, consequently, artificial intelligence fails to—it's inevitable.

Concerning labor relations, the use of algorithms can assist human resource managers in a variety of settings, and although the criteria that are used seem neutral at first glance, they may not actually be. Indirect discrimination occurs when, even though the measure, criterion, or decision appears to be neutral from a discriminatory standpoint, it has a different impact on some social groups, categories, than on other workers or subjects who do not belong to those categories.

For instance, when attendance/absenteeism is taken as a selection criterion, it can lead to almost automatically discriminating against women, since tendentially women are absent the most, even for legitimate reasons, due to parental leave or other absences related to pregnancy or family responsibilities. Thus, when this criterion is used to evaluate a worker's performance, it may automatically create an unfavorable effect, particularly on women, which can be considered an indirectly discriminatory effect of the use of algorithmics. Notwithstanding, it is crucial to note that this could also happen if a human were to choose the employees based on the same criterion.

The power of algorithmic management is that not only can modify the dynamics at work but can also modify the organization's pre-existing social and power structures, having the potential to change the dynamic between supervisors and employees (Jarrahi et al. 2021). Thus, their use can impact real-life situations, and as a result, they guide people management towards a more automated and autonomous decision-making processes (Kinowska and Sienkiewicz 2023), which were formerly handled exclusively by managers.

4 Advantages of Algorithmic Management

Algorithms are utilized by employers as instruments in labor relations management.

And why are employers increasingly using these tools? It has been shown that they save time and, therefore, resources (Jarrahi et al. 2021; Cai et al. 2024). Managers may have more time and resources to devote to strategic endeavors by automating manual operations. When combined, these can improve organizational effectiveness. Organizations which don't incorporate AI and algorithmic management into their plan risk being left behind. Algorithms driven by AI are desirable for autonomous operation and continual improvement, since they can learn from their mistakes and successes without the need for human interaction (Parent-Rocheleau and Parker 2022).

More interesting, the use of algorithms is associated with a set of advantages linked to the suppression, elimination or non-existence of situations concerning human bias and unfairness, who often lead to discrimination. Managers and practitioners seem to agree that the use of AI and algorithms in HRM may eliminate almost entirely the issues presented in the traditional HRM (Park et al. 2022).

When a company decides to use AI, its employees expect it to be efficient, objective, and unbiased, especially when used for performance evaluations or selection processes. Literature shows us that employees also generally believe that AIs work evaluations are more accurate, impartial and fair, compared to human managers (Park et al. 2021). What are the possible reasons for this? AI-driven algorithms lack human-like judgment and are not impacted by unpleasant feelings or moods—which can affect selection processes, for instance. The use of algorithms avoids all this. Algorithms can therefore produce decisions that are more equitable.

The algorithm has the advantage of allowing the criteria used to be clearly identified. These criteria are translated into computer language, but before they are translated, they are identified. Managers must select the set of criteria and information that will be made available to the algorithm so that the system can then determine what a "good" worker is. This cannot be that evident when these decisions are made by individuals (with all their prejudices and experiences). Hence, there is a potential for greater neutrality and transparency in algorithms.

Another advantage of algorithmic management is its capability to provide personalized feedback. Providing transparency on performance measures enables employees to improve. Sharing information about one's own performance helps employees understand their competitive position compared to others. Providing feedback on task performance enables future learning and improvement (Schulze et al. 2023).

The capacity of artificial intelligence algorithms to automatically and quickly assess and process enormous amounts of diverse data regarding the actions, habits, or performance of employees is one of its main advantages of its use. Algorithmics can also be used to predict future employee performance based on a variety of data sources such as past performance, current and potential projects, and upcoming training opportunities (Parent-Rocheleau and Parker 2022).

5 Disadvantages of Algorithmic Management

When making the decision to replace human decision-making with AI, managers should proceed with caution. If on the one hand algorithms minimize the risk of discrimination, on the other hand they increase the discriminatory effect (Park et al. 2022).

When it comes to selecting or evaluating a worker, a job candidate, the questions are who is the best candidate? Who is the best worker? And what's this about being the best? Whether it's the best, what it means to be the best, depends on what the employer naturally understands, so it depends on the criteria, the factors that, from the employer's point of view, are going to be relevant to that judgment, factors that are going to be entered into the system so that it gives the desired answer. But here, there are often problems with this ideal construction of the "best" worker, which then has repercussions in the construction of the algorithm, there are problems, because if the employer notes that the "best" worker is the one who is most assiduous, this will generate discrimination based on gender, or based on illness or disability.

If the relevant criterion for choosing a "better" worker is one who has had previous long-term employment relationships, therefore a more credible, more reliable worker, which is measured by this criterion, previous long-term employment relationships, this will probably result in discrimination against younger people.

Why is this so? Because systematically, younger people are the ones who have the most precarious employment relationships. What if the "best" worker, or if a criterion for determining this is geographical proximity to the company, which happens to be in the city center? This, for example, will exclude people who live further away from urban centers and may tend to exclude people on the basis of race/ethnicity. There are plenty other examples, but these are sufficient to show that the criteria that the algorithm uses, and that it will use blindly because it is an algorithm, can in fact have this impact of excluding some social categories.

The application of algorithmic management presents a complex landscape, offering both potential benefits and significant challenges (Kinowska and Sienkiewicz 2023). Algorithmic management has been found to produce predominantly negative outcomes for workers. Specifically, it tends to reduce worker autonomy and increase surveillance, which in turn lowers job satisfaction and erodes trust in the workplace (Parent-Rocheleau and Parker 2022; Kinowska and Sienkiewicz 2023).

Technological revolutions, such as the rise of algorithmic management, have a profound impact on labor markets, often sparking concerns about future employment trends. Historical and contemporary analyses suggest that the automation of processes and the integration of AI could lead to significant job displacement. For instance, Calo (2015) suggests that algorithmic management and other AI tools may displace millions of jobs, potentially driving up unemployment rates and necessitating substantial changes in infrastructure, laws, and regulations. Supporting this, numerous studies have indicated that new technologies and production automation could lead to a significant reduction in job availability, with certain roles or entire job categories at risk of being entirely phased out (Jago 2019). In response to these concerns, it is imperative for organizations to integrate AI into their operations to avoid becoming obsolete—a failure to adapt could result in being replaced by more innovative competitors.

One of the critical issues with algorithmic management is its impersonal nature, which often fails to consider the nuanced human factors crucial to effective management (Jarrahi et al. 2021). This lack of empathy and understanding can exacerbate workplace tensions and conflicts, with some scholars suggesting that the traditional "tyranny of the clock" has been replaced by the "tyranny of the algorithm" (Lehdonvirta 2018). Duggan et al. (2020) further argue that algorithmic management, by automating the monitoring, disciplining, and expectation-setting of workers, removes the interpersonal and empathetic elements of management, potentially leading to a more stressful work environment.

The reliance on algorithms can also result in biased or unfair outcomes if the data or algorithms themselves are flawed. Park et al. (2021) identified several burdens associated with the increased use of algorithms and AI in human resource management (HRM), including emotional, mental, and social burdens, as well as issues of bias and manipulation, all of which can negatively impact workplace well-being.

Moreover, the implementation of algorithmic management systems requires substantial upfront investment in technology and training. There is often resistance from employees who are apprehensive about new technologies or fear job displacement (Benlian et al. 2022). The depersonalization of management and the potential reinforcement of existing biases in decision-making processes are additional concerns (Veen et al. 2020). While algorithms are often perceived as objective, they can become "black boxes," obscuring the decision-making process and exacerbating power imbalances between management and workers. Although algorithms might reduce certain forms of discrimination, they can simultaneously introduce new biases depending on the criteria programmed into them (Benlian et al. 2022).

For instance, in hiring processes, defining the "best" candidate based on employer-driven criteria can lead to unintended discrimination. If reliability is a key criterion, this could disadvantage individuals based on gender, health, or disability. Similarly, if proximity to the workplace is a criterion, it could disproportionately exclude candidates from different racial or ethnic backgrounds, particularly those living outside urban centers. This contributes to perceptions that technological agents lack the moral authenticity of human agents (Jago 2019), and can leave workers feeling powerless in the face of such systems (Sutherland and Jarrahi 2018). Consequently, algorithmic management can lead to increased feelings of injustice and reduced job autonomy, creating a pressurized work environment that diminishes employee well-being (Duggan et al. 2020; Wood et al. 2019).

These challenges underscore the need for careful consideration and balanced implementation of algorithmic management systems. To design fair AI programs to be used in human resource management is the real challenge. For instance, companies should make the data the system uses to filter resumes and the screening process accessible for the candidates, in order to reduce the negative impacts of algorithmic unfairness (Cai and Wang 2024). To maximize their benefits while minimizing their drawbacks, it is crucial to integrate human oversight, ensure transparency, and actively work to mitigate potential biases (Parent-Rocheleau and Parker 2022).

6 Ethical-Legal Issues

In addition to the disadvantages, the use of AI tools, such as algorithmic management, presents a set of challenges related to ethical and legal aspects.

6.1 Discriminatory Nature of Algorithms and Their Potential Biases

AI undeniably holds enormous potential and offers unique added value, but it can also be misused for malicious purposes, such as creating deepfake videos or spreading false news (Lehdonvirta 2018). Additionally, concerns persist regarding AI 's potential biases and the manipulation or discriminatory nature of algorithms (Park et al. 2021). As noted earlier, algorithms can perpetuate and even amplify existing biases present in the data they are trained on, leading to discriminatory practices in hiring, promotions, performance evaluations, and other HR decisions. This disproportionately affects minorities, women, and other marginalized groups (Kinowska and Sienkiewicz 2023).

Indeed, in the context of algorithms, discrimination is often indirect (Kinowska and Sienkiewicz 2023). This form of discrimination targets specific social categories—such as gender, disability status, or religious affiliation—by creating disparities between individuals within these categories and those outside them. Essentially, indirect discrimination arises when algorithms produce outcomes that disproportionately disadvantage certain groups compared to others who do not belong to these categories. This can manifest through biased decision-making processes that perpetuate inequalities even when no explicit discriminatory intent is present (Wood et al. 2019). For instance, the data used to train algorithms for future decision-making may itself be inherently biased, perpetuating discriminatory practices. For example, consider an algorithm designed to identify the "best" workers based on evaluations provided by previous employers. These assessments, which are sometimes available on sophisticated platforms like LinkedIn, may reflect the biases of those previous employers. If these evaluations are biased—whether on the basis of gender, age, or other factors—then the data used to train the algorithm is already tainted. As a result, the algorithm may continue to propagate these biases in its future selections, leading to a cycle of ongoing discrimination.

Another significant issue arises from the representativeness of the sample data used to train algorithms. A notable example is Amazon's case, where the algorithm's training data consisted predominantly of male resumes, leading the system to favor male candidates exclusively. This illustrates a clear representativeness problem in the sample data provided to the algorithm.

Facial recognition systems present additional challenges. These systems often monitor job candidates or workers' facial expressions and mannerisms to draw conclusions. However, they may struggle with accuracy, particularly when recognizing atypical or non-standard facial features. For instance, individuals with facial anomalies or those from diverse ethnic backgrounds may not be accurately recognized if the system was primarily trained on a narrow range of typical facial characteristics. This limitation can lead to misidentification and flawed evaluations.

Moreover, there is a risk of deliberate discrimination through algorithms. If the individuals who design or control these algorithms are aware of their limitations, they could intentionally introduce biases into the training data or criteria. This results in covert discrimination that appears to be algorithmic rather than human. When algorithms are fed biased data or discriminatory criteria, the discrimination is hidden behind the algorithm's ostensibly neutral binary processes, making it harder to detect and address.

Additionally, there are compliance issues with the General Data Protection Regulation (GDPR). These regulations stipulate that individuals have the right not to be subject to decisions based solely on automated processing, including profiling, that significantly impacts their legal rights. If a worker is selected or evaluated solely through algorithmic tools, it raises concerns about GDPR compatibility, as such practices may infringe on the individual's rights under these regulations. Human oversight is essential; not only should there be a mechanism for human intervention in the evaluation process, but workers and job candidates should also have the opportunity to contest and appeal algorithmic decisions. This human oversight should involve active monitoring during the selection or evaluation process to ensure that potential biases are identified and addressed, thereby preventing unfair discrimination and safeguarding the integrity of the evaluation process.

Furthermore, a broad spectrum of entities, including governments, the International Labour Organization (ILO), and the Organization for Economic Co-operation and Development (OECD), are actively addressing the challenges associated with algorithmic discrimination. While comprehensive legislative frameworks to address these issues are still in development, some fundamental principles—such as non-discrimination and the GDPR—are already established.

Current recommendations focus on best practices to mitigate algorithmic risks, though these guidelines are not legally binding. Among these practices is the promotion of diversity within algorithm design teams. Incorporating a range of perspectives—such as those of different genders, religious and ethnic backgrounds, and age groups—can help reduce biases and enhance the sensitivity of algorithms to various social contexts. Research supports the idea that diverse teams are more effective in identifying and addressing potential biases than homogenous ones.

Additionally, the implementation of tools to detect and correct discriminatory effects in algorithms is recommended. Although translating concepts of justice and fairness into computational terms presents challenges, having mechanisms to identify and address biases is a crucial first step. Pre-market testing of algorithms by impartial, external auditors is also suggested to ensure their fairness and accuracy.

6.2 Transparency and Accountability of Algorithmic Processes

Another significant ethical and legal issue is the transparency and accountability of algorithmic processes. The decision-making mechanisms of algorithms are often opaque—a phenomenon known as algorithmic opacity—making it difficult for employees to understand how decisions are made. This "black box" nature of algorithms can lead to a lack of accountability when errors or biases occur (Duggan et al. 2020).

Workers frequently struggle to grasp the inner workings of algorithms, as algorithmic management is typically less transparent than its non-algorithmic counterpart (Kellogg et al. 2019; Möhlmann et al. 2021). Machine-learning algorithms are highly complex and constantly evolve based on real-time data inputs.

Moreover, many organizations are reluctant to disclose detailed information about their algorithms, which limits transparency and enables hidden nudging, intentional manipulation, and surveillance, while providing little opportunity to detect algorithmic bias. Indeed, when organizations use AI tools without clear communication, it might prompt a backlash from staff, who could see it negatively due to potential issues like surveillance in the workplace, which risks eroding trust, and lowering motivation and work engagement (Chamorro-Premuzic et al. 2018). This, in turn, can negatively affect employee performance indicators and in the long run organizational sustainability (Carpenter 2019; Teich 2020).

This opacity also raises concerns related to consent and informed choice, leading to frustration among workers. It creates uncertainty about their financial compensation, job assignments, and the accuracy and fairness of the algorithmic instructions they receive (Gal et al 2020; Jarrahi et al. 2021). Employees may not always be fully informed about the extent and nature of algorithmic monitoring and decision-making. This lack of informed consent raises ethical issues regarding the manipulation and control of workers.

To address these concerns and design algorithmic management more ethically, organizations should be more transparent about their data collection and storage practices (Kellogg et al. 2019; Lee et al. 2015), adhering to standards such as the GDPR (General Data Protection Regulation of the European Union). Manyika et al. emphasized that organizations before adopting AI tools must define clear and transparent policies because the absence of clear policies can be a disadvantage to employees in terms of power dynamics, as it can lead them to create negative perceptions about AI tools (Cheatham et al. 2019; Lee et al. 2015). Furthermore, organizations and managers should also explain the algorithm's logic to their workers (Möhlmann et al. 2021). One potential approach is to provide counterfactual explanations, revealing what the outcome of an algorithmic decision would have been if workers had different attributes or characteristics. This could be a crucial step toward increasing transparency in algorithmic management.

6.3 *Privacy, Surveillance, Autonomy and Control Issues*

Algorithmic management often involves extensive monitoring of employee behavior, raising significant privacy concerns and leading to dissatisfaction and decreased motivation at work (Parent-Rocheleau and Parker 2022). Continuous tracking can foster a surveillance culture, eroding trust between employees and management and threatening the positive relationship and exchange between employees and the organization.

Additionally, the use of algorithms can diminish employee autonomy by dictating tasks and closely monitoring performance. This loss of control over one's work can negatively impact job satisfaction and mental health (Sutherland and Jarrahi 2018).

Combined with the challenge of algorithmic nudging, these factors pose a threat to employees' trust and well-being. Algorithmic nudging, a fundamental aspect of algorithmic management practices, involves subtly influencing and guiding workers' behaviors based on insights from their personalized data (Möhlmann et al. 2021). For instance, organizations increasingly use gamification and push notifications to steer workers into behaviors that benefit the company, though these may be less advantageous for the workers themselves (Möhlmann et al. 2021).

However, algorithmic nudging can be designed ethically to enhance workers' well-being. Thaler and Sunstein (2008) have demonstrated that nudging can help individuals improve their health, wealth, and happiness. Examples of ethical algorithmic nudging include its application in healthcare and efforts to promote healthier eating habits (Thaler and Sunstein 2008). Other potential uses include personalized reminders that encourage climate-friendly behaviors or suggest taking breaks after extended work periods.

6.4 *Fairness and Equity*

Algorithms can facilitate efficient, optimized, and data-driven decision-making, which is a key reason for their growing adoption in managerial and organizational contexts (Lee 2018; Lee et al. 2015). However, algorithms often lack the capacity to account for individual circumstances and contextual nuances that human managers might naturally consider, potentially leading to decisions perceived as unfair or overly rigid by employees. Unlike human decision-makers, who can exercise discretion and empathy, algorithms operate based on predefined criteria and data inputs, which may not capture the full complexity of a situation. Indeed, the fact that these decisions are made by algorithms rather than by humans can shape how they are perceived, regardless of the actual quality of the outcomes (Sundar and Nass 2001). These perceptions, in turn, can significantly impact people's trust in and attitudes toward algorithmic decisions—factors that are crucial for the well-being and cohesion of workplaces. For instance, research indicated that when organizational and managerial decisions are viewed as unfair, affected employees often feel resentment and anger, which can lead to retaliatory actions against the organization (Skarlicki and Folger 1997).

For instance, algorithms might be designed to enforce strict attendance policies, automatically penalizing employees for tardiness or absenteeism without considering the reasons behind these occurrences, such as personal emergencies, health issues, or caregiving responsibilities. A human manager, on the other hand, might take these factors into account, offering flexibility or support that aligns with the employee's needs and the organization's values. The inability of algorithms to adapt to these nuances can lead to a perception of unfairness and a lack of trust in the system.

This rigidity is particularly concerning in contexts where human judgment is crucial. For example, performance evaluations conducted by algorithms might fail to recognize the unique contributions of an employee that do not fit neatly into quantifiable metrics. An employee who brings creativity, mentorship, or teamwork to the workplace might be undervalued by an algorithm focused solely on measurable outputs. This could not only demotivate employees but also stifle innovation and collaboration within the organization.

Moreover, the reliance on algorithmic decision-making can exacerbate feelings of alienation among employees, as the impersonal nature of these systems can make workers feel like mere data points rather than valued members of a team. This disconnect can lead to reduced job satisfaction, lower engagement, and higher turnover rates, as employees seek workplaces where their individuality and circumstances are recognized and respected (Park et al. 2021).

Research has shown that fairness perceptions are crucial to employee morale and productivity; when employees perceive that decisions are made fairly and with consideration for their personal situations, they are more likely to be engaged and committed to their work (Colquitt et al. 2001). Therefore, the potential for algorithmic management systems to overlook these critical aspects underscores the importance of integrating human oversight into these processes.

In addition, the lack of flexibility in algorithmic systems may also have broader implications for organizational culture. Organizations that rely heavily on rigid, algorithm-driven management practices may inadvertently cultivate a culture of strict adherence to rules at the expense of empathy, creativity, and innovation (Parent-Rocheleau and Parker 2022). This can be particularly problematic in industries where adaptability and human-centric approaches are essential to success.

To mitigate these risks, it is essential to design algorithmic management systems that are not only data-driven but also incorporate mechanisms for human intervention. This could involve setting up protocols for human review of algorithmic decisions, especially in cases where personal circumstances or unique contributions might play a significant role. Furthermore, algorithms should be designed with a degree of flexibility, allowing for adjustments based on contextual factors and the specific needs of individual employees.

Thus, while algorithms can bring efficiency and consistency to management practices, they must be carefully designed and implemented to ensure they do not inadvertently lead to unfair or rigid decision-making. Integrating human oversight and maintaining flexibility within these systems is critical to preserving fairness, fostering a positive organizational culture, and ultimately achieving better outcomes for both employees and the organization.

6.5 Job Security and Employment Practices

The implementation of algorithmic management poses substantial risks of job displacement and increased job insecurity. As algorithms assume a growing number of tasks traditionally performed by humans, there is a significant risk of workforce reduction, leading to direct impacts on livelihoods and the potential exacerbation of economic instability. Reilly (2018) underscored that while AI can offer notable benefits for business operations—such as enhanced efficiency and more informed decision-making—it also introduces serious challenges (Lee 2018). These challenges include the risk of replacing human employees with machines, which can diminish the perceived value of human labor, reduce job satisfaction, and create a disconnect between employees and their roles (Jago 2019). The inherent complexity and opacity of algorithmic systems further compound these issues, as they often obscure the decision-making process, making it difficult for workers to understand or challenge the decisions that affect their employment (Duggan et al. 2020).

In addition to the immediate threat of job loss, algorithmic management has broader implications for organizational culture and employee well-being (Kinowska and Sienkiewicz 2023). As algorithms take on a more central role in decision-making, the human elements of work—such as creativity, collaboration, and emotional intelligence—may be undervalued or neglected. This shift can foster a work environment where employees feel increasingly dehumanized, potentially leading to reduced engagement, lower productivity, and a decline in overall workplace morale (Benlian et al. 2022).

To address these risks, it is essential for organizations to pursue a balanced approach to integrating AI, one that seeks to complement human labor rather than replace it. This approach should include comprehensive reskilling and upskilling initiatives to facilitate the transition of workers into new roles. Additionally, organizations should implement policies that ensure human oversight in algorithmic decision-making processes, with a strong emphasis on ethical considerations to safeguard against potential negative outcomes (Meijerink and Bondarouk 2023; Meijerink et al. 2019).

6.6 Moral and Ethical Judgments

Algorithms lack the ability to make moral and ethical judgments. This can be problematic in situations that require empathy, understanding, and ethical considerations beyond pure data analysis. For instance, in fields such as communication and marketing, AI presents significant opportunities, but it also poses risks of misuse. For example, AI can be exploited to create decontextualized or even false content, as illustrated by the recent and controversial case of an AI-generated "interview" with Michael Schumacher for a magazine. There are other examples of unethical uses of technology, with some of the most alarming being autonomous drones capable of killing individuals. It is crucial to recognize that the increasing misuse of technology is closely tied to its growing autonomy, which magnifies the ethical challenges associated with its use. This raises the idea that machines themselves should also help prevent unethical human actions. For example, if someone instructs a program to harm humans, the program should have the capacity to refuse such instructions.

6.7 Impact on Workplace Relationships

The impersonal nature of algorithmic management can undermine human relationships in the workplace (Möhlmann et al. 2021). The reliance on data and the reduction of interpersonal interactions can weaken team dynamics, foster interpersonal conflicts, and diminish the sense of community (Benlian et al. 2022). This lack of human connection presents a significant challenge for human resources managers.

In algorithmic management, traditional manager-employee interactions are largely automated, leading workers to feel isolated, lonely, and even dehumanized. Without supervisors or team members to socialize with, workers may experience a lack of community and an increased sense of loneliness, which can decrease their organizational identification and commitment. Social relationships are crucial for many workers' well-being, motivation, work engagement, and even retention.

To address this challenge, organizations can foster a sense of community that allows employees to interact with co-workers, even within the context of algorithmic management (Möhlmann et al. 2021). For example, organizing weekly face-to-face meetings or informal gatherings can promote interpersonal contact, providing opportunities for socialization and regular interaction with supervisors and colleagues (Benlian et al. 2022). It is important to recognize that human supervisors or team members are not always superior to machines, as humans are imperfect and can be prone to biases (Meijerink and Bondarouk 2023). Some workers may even prefer working in solitude. Regardless of individual preferences, organizations should prioritize efforts to improve employees' well-being.

6.8 Legal and Regulatory Challenges

The rapid advancement of algorithmic management technologies often outpaces the development of legal and regulatory frameworks, leading to a significant legal and ethical gray area. This disparity creates an environment where practices that may be unethical or unfair can emerge and persist without adequate oversight or regulation, primarily due to the absence of specific legal provisions. As these technologies evolve at a pace that regulators struggle to match, there is a risk that companies might exploit these gaps, either deliberately or inadvertently, resulting in potential violations of workers' rights and the erosion of established labor standards.

This regulatory lag can lead to inconsistent enforcement of existing laws and a lack of accountability for organizations deploying algorithmic management systems. The absence of clear regulations increases the likelihood that these technologies could perpetuate or even exacerbate existing workplace inequalities and biases. For example, algorithms used in processes such as hiring, task assignment, and performance evaluation may unintentionally reinforce discriminatory practices related to race, gender, age, or other protected characteristics if they are not meticulously designed and continuously monitored. Without robust regulatory oversight, workers affected by these algorithmic decisions may find themselves with limited avenues for redress or contestation.

To mitigate these risks, it is imperative for policymakers to develop and implement comprehensive legal and regulatory frameworks that can keep pace with technological advancements. These frameworks should ensure that algorithmic management systems are transparent, equitable, and accountable, with clear guidelines on the ethical deployment of AI in workplace settings. Regulatory bodies should also establish mechanisms for the regular review and updating of these frameworks to accommodate the continuous evolution of technology. Moreover, given the global nature of many businesses and the technologies they utilize, international cooperation may be necessary to harmonize regulations across jurisdictions, ensuring a consistent and fair approach to algorithmic management worldwide.

In conclusion, the swift development of algorithmic management technologies underscores the critical need for legal and regulatory systems to evolve in parallel. Without adequate regulation, the likelihood of unethical practices and the exacerbation of workplace inequalities will likely increase, highlighting the urgent need for effective legal responses to ensure that technological progress is aligned with ethical standards and serves the interests of all stakeholders.

7 Final Conclusions

While the displacement of certain jobs due to technological advancements is an undeniable reality, a forward-looking perspective suggests that the overall impact may be beneficial. Historical evidence shows that technological progress has consistently driven increases in productivity, competitiveness, and consumer choice, while also generating new opportunities—some of which were once considered science fiction (e.g., Benlian et al. 2022; Duggan et al. 2020).

Despite the inherent risks and challenges, it is crucial for organizations to navigate these changes proactively rather than succumbing to populist fears. The skepticism some institutions exhibit toward the rapid growth of AI is reminiscent of past resistance to transformative technologies like electricity and the internet. Although AI will render some jobs obsolete, it will simultaneously create new roles with greater value and potential.

The "it has always been this way" mentality is no longer adequate for managing our company in today's rapidly evolving environment. Although this approach may have been effective in the past, it is unsustainable in the face of contemporary challenges. Management and work models must adapt and become more sophisticated to address the demands of the modern business landscape. While it is prudent to remain cautious about long-term outcomes, we are confident that technology will present more opportunities than challenges. When effectively monitored and controlled, the current technological revolution need not be feared. AI's ability to streamline and accelerate processes will be instrumental in liberating us from repetitive, monotonous tasks with minimal added value.

To ensure that this transition is beneficial, it is imperative to establish robust regulatory frameworks and ethical standards. AI systems must be developed and governed with a focus on ethical considerations, addressing concerns such as privacy, security, and accountability. By implementing appropriate regulations and ethical guidelines, we can harness the full potential of AI while mitigating its risks, ensuring that technological advancements lead to positive outcomes for society. Plus, emphasizing human strengths that go beyond AI capabilities—such as understanding emotional contexts, cultural nuances, technical expertise, and emotional sensitivity—will be crucial. In the ongoing debate about whether AI will replace or complement humans, we agree with Elon Musk's view that the key is "symbiosis."

Moreover, addressing the ethical and legal implications of AI is critical. For a truly symbiotic workforce, companies must implement human-centered processes that enable the retraining and upskilling of employees to meet the challenges of the technological era. It is essential to recognize that biases inherent in the data used to train algorithms can perpetuate discrimination. Ensuring that these biases are addressed is a fundamental step toward achieving a fair and inclusive technological integration.

The adoption of algorithmic management presents a complex challenge for businesses, necessitating a careful balance between harnessing its benefits and mitigating potential drawbacks, particularly regarding ethical concerns. Effectively addressing these ethical challenges requires a comprehensive strategy that includes the development of transparent and explainable algorithms, the implementation of fair and responsible data practices, the integration of ethical guidelines into AI system design, and the establishment of robust regulatory frameworks to protect workers' rights.

In summary, while AI will inevitably reshape the labor market, the focus should be on adapting to and leveraging this technology to complement human skills. This approach will help establish a balanced and productive symbiosis between humans and machines.

References

Bader V, Kaiser S (2019) Algorithmic decision-making? The user interface and its role for human involvement in decisions supported by artificial intelligence. Organization 26(5):655–672

Benlian A, Wiener M, Cram WA, Krasnova H, Maedche A, Möhlmann M, Recker J, Remus U (2022) Algorithmic management: bright and dark sides, practical implications, and research opportunities. Bus Inf Syst Eng 64(6):825–839

Burgess A (2017) The executive guide to artificial intelligence: how to identify and implement applications for AI in your organization. Springer

Cai F, Zhang J, Zhang L (2024) The impact of artificial intelligence replacing humans in making human resource management decisions on fairness: a case of resume screening. Sustainability 16(9):3840. https://doi.org/10.3390/su16093840

Cai Y, Wang C (2024) Effect of transparency of algorithmic performance management on proactive work behavior. Int J Asian Bus Inf Manag 15:1–17. https://doi.org/10.4018/IJABIM.348062

Calo R (2015) Robotics and the lessons of cyberlaw. Calif Law Rev, 513–563

Carpenter C (2019) Artificial intelligence improves seismic-image reconstruction. J Petrol Technol 71(10):65–66

Chamorro-Premuzic T, Wade M, Jordan J (2018) As AI makes more decisions, the nature of leadership will change. Harv Bus Rev 1:2–7

Cheatham B, Javanmardian K, Samandari H (2019) Confronting the risks of artificial intelligence. McKinsey Quarterly 2(38):1–9

Colquitt JA, Conlon DE, Wesson MJ, Porter COLH, Ng KY (2001) Justice at the millennium: a meta-analytic review of 25 years of organizational justice research. J Appl Psychol 86(3):425–445. https://doi.org/10.1037/0021-9010.86.3.425

Duggan J, Sherman U, Carbery R, McDonnell A (2020) Algorithmic management and app-work in the gig economy: a research agenda for employment relations and HRM. Hum Resour Manag J 30(1):114–132. https://doi.org/10.1111/1748-8583.12258

Gal U, Jensen TB, Stein M-K (2020) Breaking the vicious cycle of algorithmic management: a virtue ethics approach to people analytics. Inf Organ 30(2):100301. https://doi.org/10.1016/j.infoandorg.2020.100301

Jago AS (2019) Algorithms and authenticity. Acad Manag Discov 5(1):38–56. https://doi.org/10.5465/amd.2017.0002

Jarrahi MH (2018) Artificial intelligence and the future of work: Human-AI symbiosis in organizational decision making. Bus Horiz 61(4):577–586

Jarrahi MH, Newlands G, Lee MK, Wolf CT, Kinder E, Sutherland W (2021) Algorithmic management in a work context. Big Data Soc 8(2):20539517211020332

Junça-Silva A, Caetano A (2024) Uncertainty's impact on adaptive performance in the post-COVID era: the moderating role of perceived leader's effectiveness. BRQ Bus Res Q 27(1):40–56

Kellogg K, Valentine M, Christin A (2019) Algorithms at work: the new contested terrain of control. Acad Manag Ann 14:0174. https://doi.org/10.5465/annals.2018.0174

Kinowska H, Sienkiewicz ŁJ (2023) Influence of algorithmic management practices on workplace well-being–evidence from European organisations. Inf Technol People 36(8):21–42

Lee MK (2018) Understanding perception of algorithmic decisions: fairness, trust, and emotion in response to algorithmic management. Big Data Soc 5(1):2053951718756684

Lee MK, Kusbit D, Metsky E, Dabbish L (2015) Working with machines: the impact of algorithmic and data-driven management on human workers. In: Proceedings of the 33rd annual ACM conference on human factors in computing systems (CHI), pp 1603–1612. https://doi.org/10.1145/2702123.2702548

Lehdonvirta V (2018) Flexibility in the gig economy: managing time on three online piecework platforms. N Technol Work Employ 33(1):13–29. https://doi.org/10.1111/ntwe.12102

Meijerink J, Mischke J, Bughin J, Woetzel J, Krishnan M, Cudre S (2019) A new look at the declining labor share of income in the United States. McKinsey Global Institute Discussion Paper, 1–64

Meijerink J, Bondarouk T (2023) The duality of algorithmic management: toward a research agenda on HRM algorithms, autonomy and value creation. Hum Resour Manag Rev 33(1):100876

Möhlmann M, Zalmanson L, Henfridsson O, Gregory R (2021) Algorithmic management of work on online labor platforms: when matching meets control. MIS Quarterly. https://doi.org/10.25300/MISQ/2021/15333

Parent-Rocheleau X, Parker SK (2022) Algorithms as work designers: how algorithmic management influences the design of jobs. Hum Resour Manag Rev 32:100838. https://doi.org/10.1016/j.hrmr.2021.100838

Park H, Ahn D, Hosanagar K, Lee J (2021) Human-AI interaction in human resource management: understanding why employees resist algorithmic evaluation at workplaces and how to mitigate burdens. In: CHI'21: Proceedings of the 2021 CHI conference on human factors in computing systems, Article No: 154, pp 1–15. https://doi.org/10.1145/3411764.3445304

Park H, Ahn D, Hosanagar K, Lee J (2022) Designing Fair AI in Human resource management: understanding tensions surrounding algorithmic evaluation and envisioning stakeholder-centered solutions. In: Proceedings of the 2022 CHI conference on human factors in computing systems

Reilly P (2018) The impact of artificial intelligence on the HR function. HR papers. IES Institute for Employment Studies

Schulze L, Trenz M, Cai Z, Tan C-W (2023) Fairness in algorithmic management: how practices promote fairness and redress unfairness on digital labor platforms. In: Bui TX (ed) Proceedings of the 56th Hawaii international conference on system sciences. Hawaii International Conference on System Sciences (HICSS), pp 196–205

Skarlicki DP, Folger R (1997) Retaliation in the workplace: the roles of distributive, procedural, and interactional justice. J Appl Psychol 82(3):434

Sundar S, Nass C (2001) Conceptualizing sources in online news. J Commun 51(1):52–72

Sutherland W, Jarrahi MH (2018) The sharing economy and digital platforms: a review and research agenda. Int J Inf Manage 43:328–341. https://doi.org/10.1016/j.ijinfomgt.2018.07.004

Teich I (2020) Meilensteine der Entwicklung Künstlicher Intelligenz. Informatik Spektrum 43(4):276–284

Thaler RH, Sunstein CR (2008) Nudge: improving decisions about health, wealth, and happiness. Yale University Press

Tong APS, Vaz AP, Wittig JH, Inati SK, Zaghloul KA (2021) Ripples reflect a spectrum of synchronous spiking activity in human anterior temporal lobe. elife 10.

Veen A, Barratt T, Goods C (2020) Platform-Capital's "appetite" for control: a labour process analysis of food-delivery work in Australia. Work Employ Soc 34(3):388–406. https://doi.org/10.1177/0950017019836911

Wood AJ, Graham M, Lehdonvirta V, Hjorth I (2019) Good gig, bad gig: autonomy and algorithmic control in the global gig economy. Work Employ Soc 33(1):56–75. https://doi.org/10.1177/0950017018785616

Harmony in the Workplace: Human-Robot Collaboration and Tuning Employees' Perceptions and Emotions Through HRM Practices

Mine Afacan Fındıklı

Abstract This chapter examines the phenomenon of human-robot collaboration and the role of human resource practices in fostering positive working environment among employees. A review of the extant literature on human resource management (HRM) and human-robot interaction/collaboration revealed a paucity of research in this area. This chapter, which is constructed based on Technology Acceptance Model (TAM), aims to identify the mechanisms that underpin human-robot interaction when HRM practices are in place. A review of the literature revealed two key HRM strategies to be critical: re-skilling employees for new technological demands and fostering an inclusive, interactive work environment between humans and robots. The findings of previous studies indicate that to alleviate the negative perceptions of employees, human resources (HR) professionals should adopt more individualised practices where emotional factors and perceived competence are critical. The positive emotions that employees experience towards the use of technology have been found to enhance their perception of its usefulness. Conversely, the perception of deficiencies can lead to feelings of anxiety and a subsequent decrease in performance. In light of the practices of leading companies in business, it is imperative to address the talent gap as a priority. The positive effects of robotic-human collaboration on business effectiveness and efficiency is their prominent focus in their strategic goals.

Keywords Human resource management practices · Human–machine interaction · Human–robot collaboration · Technology acceptance model · Perceptions and emotions

---

M. A. Fındıklı
Department of Business, Istinye University, İstanbul, Turkey

M. A. Fındıklı (✉)
UBI Business School, Brussels, Belgium
e-mail: mine.findikli@ubi.edu; mine.findikli@istinye.edu.tr

C. Machado and J. P. Davim (eds.), *Challenges and Opportunities in the Artificial Intelligence Era*, https://doi.org/10.1007/978-3-031-85272-5_5

1 Introduction

The advent of AI technologies has been rapidly transforming the nature of employment in the contemporary global context. The necessity for critical and creative thinking, as well as cognitive skills, is becoming increasingly prevalent in occupations rather than previously required physical strength. This chapter presents an overview about the human-robot collaboration and the role of human resource practices in fostering positive perceptions and well-being among employees.

Technological advancements over the past century have initiated a profound transformation within our society and economy. The nature of work and business practices has experienced significant and rapid evolution. Notably, the emergence of Industry 4.0 and Society 5.0 has brought forth a multitude of innovations, including artificial intelligence, robotics, the Internet of Things, and autonomous vehicles, which have become increasingly integrated into our daily lives. The business world has supported the concept of Industry 4.0 in the production and service sectors. Nowadays this new manufacturing paradigm, which involves the integration of industrial automation and novel production technologies, has been transforming work conditions in order to increase productivity and quality in all sectors for a decade (Di Nardo et al. 2020).

Despite the apparent economic appeal of such an approach, there wight be two crucial spheres to be considered related to strategies of HRM. Firstly, the advent of 4.0 İndustry has shown a need for 're-skilling' which is not those used to date by typical employees (WEF 2024). In addition to that, it has also required an inclusive HR strategy to build a collaborative and interactive work environment between humans and robots. While robots demonstrate proficiency in tasks demanding speed, efficiency, and consistency, humans exhibit creativity, adaptability, and complex problem-solving capabilities that are challenging for robotic technologies to compensate for. This synergy has unveiled a new era of human-robot collaboration and interaction, necessitating a workforce that should be adept at operating and managing robotic systems. Therefore, in this era of digitalisation and robotics, it will be of great importance for HR professionals to apply human-centred innovative approaches not only to overcome the talent shortage, but also to overcome the difficulties that may arise in the process of human-robot congruence.

Human-robot interaction (HRI) encompasses a wide range of contexts, each differing in the desired level of social connection. Recent research indicates that participants perceive human interaction partners as more effective in taking on roles compared to robots. In other means, we can argue that interpersonal factors are more influential (Davis 2023) in this perception. The type or form of the robot is not a significant predictor of the desire for continued human- robot/AI interaction. The prominent determinants of this uncomfortable feeling are likely derived from an emotional context of oneself related to their motivations and the load of interaction's human- robot with associated with mental health and cognitive performance (Weis and Herbert 2022). It is well known that emotions influence human behaviours, some encouraging action, others hindering or altering it. However, emotions are also affected by situating and acting. Similarly, the use of technology is also a matter of human emotions (Asenbaum 2018). In this context, if users believe that the benefits of a particular technology will enable them to improve their work performance in business life, the perceived usefulness of the technology may blossom into positive emotions towards the use of technology (Toker et al. 2023). In contrast, if the person perceives a deficiency in his/her own competences and skills compared to the robot, this bias may lead individuals to depression, anxiety, and attention-deficit/hyperactivity disorder, as well as decrease of cognitive performance (Weis and Herbert 2022). In today's business environment, where employee well-being is highly valued, such a dilemma can threaten job performance and the harmonious functioning of the organisation. Although in Industry 4.0, IoT and AI technologies are expected to provide promising transformative solutions for the many of existing industrial systems, it should not forget that technology has emerged with people's innovative skills to enhance people's cognitive capabilities and efficiency in business output. Furthermore, although the general opinion regarding team members is quite positive that robots will succeed as teammates alongside humans, recent studies have been evaluating the potential of robots to meet the requirements of successful teammates. It is argued that the absence of human-like mental models and a sense of self in robots may render them untrustworthy and result in their rejection from human teams (Groom and Nass 2007).

In this perspective, it can be argued that 'harmony in the workplace' as a means of maintaining and enhancing employee well-being will be one of the main focuses of HRM professionals in the era of transformation and digitalisation. This is because the concept of harmony and collaboration between employees and robots is not only focused on increasing productivity. It also aims to create a workforce that is flexible, adaptable and able to cope with future changes.

Based on the tenets of Technology Acceptance Model (TAM) the aim of this chapter is to understand the mechanisms of human-robot interaction supported by HRM practices. Within this aim, the question of this study is "*How do HRM practices ensure the employee well-being in successfully maintaining human-robot interaction and collaboration?*".

The first section of the chapter begins with an overview of 4.0 Industry and Human-Robot Interaction, and the second section gradually narrow down to specific studies and findings related to human-robot collaboration and employees' perceptions. this section is planned to interpret human-robot interaction/collaboration in the workplace, and the relationship between HRM practices and human-robot collaboration in the context of the existing literature. The third section discuss the implications of recent and studies for HRM Practices and Human- Robot Collaboration. This section is designed for emphasising HRM practices in terms of human-robot congruence concept. The conclusion section summarizes the key points of the chapter.

2 4.0 Industry and Human- Robot Interaction

The advent of Industry 4.0 technologies has enabled the integration of the next generation of workers, designated as O4.0, into manufacturing operations and equipment through the utilisation of Human-Cyber-Physical Systems (H-CPSs). These innovations not only provide a comprehensive toolbox to support workers but also reposition humans at the core of production. The primary objective of this period is to address the flexibility requirements for an optimal collaborative working system that integrates human operators and human-robot systems, with the goal of developing a socially sustainable production workforce, which is termed Operator 5.0 (Gladysz et al. 2023).

With this new paradigm shift from Industry 4.0 to Industry 5.0 (and the accompanying Society 5.0), skills-based technological innovations have been gradually transforming the skill profile of current and future occupations. As previously stated, this digital transformation will not eliminate the need for human interaction; rather, it will alter the manner in which humans interact with computers, both in the performance of tasks (Kolade and Owoseni 2022) and in the improvement of process efficiency, services, and products (Ciccarelli et al. 2023). A number of technological innovations, including collaborative robots, exoskeletons, smart wearable devices, and collaborative technologies, have been developed to assist operators and technicians in performing their duties, addressing both physical and cognitive aspects of the job (Romero et al. 2021). Similarly, while previous studies have highlighted the impact of automation on the reduction in the demand for low-skilled workers in routine tasks and manual and cognitive routine work (Wolcott 2021), recent data on robotics indicates that the share of robotic capital has increased dramatically by approximately 40% from the 1990s to the end of the decade (Battisti et al. 2021). The ILO Report (2023) and the WEF survey of large corporations (2023) also indicate that there has been a significant increase in the use of automation and digital transformation in clerical and administrative work (Gmyrek et al. 2023).

Together with the convergence of human and AI-equipped robots in the same working environments the human and the robot agent can no longer be considered separately and that tasks are shared between them and they work as a team in cooperation towards the goal (Hoc 2000). Robot teammates are designed with high levels of autonomy and well-developed coordination skills to assist humans in unpredictable environments (Groom and Nass 2007). It is even argued that AI robots are also increasing the value of engineers and managers, and some of the most automated environments—the factory and other industrial settings—are experiencing a renaissance of human labour because in many cases, AI is freeing up time, creativity and human capital, essentially allowing people to work more like humans and less like robots (Daugherty and Wilson 2018).

For instance, Hitachi employs AI to analyse large data sets and workers' routines in order to inform its robots, which deliver instructions to employees in order to meet fluctuating demand and on-site kaizen objectives. In a pilot study, the company observed an 8 percent improvement in productivity in logistics tasks. At Siemens, a multitude of spider-like 3-D printed robots utilise AI to communicate and collaborate in order to build things in the company's Princeton, New Jersey, laboratory. Each robot is equipped with vision sensors and laser scanners. Collectively, they are capable of manufacturing on the go. At Inertia Switch, robotic intelligence and sensor fusion enable robot-human collaboration. The manufacturing firm utilises Universal Robotics' robots, which are capable of learning tasks on the go and can flexibly move between tasks, making them useful assistants to humans on the factory floor. Coca-Cola, which operates a vast network of 16 million cooler cabinets that maintain the refrigeration of its soft drinks at retail outlets worldwide, has initiated a proof-of-concept project utilising AI to manage the coolers. The project calls for the deployment of a new AI capability, called Einstein, from customer relationship management (CRM) vendor Salesforce. This capability employs computer vision, deep learning, and natural-language-processing technologies. Based on thistechnology, Einstein generates a restocking order, using CRM data and other information, including weather forecasts, promotional offers, inventory levels, and historical data to account for seasonal fluctuations and various other factors. The Einstein project has shown that AI has both automated employee tasks and enhanced the capabilities of workers (Daugherty and Wilson 2018).

Parallel to these rapid developments in business life, scientific research has shifted from studying human-computer interaction, which focused on fully controllable systems, to studying dynamic, highly complex human-robot systems, which has started the process of incorporating human-robot collaboration (Jacko 2012; Bolton et al. 2018; Obaigbena et al. 2024). In order to understand the main research trends in human-robot interaction and collaboration, a bibliometric analysis was conducted.

At the first step of data extraction phase, a search in SCOPUS using the keywords "human-robot collaboration" or "human-robot interaction" revealed that 2720 studies have been carried out in "(1) *Business Administration*, (2) *Psychology*, (3) *Multidisciplinary*, (4) *Social Sciences*" *areas in English.* All searches spanned from data base inception until 2024. The graphs of the study classified by years, countries, and subject areas to understand the general descriptives is presented below (Figs. 1, 2 and 3). As can be seen from the graph, studies on AI are gradually increasing in these three fields.

The line graph describing a trend of published papers related to human-robot interaction/collaboration from 1990 to 2026 with a significant rise starting around 2010. The y-axis likely represents values ranging from 0 to 500, with a sharp increase after 2017, reaching its peak between 2021 and 2022.

A horizontal bar chart describing the number of published papers related to human-robot interaction/collaboration by country. The x-axis ranges from 0 to 1000 papers, with each country's bar reflecting its relative contribution. The United States leads with the highest number of publications, followed by Germany, the United Kingdom, Italy, China, Japan, France, the Netherlands, Sweden, and Australia.

It is observed that the majority of work in these three areas is carried out in the USA. Furthermore, only 4.5% of these studies are in the field of business management.

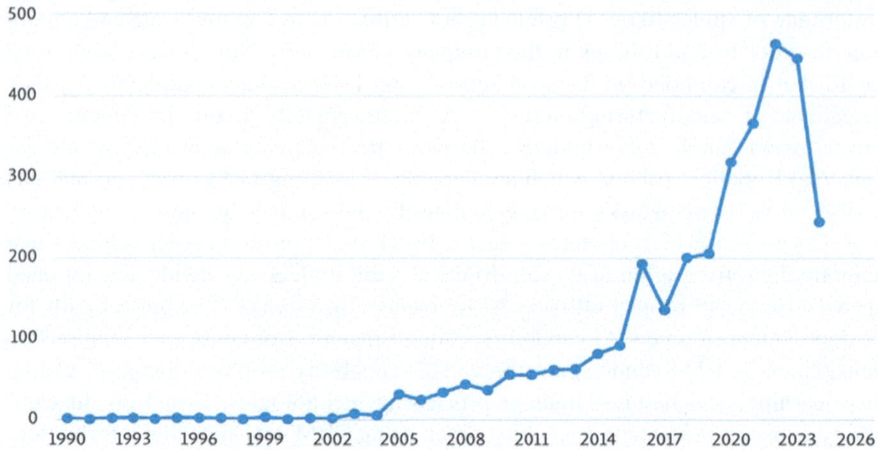

Fig. 1 Published papers related to human-robot interaction/collaboration by year (1993–2024)

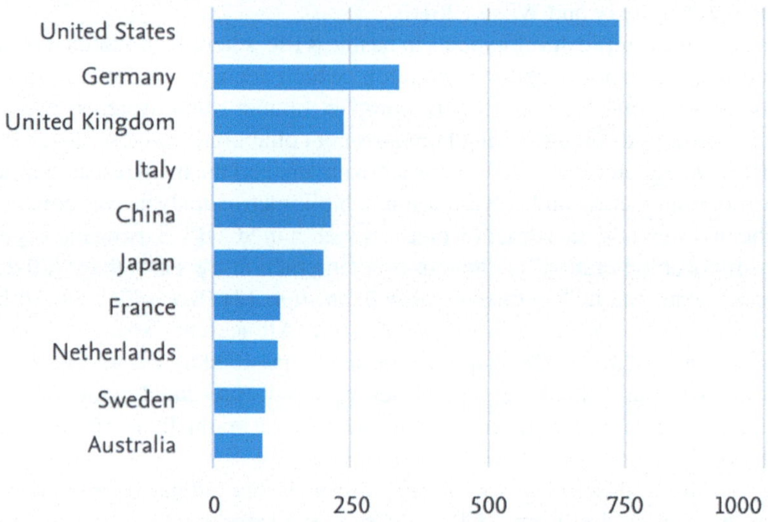

Fig. 2 Published papers related to human-robot interaction/collaboration by country

A pie chart displaying the distribution of studies across various disciplines related to human-robot interaction/collaboration. The largest share of studies is in Computer Science (24.0%), followed by Social Sciences (21.8%), Psychology (14.0%), and Engineering (12.2%). It is noted that the majority of work in these areas is conducted in the USA, and only 4.5% of these studies focus on Business Management.

In order to focus human- robot interaction and collaboration this research focuses on HRM practices, thus *Psychology, Interdisciplinary, Social Sciences* articles were excluded, and "Human Resources Management" term was added in the keywords

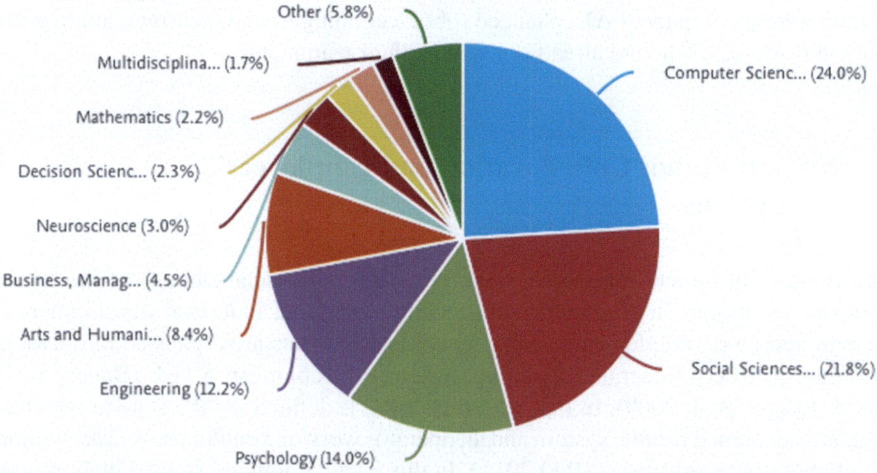

Fig. 3 Published papers related to human-robot interaction/collaboration by subject erea

as a third one. Concordantly, it was observed that there were very few studies in the time period of the research (such as; Li et al. 2023; Macpherson and Werner 2023; Pasparakis et al., 2023; Akay et al. 2022; Parvez et al. 2022; Antakli et al. 2023). Among the studies identified, only three have been related to the topic of human resource management (HRM) practices.

Parvez et al. (2022) aimed to extend the Technology Acceptance Model (TAM) to examine whether the introduction of robots influences employees' behavioural intentions to use robots and their perceptions of robots to promote human-robot collaboration (HRC). The role of strategic human resource management (HRM) involvement as a moderator in the perception of robots as team members was also investigated.

Akay et al. (2022) focused on the challenges faced by human resource management (HRM) leaders and departments in contemporary organisations due to the close interaction between artificial intelligence (AI) (primarily robots) and human workers, especially at the team level. They also discussed important potential strategies that may be useful in addressing these challenges, based on a conceptual review of existing research.

Pasparakis et al. (2023) found that the introduction of human-robot collaboration positively affects job satisfaction for the contrasting collaboration dynamics of (i) gaining control (the human leading the robot) and (ii) relinquishing control (the human following the robot). This positive effect is stronger when the human follows the robot. They also find that following the robot has a positive effect on pickers' self-esteem, and that self-efficacy related to human-robot interaction benefits from the introduction of collaborative robotics, regardless of the setup dynamic. It can be argued that this systematic literature review demonstrates the necessity of questioning the impact of AI-enhanced robot technologies and their interaction with human resources, who are already or will be their teammates.

3 Human–Robot Collaboration and Employees' Perceptions

The concept of human-robot collaboration (HRC) is a crucial element of the smart industry paradigm. In alignment with technological and industrial developments, human operators -employees- and an AI-enhanced robots are organised to interact, forming a closely integrated dynamic system to accomplish a task (Bauer et al. 2008; Krüger et al. 2009). In line with this, HRC is defined as "the state in which a specially designed robotic system and an operator work on simultaneous tasks within a collaborative workspace" (ISO 2011). In this context, human- robot collaboration can be defined as to the process of agents working in concert to achieve a shared objective.

While, in the past, humans and robots were typically situated in separate workspaces, in a smart industry context, there is a direct interaction and collaborative work between humans and AI. Therefore, the robot as part of the team takes on the explicit or implicit intention of the team as its own in order to perform and to achieve a common goal (Molitor 2022). In other means, the optimal level of teamwork is achieved when members of the team can comprehend one another's perspectives.

In the context of the contemporary transformation towards a human-centric, sustainable and resilient production paradigm of Industry 5.0, industrial enterprises strive to attain a state of transformable production, whereby manufacturers can expeditiously introduce new products. The developments in production under Industry 5.0 have resulted in the necessity for humans and robots to work together in harmony. In parallel with the developments of the industries, over the past decade, numerous academic studies have examined the potential of human-robot collaboration (HRC) in a range of production contexts. Thus, they have identified three distinct roles that human and robotic agents can assume at different stages of task execution which are (Baratta et al. 2023);

(1) an active role, which is the dominant decision maker,
(2) a supporting role, which performs assisted operations desired by the teammate,
(3) an inactive role, which acts as an idle spectator, trusting the teammate's manipulation.

Additionally, several types of HRC are defined, including the following four categories:

(1) Coexistence: the employee and the robot share the same work environment but do not interact with each other.
(2) Synchrony: the employee and the robot share the same work environment but at different time steps.

(3) Cooperation: the employee and the robot work together on the same task. The robot and the human operator share the same work environment simultaneously, with each entity focusing on distinct tasks.
(4) Collaboration: The employee and the robot perform tasks together, with the actions of one entity influencing and having immediate repercussions on those of the other entity. Consequently, the optimum of adaptation between the employee and robot can be achieved by shared activity, ad goal-oriented intention and action (Li et al. 2023).

Although, this bi-directional collaboration has been incorporated into production and assembly processes to promote system flexibility, changeability and adaptability, the employees' perceptions, emotions, and well-being remain important aspect as they navigate this technologically advanced and demanding process. Human-robot collaboration challenges arise from the inherent differences between individual team members, both in terms of their mental and computational abilities, their physical characteristics (Hiatt et al. 2017), as well as their perceptions. According to previous studies Artificial intelligence (AI) matches or outperforms humans in any number of strategic games, standardized tests, and cognitive tasks that involve high-level thinking and strategic reasoning. It is also argued that "digital intelligence" will inevitably surpass human "biological intelligence" due to the cognitive and computational limitations of humans (Felin and Holweg 2024).

It is well known that emotions influence human behaviour, some encouraging action, others hindering or altering it. Similarly, the use of AI technology or robotics is also a matter of human perceptions, and emotions. In this context, if users believe in their capabilities and the benefits of a particular technology will enable them to improve their work performance in business life, they can feel positive emotions towards the use of technology (Asenbaum 2018). Based on the TAM theory, technology's usefulness and ease of use (Kim 2009) can generate positive emotions in individuals. According to Pelegrín-Borondo et al. (2020), affective and normative factors significantly influence the acceptance of new technologies. At the affective level, positive emotions are most likely to affect accepting new technology. The Technology Acceptance Model (TAM) indicates that individuals accept and use new technology if they accept the usefulness and the ease of technology use (Marangunić and Granić 2015). This may encourage positive attitudes to Robots as companions, too.

Molitor and Renkema (2022), drawing from the assumptions of the Technology Acceptance Model (TAM), proposed that six factors influence the intention to collaborate: (1) performance expectancy, (2) trust, (3) effort expectancy, (4) social support, (5) organizational support, and (6) computer anxiety. They defined performance expectancy as the belief that a system or technology will enhance job performance. If employees perceive that a particular technology boosts their job performance, they are more likely to accept collaboration. The researchers also highlighted that trust plays a crucial role in technology acceptance, impacting how individuals perceive, interact with, and collaborate with the technology. Moreover, they found that effort expectancy, which is assessed by the extent to which collaborative efforts reduce individuals' collective effort, can positively or negatively influence acceptance and collaboration with the system. Utilizing the TAM and Theory of Planned Behaviour (TPB), the study demonstrated that acceptance and collaboration with robots are influenced by the social environment and that organizational support can facilitate this process. Finally, they emphasized the significance of computer anxiety, suggesting that it is shaped by individuals' computer skills. They argued that while basic cognitive, physical, and manual skills may decline in the coming years, the demand for technological skills, such as computer proficiency, will rise.

As previously stated, the digital transformation will not eliminate the necessity for human interaction; rather, it will alter the manner in which humans interact with computers and robots, both in the performance of tasks (Kolade and Owoseni 2022) and in the improvement of process efficiency, services, and products (Ciccarelli et al. 2023). Concurrently, this rapid evolution presents challenges for highly skilled professionals capable of engaging in non-routine cognitive tasks, encompassing analytical and interpersonal abilities. For example, the workforce is compelled to reexamine their competencies, occupational roles, industry requirements, and conventional career trajectories. This can engender feelings of uncertainty and trepidation regarding the future trajectory of their careers (Chetty 2023). Similarly, the extant literature has highlighted the existence of skill mismatches, which are increasingly recognised as a significant challenge in the contemporary labour market (Lincaru et al. 2022). These developments can impose a significant cognitive load on the individual for the employee to adapt to these systems and work in harmony (Haslgrubler et al. 2018). The principal causes of the cognitive load can be attributed to the advent of sophisticated robotics and automated machinery on the factory floor, coupled with a growing scarcity of proficient operators (Mangler 2021). The complexity of tasks, the type of tasks, time pressure, speed, and the quality of instructions may intensify the effort and cognitive load for operators, thereby increasing their mental effort and psychological stress levels (Lagomarsino 2022). These individuals experience feelings of insecurity and work overload and dedicate additional time to demonstrate their value and protect their employment status. Because of the aforementioned factors, stress, anxiety, fatigue, hypertension, and sleep disorders may become an integral part of their daily lives (Mangler 2021). In order for both reskilling one's competencies and being in harmony with robots to be achieved, it is necessary for HRM practices to be reassessed in order to address the challenges of the 5.0 era.

4 HRM Practices and Human- Robot Collaboration

The increasing prevalence of artificial intelligence (AI) in business practices transform the way organizations compete in the market and reshape their workforces (Chowdhury et al. 2023). With this rapid and challenging change, the role of the human resources professionals becomes increasingly important. Although the functions of HRM is still to undertake a number of classical activities (Dessler 2007), in parallel with the implementation of AI technology in decision—making and management, the processes of recruitment, training, performance management and employee engagement, as well as others functions within the domain of human resource management need a shift to support and facilitate the acceptance, adoption and collaboration with new technologies such as AI technologies and robots. Artificial intelligence plays a pivotal role in the integration of human resource management functions, facilitating and optimizing human-robot collaboration. Artificial intelligence facilitate the provision of data from internal data analysis and non-market data to human resources management, thereby enhancing the effectiveness of all HRM functions. These include the rapid evaluation of candidates, the matching of their skills and knowledge with suitable positions, and the measurement of their performance. This contributes to the added value of the organization (Berhil et al. 2020).

The effective utilization of artificial intelligence in human resources management confers benefits across the entire spectrum of HR activities, including recruitment, training, planning, performance management, and forecasting labor market trends (Al-Jawder et al. 2022). Moreover, the effectiveness of HRM is not contingent on its compatibility with artificial intelligence technology alone. The integration of advanced technology with human work processes is also essential to support employees in such environments, ensuring a balance between efficiency and employee well-being.

To achieve the balance in the integration of AI and HRM practices, human resource professilonals have to overcome some challenges which are mainly: (1) planing AI-based training programs that can leverage employees' learning styles and paces, allowing them to learn new skills and improve performance, (2) forming a clear communication channels to provide personalized and timely feedback, recommendations, and support, (3) optimizing HR processes such as performance management, succession planning, and employee retention by analyzing employee data and feedback (Sabil et al. 2023). Briefly, in order to ensure and maintain employee well-being in line with human-robot interaction and collaboration, it is necessary for organisations to free up HR staff to focus on higher-level tasks such as developing HR strategies, building relationships with employees, and providing personalised support (Zehir et al. 2020). Because their high-complexity tasks require their adaptability to collaborate, cooperate efficiently.

A report published by the World Health Organization (WHO 2005) indicated that the utilisation of information and communication technology (ICT) has led to a transformation in the work patterns of employees (To et al., 2013). While there is evidence that productivity and efficiency have been enhanced thanks to human-robot interaction, it has also been revealed that stress among employees or increased mental workload, which may lead to several detrimental fallouts such as mental exhaustion from work, commitment issues and turnover intentions. The causes of this stress are found due to the numerous and constant connectivity, the use of a variety of new applications multitasking, information overload, a high level of uncertainty, job insecurity and technical problems (Malik et al. 2022).

Previous studies have indicated that the introduction of human-robot collaboration may result in a reduction in communication and interaction among employees when compared to traditional collaborative work processes (Savela et al. 2021). Moreover, human employees have reported feelings of emotional exhaustion, which can result in a lack of attention to their work duties and a reduction in their willingness to interact with others in a friendly manner (Lv 2024). Consequently, if human resources managers are unable to provide adequate support to employees, the adoption of new technologies can become a source of stress, which may ultimately result in employee turnover. Eventually, it is unsurprising that humans may experience difficulties in the face of robots' emotionless and analytical decisions, given that humans are limited to their own evaluations and skills.

In order for employees to adopt technologies and work effectively together, human resource management practices should provide a combination of training, empowerment, autonomy, and incentives to employees. It would be beneficial for organisations to design training programmes in a way that enhances innovative capability and learning. This would help to strengthen employee awareness and skills, and could be achieved through collaboration with external partners such as educational institutions to create innovative learning opportunities. Additionally, performance appraisals can facilitate learning and innovation, as well as workforce empowerment, and the creation of incentives reflecting the contribution of employees to the company.

In the context of human resources management (HRM), the functions of recruitment and selection are of particular importance when hiring for roles that involve significant interaction with AI and robots. In such cases, it might be beneficial for HR to prioritize candidates with strong technical skills and an advanced technology knowledge. In order to evaluate how candidates interact with AI technologies and respond to HMI scenarios, it would be beneficial for them to undergo a simulation-based assessment. Additionally, continuous training and development programmes, which are designed to align with the evolving technology landscape, can facilitate the maintenance of employee proficiency with the latest HMI tools and techniques. In particular, the use of virtual reality (VR) technology can leverage the efficiency to create simulated human-machine interactive environments. Such an approach enables HR to provide employees with assistance in addressing a range of issues, including those related to cognition, emotion and practical matters (Molitor 2022).

Leading businesses across a range of industries are setting the standard for best practices implementation in order to ensure successful Human-Robot Collaboration (HRC). These businesses have effectively incorporated AI and sophisticated robotics into their operations, creating a collaborative atmosphere that boosts output, effectiveness, and worker satisfaction. The following is a summary of five companies' announcements about human-robot collaboration.

The announcements on their websites highlight the current situation of jobs in a major transformation phase towards digitalisation and cyborgysation in the human-robot co-creation of production.

First important implication from company announcements is that "Robots and humans will work in total efficiency and harmony."

Amazon uses a massive network of robots that collaborate with human workers to speed up the picking, packing, and shipping procedures (Amazon 2023).

> 750,000 Amazon robots are doing the heavy lifting for our employees so they can deliver for customers. With the latest in AI, our technology makes our sites safer.

Siemens has implemented the Digital Factory concept, integrating AI and robotics to create a highly automated and flexible production environment. The company's workforce is continuously trained to ensure effective collaboration with advanced technologies. Furthermore, Siemens uses cobots designed to work safely alongside human workers, enhancing productivity and precision in manufacturing processes (Siemens 2024).

> "Once this channel of communication has been opened, it can be used to control anything you want." From robots that are trained to assist neurosurgeons during complicated brain surgery, to factory robots that take on the lifting and mixing of chemicals in a factory—vital tasks that can be hazardous to humans. The opportunities for human-robot collaboration are endless.
>
> "Eventually robots will be able to understand human intention," says Zi Jian. If someone falls in the workplace a robot will be able to recognize they need help and come to their aide. Or if someone drops a tool the robot will be able to pick it up and hand it back, without being asked to.

BMW employs a combination of industrial robots and collaborative robots (cobots) in its manufacturing plants, allowing for a flexible and efficient production process.

> BMW aims to deploy humanoid robots at its Spartanburg factory

Ford employs a combination of robotic and collaborative robots (cobots) in its assembly lines to enhance efficiency and precision in vehicle manufacturing.

> Removing the barriers to success: KUKA robots work collaboratively with humans

The second implication from company announcements is that "The skills and competencies of the workforce need to be reshaped quickly and effectively to cope with today's technological developments."

Amazon invests heavily in training programs to ensure employees are proficient in operating and interacting with robots safely. Amazon's robots handle repetitive and physically demanding tasks, reducing the physical strain on human workers and allowing them to focus on more complex and cognitive tasks (Amazon 2023).

> Amazon is working to close the skills gap and train employees for jobs of the future
>
> "We encourage companies and academic institutions to be thinking about new ways to help people find new skills and passions," Dresser added. "Our robotics team is just one example of many teams working in technical and skilled trades that are delivering every day for customers around the globe."

BMW employs a combination of industrial robots and collaborative robots (cobots) in its manufacturing plants, allowing for a flexible and efficient production process. The company's human-centric approach prioritizes ergonomics and employee well-being, with robots being used to handle tasks that are hazardous or physically demanding.

> BMW offers extensive training programmes to ensure workers are comfortable and skilled in working with robotic systems, fostering a culture of innovation and collaboration (BMW 2013, 2024).

Fanuc, a prominent manufacturer of industrial robots, incorporates artificial intelligence (AI) into its robotic systems, thereby enhancing their capacity to operate in collaboration with humans across a range of industrial sectors. *Fanuc provides comprehensive training and support services to its customers*, thereby ensuring the effective implementation and maintenance of HRC in their operations. The company is committed to the continuous innovation of its product range with the objective of enhancing the safety and efficiency of human-robot collaboration.

Ford employs a combination of robotic and collaborative robots (cobots) in its assembly lines to enhance efficiency and precision in vehicle manufacturing. Ford invests in training programmes that equip employees with the skills necessary to work alongside and manage robotic systems effectively.

***The third implication from company announcements is that* "The co-creation of humans and robots will be more than the sum of its parts."**

Ford prioritizes the design of workstations where robots undertake heavy lifting and repetitive tasks, thereby reducing the risk of injury and improving worker comfort with the understanding of *"Humans and robots augmenting each other's strengths"*.

> In a Ford Motor Company factory in Cologne, Germany, KUKA's LBR iiwa robot is helping to transform their production line into Industry 4.0—the 4th industrial revolution—in which humans work hand-in-hand with robots and factories become smarter.

BMW tests how general-purpose robots could improve factory productivity as part of a multi-stage deployment deal. Based on their announcement (2024):

> BMW signed a commercial agreement to deploy general-purpose humanoid robots in the automaker's manufacturing facilities built by Figure, a Silicon Valley-based autonomous robotics company, according to a press earlier this month.

Fanuc, according to their statement titled "Human-robot collaboration", investigates Collaborative robots' technology.

> How does human-robot collaboration benefit your business?
>
> Human-robot collaboration can add benefit your business in many ways. One of these is improved working conditions for humans. With collaborative robots on the team, humans no longer need to complete physically demanding tasks and are free to focus on more rewarding work. As a result, humans stay physically healthy for longer and issues, such as repetitive strain and other work-related injuries, cease to be a problem. Human-robot collaboration also goes some way to easing the problems associated with ageing populations in industrial societies.

It will not be much of a fortune telling exercise to predict the strategic importance of HRM practices by being aware about all this rapid change.

5 Conclusion

This chapter aimed at exploring the potential perceptions of employees in the process of human-robot collaboration and the impact of HR strategies in generating the human-robot collaboration congruence and altering the employee wellbeing.

The chapter unveiled that there are relatively few studies conducted on employees' perceptions and emotions in regard to human-robot interactions in workplace. As a result of the literature review, most studies address how the workplace should be set up to facilitate human-machine collaboration and how AI technologies and robots can speed up and improve the efficiency of the workforce. However, there is currently limited research on the potential psychological and cognitive costs of this collaboration for employees, who are an integral part of the process and witness this rapid digital transformation.

Important questions that emerged from this chapter and that needs further exploration as discussed as below:

1. HRM professionals' thoughts, opinions and limitations regarding employees' attitudes and feelings towards adopting technology.

   According to recent studies, it is argued that humans are more willing to collaborate with humans' co-workers than machines. We can counter that interpersonal elements have a greater influence on this view. The main causes of this perception are probably generated from an emotional context of oneself that is connected to their motives and the amount of human-robot interaction that is linked to mental health and cognitive function. Relatively more is known regarding the productivity and organizational outcomes of human-robot collaboration. More studies needed to predict the antecedents and triggers of resistance to collaborate or negative emotions, from the employees' side.
2. İnvestigating the mechanisms and boundary constraints of human-robot collaboration.

   As we quickly move towards digital and AI-supported artificial intelligence technologies, HRM practices should be expanded to be more inclusive and human-centered, considering workers' emotions and cognitive burdens. Future research should focus on comprehending the mechanisms and boundary constraints relating to the congruence of human-robot collaboration in HRM practices. HRM professionals ideas, opinions and limitations on employee attitudes and feelings towards technology adoption can be a different angle of this area to research.
3. Understanding the antecedents of employees' willingness to collaborate with social robots, investigate the moderator role of HRM practices.

   Based on Technology Acceptance (TAM), Conservation of Resources (COR) and ability (A), motivation (M) and opportunity (AMO) Theory the blurred relationships between skill-enhancing, motivation-enhancing and opportunity-enhancing bundles of HRM practices and employees' congruence with AI technology can be investigated.

References

Akay S, Arslan B, Bagci SC, Kanero J (2022) "My robot friend": application of intergroup contact theory in human-robot interaction. In: 2022 17th ACM/IEEE international conference on human-robot interaction (HRI). IEEE, pp 665–668

Al-Jawder M, Hamdan A, Roboe A (2022) The impact of artificial intelligence on enhancing human resource management functionality. In: International conference on business and technology, vol 620, pp 509–515. https://doi.org/10.1007/978-3-031-26953-0_46.

Antakli A, Kazimov A, Spieldenner D, Rojas GE, Zinnikus I, Klusch M (2023, July) Ajan: an engineering framework for semantic web-enabled agents and multi-agent systems. In: International conference on practical applications of agents and multi-agent systems. Cham, Springer Nature Switzerland, pp 15–27

Asenbaum H (2018) Cyborg activism: exploring the reconfigurations of democratic subjectivity in Anonymous. New Media Soc 20(4):1543–1563

Baratta A, Cimino A, Gnoni M, Longo F (2023) Human robot collaboration in industry 4.0: a literature review. In: 4th International conference on industry 4.0 and smart manufacturing, procedia computer science, vol 217, pp 1887–1895

Battisti M, Del Gatto M, Gravina AF, Parmeter CF (2021) Robots versus labor skills: a complementarity/substitutability analysis (No. 202104). Centre for North South Economic Research, University of Cagliari and Sassari, Sardinia

Bauer A, Wollherr D, Buss M (2008) Human–robot collaboration: Asurvey. Int J Humanoid Rob 5(01):47–66

Berhil S, Benlahmar H, Labani N (2020) A review paper on artificial intelligence at the service of human resources management. Indonesian J Electr Eng Comput Sci 18(1):32–40

Bolton C, Machová V, Kovacova M, Valaskova K (2018) The power of human–machine collaboration: artificial intelligence, business automation, and the smart economy. Econ Manage Financ Markets 13(4):51–56

Chetty K (2023) AI literacy for an ageing workforce: leveraging the experience of older workers. OBM Geriatrics 7(3):243. https://doi.org/10.21926/obm.geriatr.2303243

Chowdhury SD-E, Bhattacharya S, Rodriguez-Espindola O, Abadie A, Truong L (2023) Unlocking the value of artificial intelligence in human resource management through AI capability framework. Hum Resour Manag Rev 33(1):100899

Ciccarelli M, Papetti A, Germani M (2023) Exploring how new industrial paradigms affect the workforce: a literature review of operator 4.0. J Manuf Syst 70:464–483. https://doi.org/10.1016/j.jmsy.2023.08.016

Daugherty PR, Wilson HJ (2018) The self-aware factory floor: AI in production, supply chain, and distribution, in Human+ machine: reimagining work in the age of AI, vol 38(1). Harvard Business Press

Davis JL (2023) Role-taking and robotic form: an exploratory study of social connection in human-robot interaction. Int J Human-Comput Stud 178–187

Dessler G (2007) Human resource management. 11thedn, Prentice-Hall, Englewood Cliffs

Di Nardo M, Forino D, Murino T (2020) The evolution of man–machine interaction: the role of human in Industry 4.0 paradigm. In: Di Nardo M, Forino D, Murino T (eds) Department of Chemical, Materials and Industrial Production Engineering, University of Naples Federico II, Naples, Italy ABSTRACT Ind. Production & Manufacturing Research, pp 20–34. https://doi.org/10.1080/21693277.2020.1737592

Felin T, Holweg M (2024) Theory is all you need: AI. Human Cognition, and Decision Making. https://doi.org/10.2139/ssrn.4737265

Gladysz B, Tran TA, Romero D, van Erp T, Abonyi J, Ruppert T (2023) Current development on the Operator 4.0 and transition towards the Operator 5.0: a systematic literature review in light of Industry 5.0. J Manuf Syst 70:160–185. https://doi.org/10.1016/j.jmsy.2023.07.008

Gmyrek P, Berg J, Bescond D (2023) Generative AI and jobs: a global analysis of potential effects on job quantity and quality. ILO Working Paper 96 (Geneva, ILO), https://doi.org/10.54394/FHEM8239

Groom V, Nass C (2007) Can robots be teammates? Benchmarks in human–robot teams. Interact Stud 8(3):483–500

Haslgrubler M, Gollan B, Ferscha A (2018) A Cognitive assistance framework for supporting human workers in industrial tasks. IT Professional 20(5):48–56. https://doi.org/10.1109/MITP.2018.053891337

Hiatt L, CNarber C, Bekele E, Khemlani S, Trafton G (2017) Human modeling for human–robot collaboration. Int J Robot Res 36(5–7):580–596. https://doi.org/10.1177/0278364917690592

Hoc J-M (2000) From human—machine interaction to human—machine cooperation. Ergonomics 43(7):833–843. https://doi.org/10.1080/001401300409044

ISO (2011) ISO 10218–1: robots and robotic devices—safety requirements for industrial robots—Part 1: Robots

Jacko JA (2012) Human computer interaction handbook: fundamentals, evolving technologies, and emerging applications. CRC Press, Taylor & Francis Group, Third Edition, p 1375

Kim YJ (2009) Investigating the role of attitude in technology acceptance from an attitude strength perspective. Int J Inf Manage 29(1):67–77. https://doi.org/10.1016/j.ijinfomgt.2008.01.011

Kolade O, Owoseni A (2022) Employment 5.0: the work of the future and the future of work. Technol Soc 71. 102086. https://doi.org/10.1016/j.techsoc.2022.102086

Krüger J, Lien TK, Verl A (2009) Cooperation of human and machines in assembly lines. CIRP Ann Manuf Technol 58(2):628–646

Lagomarsino ML (2022) An online framework for cognitive load assessment in industrial tasks. Robot Comput-Integr Manuf 78, 102380. https://doi.org/10.1016/j.rcim.2022.102380

Li S, Pai Zheng P, Liu S, Wang Z, Wang X, Zheng LW (2023) Proactive human–robot collaboration: mutual-cognitive, predictable, and self-organising perspectives. Obotics Comput-Integr Manuf 81:1–30. https://doi.org/10.1016/j.rcim.2022.102510

Li X, Lu Q, Chen J, Jiang N, Li K (2023) A robust region control approach for simultaneous trajectory tracking and compliant physical human–robot interaction. IEEE Trans Syst Man Cybern: Syst 53(10):6388–6400

Lincaru C, Pîrciog S, Grigorescu A, Tudose G (2022) Spatio-temporal patterns of the talents labour market across European countries. Rom J Reg Sci 16(2)

Lv XS (2024) My colleague is not "human": will working with robots make you act more indifferently? J Bus Res 176:114585

Macpherson WE, Werner A, Mey MR (2023) Talent approaches for the South African automotive industry. SA J Hum Resour Manag 21:2224

Malik N, Tripathi SN, Kar AK, Shivam G (2022) Impact of artificial intelligence on employees working in industry 4.0 led organizations. Int J Manpower, Bradford 43(2):334–354. https://doi.org/10.1108/ijm-03-2021-0173

Mangler JD-M (2021) Sustainability through cognition aware safety systems. Next level human-machine-interaction. https://doi.org/10.48550/arXiv.2110.07003

Marangunić N, Granić A (2015) Technology acceptance model: a literature review from 1986 to 2013. Univ Access Inf Soc 14:81–95. https://doi.org/10.1007/s10209-014-0348-1

Molitor Ma (2022) Human-robot collaboration in a smart industry context: does HRM matter? In: Bondarouk T, Olivas-Luján M (eds) Smart industry—better management (advanced series in management, vol 28. Emerald Publishing, pp 105–123

Molitor M, Renkema M (2022) Human-robot collaboration in a smart industry context: does HRM matter? In: Smart industry–better management. Emerald Publishing Limited, pp 105–123

Obaigbena A, Lottu OA, Ugwuanyi ED, Jacks BS, Sodiya EO, Daraojimba OD (2024) AI and human-robot interaction: a review of recent advances and challenges. GSC Adv Res Rev 18(2):321–330

Parvez MO, Öztüren A, Cobanoglu C, Arasli H, Eluwole KK (2022) Employees' perception of robots and robot-induced unemployment in hospitality industry under COVID-19 pandemic. Int J Hosp Manag 107:103336

Pasparakis A, De Vries J, De Koster R (2023) Assessing the impact of human–robot collaborative order picking systems on warehouse workers. Int J Prod Res 61(22):7776–7790

Pelegrín-Borondo JA-O, Souto-Romero M (2020) Does ethical judgment determine the decision to become a cyborg? J Bus Ethics 161(1):5–17. https://doi.org/10.1007/s10551-018-3970-7

Romero DW, Keepers M, Cavuoto LA, Megahed FM (2021) Smart wearable and collaborative technologies for the Operator 4.0 in the present and post-COVID digital manufacturing worlds. Smart Sustain Manuf Syst 5(1):148–166

Sabil S, Bangkara BA, Mogea T, Niswan E, Timotius E (2023) Identification of HRM improvement strategy using artificial intelligence in modern economic development. Int J Profess Bus Rev 8(6):10

Savela N, Kaakinen M, Ellonen N, Oksanen A (2021) Sharing a work team with robots: the negative effect of robot co-workers on in-group identification with the work team. Comput Hum Behav 115:106585

TO O, MA O, AA A (2013) Information and communications technology (ICT) and health workers proficiency as a determinant of health information management: a case study of health facilities Ogun Southwestern Nigeria. Am Acad Sch Res J 5(4)

Toker K, Afacan Findikli M, Gozubol ZG (2023) To be a cyborg or not: exploring the mechanisms between digital literacy and neural implant acceptance. Kybernetes

WEF (2024) Reskilling revolution: preparing 1 billion people for tomorrow's economy. Retrieved from https://www.weforum.org/impact/reskilling-revolution-reaching-600-million-people-by-2030/

Weis P, Herbert C (2022) Do I still like myself? Human-robot collaboration entails emotional consequences. Comput Human Behavior 127. https://doi.org/10.1016/j.chb.2021.107060

Wolcott EL (2021) Employment inequality: Why do the low-skilled work less now? J Monet Econ 118:161–177. https://doi.org/10.1016/j.jmoneco.2020.09.004

Zehir C, Karaboğa T, Başar D (2020) The transformation of human resource management and its impact on overall business performance: big data analytics and AI technologies in strategic HRM. Digital business strategies in blockchain ecosystems: transformational design and future of global business, pp 265–279

Websites

AMAZON (2023) https://www.aboutamazon.com/news/operations/how-amazon-deploys-robots-in-its-operations-facilities

https://www.siemens.com/global/en/products/automation/topic-areas/digital-enterprise/partner-ecosystem.html?acz=1&gad_source=1&gclid=CjwKCAjwm_SzBhAsEiwAXE2Cv9KMFKDEKeEbXYP-egotx96i8_1lFwqn0POfrRpbxBwVtWoxdV888hoCEwMQAvD_BwE

https://www.siemens.com/mea/en/company/jobs/what-we-do/working-with-robots.html

https://www.press.bmwgroup.com/global/article/detail/T0209722EN/innovative-human-robot-cooperation-in-bmw-group-production?language=en

https://www.automotivedive.com/news/bmw-autonomous-humanoid-robots-spartanburg-factory-figure-bots/705680/

https://www.fanuc.eu/il/en/robots

https://www.fanuc.eu/be/nl/wie-zijn-wij/news-and-events/press_release_human-robot-collaboration

https://www.kuka.com/en-de/company/press/news/2016/08/kuka-roboter-und-menschen-arbeiten-hand-in-hand

AI in Finance: Applications and Challenges

Benilde Oliveira and Cristiana Cerqueira Leal

Abstract This chapter discusses the most important challenges of delivering transparency for black-box models in the context of the latest explainable AI literature and the regulatory framework introduced by the European Union AI Act. The key AI technologies in Finance are presented. Recent advances in AI applied to finance are mainly credited to Machine Learning techniques based on Deep Neural Networks. As AI becomes more integrated into the financial sector, a significant challenge emerges from the limited human ability to comprehend the complexities of the black-box models. Recent legislation, such as the European AI Act, emphasises the importance of AI systems transparency, particularly in high-risk areas. There is a growing demand for explainable AI to ensure that the decision-making processes of AI systems are clear and well-documented to meet regulatory transparency requirements. However, there is no agreement on how to promote the transparency of AI models. While post-hoc explanatory models can be useful in many situations, they also have limitations and therefore, especially in high-stakes decision-making contexts, interpretability should be favoured over explainability.

Keywords AI in finance · EU AI Act · Black-box models · Transparency · Explainable AI · Explainability · Interpretability

1 Introduction

Based on a survey applied to a comprehensive and representative sample of Artificial Intelligence (AI) experts, Grace et al. (2018) concluded that researchers believe there is a 50% chance of AI outperforming humans in all tasks by 2061 and of automating

B. Oliveira (✉)
Management Department, School of Economics, Management and Political Science, University of Minho, Braga, Portugal
e-mail: benilde@eeg.uminho.pt

C. C. Leal
Centre for Research in Economics and Management (NIPE) and Management Department, School of Economics, Management and Political Science, University of Minho, Braga, Portugal

C. Machado and J. P. Davim (eds.), *Challenges and Opportunities in the Artificial Intelligence Era*, https://doi.org/10.1007/978-3-031-85272-5_6

all human jobs by 2138. By 2028, AI is estimated to power 95% of all customer interactions, and consumers will eventually prefer artificial intelligence and chatbots to human interaction (Nirale 2018).

Although AI has been used in Finance since the 1950s (Ng 2020), most recent developments in this field have assumed a transformative role in reshaping finance practices. In the early days, AI systems were relatively easy to understand. However, rapid advancements in AI techniques have led to more complex models over the last two decades. AI-driven technologies such as Natural Language Processing (NLP), Cognitive Robotic Process Automation (CRPA) and Deep Neural Networks (DNNs) are revolutionising traditional financial processes (Berdiyeva et al. 2021).

1.1 Automation in Finance

In the mid-twentieth century, the arrival of computers marked a significant turning point in the automation of the finance sector. Initially, computers were used for fundamental operations, such as basic calculations and data management. However, these early systems were limited by their inability to perform tasks beyond their pre-programmed capabilities, lacking the capacity for autonomous decision-making or adaptation to new available information. Reducing manual labour and minimising errors in data processing were the main goals in this initial phase.

Later on, during the 1970s, further significant technological developments transformed the financial landscape, giving rise to the arrival of electronic trading systems and market data platforms. Stock exchanges began implementing computerised trading, allowing quicker and more efficient trade execution. The NASDAQ, launched in 1971, was among the first electronic stock markets, offering real-time price quotes. At this point, financial institutions began to invest in developing computer-based methods to follow pre-set trading instructions based on specific criteria and market conditions. This ultimately led to the development of algorithmic trading. Although early trading algorithms were basic compared to today's, they established the foundation for the sophisticated AI-driven trading strategies that followed in subsequent years.

Despite significant progress in the initial phases of computerisation within the finance sector, decision-making remained mainly the responsibility of human experts. Finance experts relied on computers as instrumental tools rather than autonomous systems capable of independent decision-making. While computers surpassed in processing data at a speed that exceeded human capability, they could not adapt to new information or learn from previous experiences. The role of human experts was still critical in interpreting the data processed by computers and making informed decisions based on their expertise and experience.

The development of electronic trading in the 1980s enabled faster and more efficient transactions in financial markets. At the same time, the concept of Expert Systems (ES) began to expand into financial services as the industry recognised their potential to perform tasks requiring specialised knowledge, such as credit risk assessment and investment advisory. Early uses of AI in finance focused on automating decision processes for tasks like credit risk assessment in the context of loan approval and fraud detection, providing a consistent and efficient application of expert knowledge (Jackson 1990).

1.2 *Data-Driven Technologies and the Rising of Machine Learning in Finance*

The Internet boom in the early 1990s promoted the development and widespread use of online trading platforms, which significantly increased accessibility to financial markets for individual investors. More advanced AI methods, such as neural networks and decision trees, were also developed in the 1990s and applied to address more complex financial challenges, such as predicting stock prices and optimising portfolios.

As the finance industry demonstrated a growing interest in developing systems that could provide deeper insights for more informed decision-making, the integration of data-driven approaches and advanced algorithms gradually replaced traditional methods. This laid the basis for further development of AI technologies in finance, introducing capabilities such as predictive analytics, Machine Learning (ML), and advanced algorithmic trading.

During the first decade of the 2000s, there was a notable increase in the implementation of AI technologies in finance. This allowed financial institutions to develop models that could learn from data and improve their performance over time. Unlike rule-based systems, ML models could extract insights from historical data, making them more adaptable and thus superior to rule-based systems in areas such as credit scoring, risk assessment, and customer segmentation (e.g. Khandani et al. 2010; Lessmann et al. 2015).

The developments in ML have had a positive impact on advanced algorithmic trading. AI-based technologies have enabled traders to significantly increase the speed and volume of their trades, thereby improving market liquidity and efficiency (Hendershott et al. 2011). However, events like the Flash Crash in 2010 (Kirilenko et al. 2017), one of the most rapid and severe disruptions in U.S. stock market history, raised serious concerns about the impact of AI-based trading on the stability of financial markets. Following the event, the US Securities and Exchange Commission (SEC) investigated the possible causes of the unexpected market crash. In September 2010, the SEC published a report containing the findings of its investigation (SEC/CFTC 2010). According to the report, the markets were particularly fragile and exposed to extreme turbulence before the flash crash. A single large selling order of E-Mini S&P contracts, followed by aggressive selling orders executed by high-frequency trading algorithms, triggered a massive decline in market prices. Although the decline was already underway due to prevailing negative market trends, different studies on the 2010 Flash Crash concluded that high-frequency trading algorithms played a significant role in the crash. The aggressive trading activities of large volumes of securities led to enormous price volatility in the financial markets. At the very least, the activities of high-frequency traders based on AI technology worsened the effects of the crash (Kirilenko et al. 2017).

1.3 The Big Data Era

The Big Data era began to take shape in 2010. Before this period, financial institutions primarily relied on structured data from traditional sources such as stock prices, transactions, and economic reports. The development of technologies like Hadoop (White 2012) and cloud computing enabled financial firms to efficiently store, manage, and process considerable amounts of structured data from markets and financial institutions, as well as unstructured data like social media news and customer reviews. Financial experts have started to rely on AI technologies to examine big data and improve their intelligence on market trends, customer behaviour, and risk management. By enabling a significant increase in the volume, variety, and velocity of data accessible to financial institutions, the emergence of Big Data revolutionised the financial industry. It created new opportunities for data-driven insights and decision-making.

Over the past decade, financial technology (Fintech) has significantly transformed the financial industry (Gomber et al. 2018). Innovations like mobile banking, peer-to-peer (P2P) lending, and robot advisors have made banking and investment services more accessible to a broader audience. Mobile banking has simplified financial management by providing users with convenient smartphone and tablet access. P2P lending platforms such as Zopa (UK) and Auxmoney (Germany) directly connect borrowers with investors, bypassing traditional intermediaries, to provide credit to individuals and small businesses. Robo-advisors, such as Nutmeg (UK) and Finanbest (Spain), leverage technology to offer automated investment management services at a reduced cost, with minimal human intervention. These platforms employ algorithms to provide tailored financial advice and manage investment portfolios based on individual goals and risk tolerance, ultimately making wealth management more accessible with lower fees than traditional financial advisors (Gomber et al. 2018).

As financial institutions generate more data and technology advances, it is anticipated that the use of AI in finance will increase in the coming years. With technological advancements, the finance industry is facing significant pressure to increase profitability, increase service quality, reduce costs, and improve efficiency.

2 Key AI Technologies in Finance

AI involves several technologies that focus on different aspects of creating intelligent systems. Although diverse, these technologies often overlap and complement each other in AI applications. In finance, AI technologies such as ML, ES, NLP, and CRPA are being applied in different areas and are performing a key role in transforming the industry by changing the way financial institutions operate, make decisions and interact with their stakeholders.

2.1 Machine Learning

ML is a foundational technology of AI that involves the construction of models that can generalise from training data to new, unseen data. It focuses on developing algorithms that enable computers to learn from and make predictions or decisions based on data without being explicitly programmed for each task.

ML methods are divided into several classes depending on the learning method and purpose: supervised, unsupervised, reinforcement, and deep learning.

Supervised learning methods solve classification or regression issues. A model is trained in supervised learning using labelled data, where each input is paired with the correct output. The model learns to map inputs to outputs, and once trained, it can predict outcomes for new, unlabelled data. Supervised learning is widely used in applications such as financial prediction, portfolio management, credit rating, and fraud detection (e.g. Krauss et al. 2017; Kvamme et al. 2018; Zhong and Enke 2019).

The primary objective of unsupervised learning is to understand the data's underlying structure. Therefore, it focuses on identifying hidden patterns, anomalies, and imbalances in data that lack predefined labels. Unsupervised learning has several applications, including anomaly detection, customer segmentation, and market analysis (e.g. Bao et al. 2019; Gomes et al. 2021; Mittal and Tyagi 2019; Umuhoza et al. 2020). However, interpreting and validating results can be more challenging, as no predefined labels guide the process (Lee and Shin 2020).

Unlike supervised and unsupervised learning, reinforcement learning (RL) is based on learning through repeated experience gained by interacting with the environment, with the agent making decisions that lead to rewards or penalties. Reinforcement learning is beneficial in situations where the optimal actions are unknown, such as order execution, portfolio optimisation, and dynamic pricing in financial services (Culkin and Das 2017; Nevmyvaka et al. 2006; Yu et al. 2019; Zhang et al. 2020).

Compared with traditional ML techniques, such as support vector machines, Deep Learning (DL) offers the advantage of unsupervised feature learning. This means that DL algorithms can automatically discover the features or representations of the data that are most useful for learning without human intervention. This is a significant advantage over traditional ML, where feature engineering is time-consuming and often subjective. DL also presents strong generalisation capability, meaning it can perform well on new, unseen data and robust training power for big data.

Common applications of DL techniques in finance include stock price prediction (e.g. Zheng et al. 2019; Matsubara et al. 2018), risk management, credit scoring (e.g. Wang et al. 2018), and portfolio management (e.g. Song et al. 2017). DL-based models use large historical datasets to forecast stock prices and future trends to improve investment decisions. Additionally, DL has transformed risk management in the finance industry by employing sophisticated algorithms to analyse vast amounts of data and improve risk-scoring models.

2.2 *Expert Systems*

An ES is an AI system encompassing a well-organized body of knowledge, emulating expert problem-solving skills within a specific domain of expertise. Since its performance depends on the quality of the knowledge base and the rules used by the inference engine, which can affect its accuracy and effectiveness, an expert system can be resource-intensive and expensive to create.

ES comprises three main components: the knowledge base, the inference engine, and the user interface components (Metaxiotis and Psarras 2003; Sotnik et al. 2022). The knowledge base contains the necessary information to solve specific problems. It is a repository created by human experts, containing domain-specific information and heuristic rules. Knowledge can be represented using different techniques (e.g., semantic nets, frames, predicate logic). The inference engine is the processing unit that utilises information from the knowledge base to make decisions or recommendations. In a consultation session, the inference engine evaluates the current status of the knowledge base, manages its content, and determines the order in which inferences are made. At the same time, the user interface plays a key role in facilitating interaction between the system and the user by including several components, such as displays, dialogues, and explanations, that help users understand and effectively use the system's recommendations (Metaxiotis and Psarras 2003). ES are particularly useful in areas where expert knowledge is complex and not easily accessible.

In the finance area, ES applications include financial forecasting (e.g. Petropoulos et al. 2008; Zarandi et al. 2009; Hossain et al. 2022), credit risk assessment (e.g. Holsapple et al. 1988; Tsai and Wu 2008; Sreekantha and Kulkarni 2012), and portfolio management (e.g. Freitas et al. 2009; Shiue et al. 2008; Yunusoglu and Selim 2013).

2.3 *Natural Language Processing*

NLP is a subfield of AI dedicated to developing algorithms and models for processing, analysing, and comprehending human languages. It is focused on facilitating communication between humans and computers within the AI domain. NLP encompasses a range of computational techniques for analysing and representing texts at one or more levels of linguistic analysis to enable human-like language processing for a range of particular tasks or applications (Liddy 2001). NLP attempts to address the inherent problem that while human communications are often ambiguous and imprecise, computers require unambiguous and precise messages to enable understanding.

The finance industry generates and utilises substantial amounts of information in the form of news articles, financial reports, and other types of textual data. The increasing availability of financial text data and the growing demand for automation in the finance industry have enhanced the development of NLP applications in finance. Advances in computer science, linguistics and ML have driven the evolution of NLP in finance. As the volume of financial data continues to increase, traditional analytical approaches are often insufficient to meet the demands of contemporary financial organisations. NLP addresses this challenge by enabling real-time processing and interpretation of unstructured data sources like news, reports, financial statements, and social media comments. Consequently, financial institutions and technology firms successfully use NLP in algorithm trading, fraud detection, customer service, information extraction, market analysis, and investment decisions.

In algorithmic trading, NLP can process news articles, press releases, and social media data to make automatic trading decisions. Trading algorithms can react to market-moving news faster than human traders, making trades based on the sentiments and information extracted from textual sources (Hagenau et al. 2013).

Financial institutions increasingly turn to virtual assistants, like chatbots powered by natural language processing, to enhance customer service. These tools allow better customer interaction, improving experience while decreasing the reliance on humans. Both fintech and traditional financial institutions are leveraging these NLP-based systems to improve their customer´s experience. They offer tailored investment advice and financial products, such as saving plans or loan products, based on individual risk profiles and financial goals. They may also employ nudging strategies to offer sound financial decision support in a sustainable and long-term manner, contributing to the individual's financial well-being over time (Leal and Oliveira 2024).

NPL is also being intensely used for risk management and fraud detection purposes, as it is beneficial for identifying potential risks or fraud by identifying inconsistencies in financial disclosures. Traditional fraud detection systems often struggle to detect fraud on time. Compared to traditional methods, AI-based fraud detection approaches provide a more efficient strategy by offering complex fraud pattern detection and real-time analysis. This reduces costs and increases the effectiveness of fraud detection systems (Adeyeri 2024).

NLP is also highly beneficial for information extraction as it automatically summarises lengthy financial documents, including earnings reports, Environmental, Social, and Governance (ESG) reports, and regulatory filings. By reducing the time human, financial analysts spend processing and reading the data, it allows them to extract key information and make quality decisions in real-time. By analysing large datasets with speed and precision, AI algorithms enhance the reliability of financial information, enabling stakeholders to make informed decisions based on real-time reports (Adeyeri 2024).

Recent developments in NLP have significantly enhanced sentiment extraction from financial news and texts (e.g. Agaian and Kolm 2017; Zhao et al. 2021). Quickly identifying positive or negative sentiments from the news is crucial for traders, portfolio managers, and investors when making investment decisions, including in the context of sustainable investing (Oliveira and Leal 2024). Sentiments expressed in news and tweets significantly impact stock prices and brand reputation, making constant measurement and tracking of these sentiments one of the most essential activities for investors. However, the financial industry's unique vocabulary necessitates specialised sentiment analysis. Generic sentiment analysis is inadequate for finance because many terms have different meanings in this context. For example, "liability" is generally negative but neutral in finance. Similarly, "share" typically has a positive connotation, but in finance, it simply represents a financial asset or stock, making it neutral. Moreover, "bull" is generally neutral but positive in finance, while "bear" is neutral in general but negative in finance. These examples emphasise the need for dedicated models to extract sentiments from financial texts.

2.4 Cognitive Robotic Process Automation

Robotic Process Automation (RPA) can be defined as "the use of a preconfigured software instance that uses business rules and predefined activity choreography to complete the autonomous execution of a combination of processes, activities, transactions, and tasks in one or more unrelated software systems to deliver a result or service with human exception management" (IEEE 2017). RPA involves using software "robots" to mimic human actions and automate processes. This type of software uses rules and predefined logic to automate repetitive computer-based tasks with minimal human involvement. RPA is, therefore, a technology that uses robotic software to replace humans in performing ordinary and repetitive tasks on computers.

Most recently, RPA technology has been going through a major change being incorporated with AI. CRPA, also known as Intelligent Process Automation (IPA), refers to a combination of RPA and AI, and the finance industry has been exploring intelligent automation.

Traditional RPA automates rule-based tasks using structured data but cannot directly manage unstructured data. In contrast, CRPA employs advanced AI capabilities to process unstructured data inputs, significantly expanding the range of applications. CRPA is automation powered by cognitive computing technologies that give the system human-like capabilities, such as judgment-based decision-making. In CRPA, machines learn from data, suggest courses of action, and make intelligent decisions like humans. Therefore, compared to traditional RPA, CRPA presents essential differences in underlying technologies, methodology, data processing capabilities and scope of application. Traditional RPA uses a process-based approach that automates rules-based actions, which requires technologies such as workflow automation, screen scraping, and macro scripts. On the other hand, CRPA uses ML, NLP, and several other complex AI technologies to augment automation capabilities (Villar and Khan 2021).

In the finance area, CRPA systems are being successfully applied in different areas such as accounting and auditing (Zhang 2019; Gotthardt et al. 2020; Langmann and Kokina 2021), banking (Tatikonda et al. 2022; Joseph 2023; Shidaganti et al. 2023) and insurance (Lamberton et al. 2017; Marek et al. 2019).

3 The Black-Box Problem

According to Statista (2024), global spending on AI in the financial sector was estimated to be $35 billion in 2023. This figure is projected to increase to $97 billion by 2027, representing a total growth of 177% over four years. This translates to an annual growth rate of 29%. In 2023, significant investments in AI were primarily observed in the banking and retail industries. The banking sector represented approximately 59% of total AI investments, amounting to about 20.6 billion U.S. dollars, while the retail sector accounted for around 56%, or 19.7 billion U.S. dollars (Statista 2024). These figures highlight the competitive landscape of AI investments and indicate the growth potential of AI-based systems in the financial industry in the near future.

3.1 The Modern AI Revolution: Deep Neural Networks

Over the last decade, DL has emerged as one of the most promising branches of the modern AI revolution and is the fastest-growing AI sub-domain (Szczepanski 2019). It is an advanced technique of ML based on Artificial Neural Networks (ANNs) that were initially inspired by mechanisms of learning and information with structure and function similar to the processing in the human brain.

In 2024, The Royal Swedish Academy of Sciences awarded the Nobel Prize in Physics to John J. Hopfield from Princeton University (USA) and Geoffrey E. Hinton from the University of Toronto (Canada). They were recognised "for foundational discoveries and inventions that enable machine learning with artificial neural networks" (Nobel Prize Outreach AB 2024). This acknowledgement not only honours the significant contributions of these researchers but also emphasises the growing importance of DL in driving innovation and progress across various fields, including finance.

DL algorithms differ from conventional ML because they can enhance performance through repetition without human feedback. These algorithms utilise structures known as artificial neural networks, which consist of multiple layers of computing units called neurons. Information flows through these networks in a non-linear manner, mimicking the way our brains handle data. One of the key benefits of deep architectures is their ability to tackle tasks using an end-to-end approach. Without human-designed intermediate steps, the network learns the entire process, from input to output. This method lessens the need for extensive data preprocessing, as the input to the network can be a raw signal or image vector, allowing the network to autonomously detect patterns that relate the input to the desired output. This functionality significantly eases the burden on researchers. However, DL relies on large and varied datasets, often including unstructured data, in contrast to traditional ML methods, which can operate effectively with smaller datasets.

The term "deep" in DL refers to the multi-layered architecture of the neural networks. Therefore, DNNs are ANNs with multiple hidden layers, making them more complex and resource-intensive than conventional neural networks. According to Arrieta et al. (2020), the empirical success of DNNs can be attributed to a combination of efficient learning algorithms and their expansive parametric space with hundreds of layers and millions of parameters.

Although DL was developed in computer science, its adaptability to various fields, including finance, ensures its versatility and potential (Chai and Ngai 2020). The ability of DL-based models to learn directly from complex datasets without the need for human manual intervention has led to significant breakthroughs in various fields, including finance. DL-based technologies are not just valuable tools for developing new financial products and services in finance but also efficient risk managers, ensuring compliance and enhancing fraud detection and prevention (Hu and Peng 2023). DL has revolutionised fraud detection by improving the accuracy of transaction pattern recognition. Models trained on transaction data can identify anomalies that suggest suspicious fraudulent activities. Another area significantly benefiting from recent advancements in DL is algorithmic trading (Koppisetti 2024). These models analyse both historical and real-time data to predict market trends and execute trades with minimal human intervention. Programmed algorithms optimise trading systems to maximise returns.

3.2 *The Challenge of Transparency*

Despite its significant potential and success, no comprehensive theoretical understanding of the optimisation process or the internal organisation of DNNs exists. As a result, they are often referred to in the literature as black-box models.

According to Rudin (2019), an AI model is classified as a black-box when it is too complex for any human to understand. Highly recursive DL models are frequently characterised as black-box models due to their significant complexity and the opaque nature of their operational mechanisms. This perception is attributed to several factors, including the high complexity inherent in DNNs, involving billions of parameters and engaging in complex non-linear interactions. Therefore, a significant challenge in this field is the lack of transparency concerning the features the model considers important during training. Moreover, using non-linear activation functions increases the difficulty of rationalising the model's functioning from input to output and, consequently, the understanding of the decision-making mechanisms used by these models.

The lack of transparency in black-box models makes the assessment or improvement of these models challenging, as their internal mechanisms are not readily visible. This concern is especially critical in areas like finance and other high-stakes areas, where potential errors can lead to significant consequences.

4 European Union AI Regulatory Framework

As AI becomes more prevalent, efforts to regulate the black-box models are increasing. At a regulatory level, the challenge lies in creating a regulatory framework that ensures the trustworthiness of AI systems but still allows for faster innovation, which is an inherent characteristic of the AI field. Achieving this requires a careful consideration of the interests of the different stakeholders.

In 2018, The European Commission appointed a group of 52 experts to provide advice and support the development and implementation of the European Union's (EU) AI strategy. The High-Level Expert Group on AI (AI HLEG) consists of academia, business, and civil society representatives.

4.1 The Foundations of Trustworthy AI: Ethical Principles

EU policymakers have consistently aimed to promote trustworthy, responsible, and 'human-centric' innovation in AI. On 8 April 2019, the High-Level Expert Group on AI (AI HLEG) presented Ethics Guidelines for Trust-worthy Artificial Intelligence.

The Ethics Guidelines establish the foundations of "Trustworthy AI", grounded in fundamental rights and summarised by four ethical principles that must be followed to ensure ethical and robust AI (AI 2019):

1. *Respect for Human Autonomy*: AI should empower human choice and support self-determination without coercion or manipulation.
2. *Prevention of Harm*: AI systems should neither cause nor exacerbate harm. They must be safe and secure. In the development, deployment and use of AI systems, vulnerable persons should receive greater attention. Preventing harm also requires consideration of the natural environment and all living beings.
3. *Fairness*: AI systems development, deployment, and use must be fair. AI development and use must ensure equal and just distribution of benefits and costs

and ensure that individuals and groups are free from unfair bias, discrimination and stigmatisation. Using AI systems should not cause people to be misled or have their freedom of choice unfairly restricted. The procedural dimension of fairness entails the ability to contest and seek effective redress against decisions made by AI systems and by the humans operating them. In order to do so, the entity accountable for the decision must be identifiable, and the decision-making processes should be explicable.

4. *Explicability*: AI processes must be transparent processes. The capabilities and purpose of systems must be openly communicated, and decisions, whenever possible, should be explained to those directly and indirectly affected. Explicability is crucial for building and maintaining users' trust in AI systems. In the case of black-box models, when explaining why a model produces a specific output is not feasible, other measures like traceability, audibility, and clear communication may be necessary, provided that the system respects fundamental rights. The need for explicability varies based on context and the potential impact of inaccurate outputs.

4.2 Requirements to Develop and Implement Trustworthy AI

In addition, Ethics Guidelines provide direction on how to implement and realise trustworthy AI based on a set of seven requirements that should be fulfilled, deriving from the four principles previously outlined (AI 2019):

1. *Human Agency and Oversight*: AI systems should enhance human autonomy and decision-making while respecting fundamental rights. AI systems have the potential to both enhance and inhibit individual rights. Therefore, conducting thorough impact assessments before development is essential to identify and address potential risks. Empowering users to make informed decisions is crucial, as is implementing safeguards to prevent manipulation. To maintain human autonomy and prevent harm, effective oversight is necessary. This can be achieved through human-in-the-loop and human-in-command approaches. The level of oversight required depends on the specific application of the AI system and its associated risks. Ultimately, finding a balance between AI capabilities and human control is key to ensuring these technologies serve society without compromising individual freedoms or safety.
2. *Technical Robustness and Safety*: A key component of achieving Trustworthy AI is technical robustness, which requires AI systems to be developed with a preventative approach to risks and in a manner such that they reliably behave as intended while minimising unintentional and unexpected harm and preventing unacceptable harm. This should also apply to potential changes in their operating environment or the presence of other agents (human and artificial) that may interact with the system. In addition, the physical and mental integrity of humans should be ensured. Protecting AI systems against vulnerabilities and misuse is crucial to preserve their integrity and prevent damage. Safety measures should be

fitted to the risk level of each AI system. This includes implementing emergency protocols that allow for human intervention or a switch to rule-based operations if necessary. Accuracy and consistency in results across various inputs are also essential, especially in high-stakes areas. Finally, AI systems' results must be reproducible and reliable. Reproducibility describes whether an AI experiment exhibits the same behaviour when repeated under the same conditions. This enables scientists and policymakers to describe what AI systems do accurately. To ensure reliability and reproducibility, developers should implement methods enabling systematic testing and AI performance verification. Replication files can facilitate the process of testing and reproducing behaviours.

3. *Privacy and Data Governance*: AI systems must prioritise privacy and data protection throughout their entire lifecycle. This includes the information initially provided by users and any data generated about them during their interactions with the system. The quality of the datasets used is crucial for the performance of AI systems, and these datasets should be thoroughly evaluated before training. Furthermore, it is essential to maintain data integrity, as introducing malicious data can alter the behaviour of AI systems, particularly self-learning. All processes and datasets must be tested and documented at each stage, including planning, training, testing, and deployment. Clear data access protocols should be established in organisations that manage individuals' data. Only qualified personnel with the necessary competencies and a legitimate need to access an individual's data should be permitted to do so.
4. *Transparency*: The datasets and processes contributing to an AI system's decisions, including data gathering, data labelling, and the algorithms used, should be documented to the highest possible standard. This documentation will enable traceability and, consequently, enhance transparency. Explainability is also key in improving transparency, as it involves clarifying an AI system's technical processes and related human decisions. Technical explainability means that the decisions made by an AI system should be understandable and traceable by people. Furthermore, there may be trade-offs between improving a system's explainability, which could reduce its accuracy and increasing its accuracy, which might compromise explainability. AI systems should not pose as humans to users, and individuals have the right to know they are interacting with an AI system. This means that AI systems must be identifiable as such.
5. *Diversity, Non-discrimination, and Fairness*: Data sets used by AI systems may suffer from inadvertent historical bias, incompleteness, and poor governance models. Whenever possible, identifiable and discriminatory bias should be eliminated during the data collection phase. Additionally, unfair bias may also affect the development of AI systems. To mitigate this, control processes should be established to review and address the system's purpose, constraints, requirements, and decisions clearly and transparently. Hiring individuals from diverse backgrounds, cultures, and disciplines can promote a variety of perspectives and should be actively encouraged. Particularly in business-to-consumer domains, AI systems should be designed to accommodate all individuals, regardless of their

age, gender, abilities, or characteristics. AI systems should not have a one-size-fits-all approach and should consider Universal Design principles addressing the broadest possible range of users. Consulting with stakeholders whom the system may directly or indirectly impact throughout its lifecycle is recommended to create trustworthy AI systems.

6. *Societal and Environmental Well-being*: AI systems should promote sustainability and ecological responsibility. Research on how AI can help with global issues like the Sustainable Development Goals should be encouraged. Ideally, AI systems should benefit all human beings, including future generations. While AI can improve social skills, it can also negatively impact them, which can affect people's physical and mental health. Therefore, it is recommended that the effects of these systems be carefully monitored and assessed. Beyond assessing the impact of an AI system's development, deployment and use on individuals, this impact should also be assessed from a societal perspective, considering its effect on institutions, democracy and society in general. The use of AI should be considered carefully, especially in democratic processes, including political decisions and elections.
7. *Accountability*: The requirement of accountability complements the above requirements and entails implementing mechanisms to ensure responsibility and accountability for AI systems and their outcomes before and after their development, deployment and use. Key points include making algorithms transparent and conducting independent audits for applications that affect people's rights. Getting evaluations from internal and external auditors, along with their reports, helps build trust in AI systems. Identifying and reducing any negative impacts is important, especially for those who may be indirectly affected by the systems. There should be protection for whistle-blowers, NGOs, trade unions, and others when they report valid concerns about an AI system. Conflicts may arise when putting the abovementioned requirements into practice, leading to necessary compromises. These compromises should be recognised and assessed regarding their potential impact on ethical standards, particularly fundamental rights. If it becomes impossible to find any ethically acceptable compromise, the development, deployment, and use of the AI system in its current form should be ceased. Decisions about which compromises to pursue should be well-reasoned and thoroughly documented. The decision-maker should take responsibility for how these compromises are determined and consistently evaluate whether the resulting decisions remain appropriate, allowing adjustments to be made to the system as needed.

The Ethics Guidelines, presented by the AI HLEG in 2019, establish the context for the EU strategy for regulating AI. The guidelines present the concept of Trustworthy AI, which has become a key element of the EU approach to AI. The four ethical principles defined in the Ethics Guidelines, which expanded into seven key requirements for trustworthy AI, establish the framework that significantly shaped the EU AI Act (EU 2024b). The EU AI Act classifies AI systems according to the level of risk they pose to people's rights and safety.

4.3 European Union AI Act and the Risk-Based Approach

The EU was the world's first jurisdiction to create and approve legislation to regulate AI systems. While other countries may have some AI-related regulations or guidelines, the EU AI Act was the first comprehensive AI legislation developed and approved by any significant jurisdiction, setting the groundwork for future global regulatory standards.

4.3.1 Risk-Based Classification of AI Systems

In line with the Ethics Guidelines for Trustworthy Artificial Intelligence presented by the AI HLEG in 2019, the EU AI Act highlights the need to regulate high-risk AI systems. Overall, the EU AI Act translates various ethical principles and considerations from the Ethics Guidelines 2019 into a structured legal framework.

In the context of the EU AI Act, an AI system is defined as "a machine-based system that is designed to operate with varying levels of autonomy and that may exhibit adaptiveness after deployment, and that, for explicit or implicit objectives, infers, from the input it receives, how to generate outputs such as predictions, content, recommendations, or decisions that can influence physical or virtual environments" (EU 2024b, Chapter I, Article 3).

The EU AI Act introduces a risk-based approach to classify AI systems into four risk levels, with each level subject to different degrees of regulations and requirements:

1. ***Unacceptable Risk***: AI systems threatening safety, livelihoods, or other fundamental rights are prohibited. The following specific types of AI systems are prohibited (EU 2024b, Chapter II, Article 5):
   (a) AI system that deploys subliminal, manipulative, or deceptive techniques to distort behaviour and impair informed decision-making, causing significant harm.
   (b) AI systems that exploit any vulnerabilities related to age, disability, or socio-economic circumstances to distort behaviour, causing significant harm.
   (c) AI systems for social scoring, like evaluating or classifying individuals or groups based on social behaviour or personal traits, causing detrimental or unfavourable treatment of those people.
   (d) AI systems are used to make risk assessments of a natural person committing criminal offences only based on profiling or personality traits. An exception is accepted if the AI system supports human assessments based on objective, verifiable facts directly linked to criminal activity.
   (e) AI systems that create or expand facial recognition databases by untargeted scraping of facial images from the internet or CCTV footage.

(f) AI systems to infer the emotions of a natural person in the areas of workplace and education institutions, except where the use is intended to be put in place for medical or safety reasons.

(g) AI systems for biometric categorisation based on sensitive attributes such as race, political opinions, trade union membership, religious or philosophical beliefs, sex life, or sexual orientation, unless it involves labelling or filtering lawfully acquired bio-metric datasets or when law enforcement categorises biometric data.

(h) AI systems for 'real-time' remote biometric identification (RBI) in publicly accessible spaces for law enforcement purposes, except when:

   - searching for missing persons, abduction victims, and people who have been human trafficked or sexually exploited;
   - preventing substantial and imminent threats to life or terrorist attacks;
   - identifying suspects in crimes listed in Annex II of the Act and punishable in the Member State concerned by a custodial sentence or a detention order for a maximum period of at least four years. Some examples of such crimes are terrorism, trafficking in human beings, sexual exploitation of children, rape, environmental crime and sabotage.

2. ***High-Risk***: According to the EU AI Act (EU 2024b, Chapter II, Article 6), an AI system is considered high-risk when it is used as a safety component of a product or when it is a product itself that is covered by EU harmonisation legislation listed in Annex I of the Act, that must undergo a third-party assessment before they can be sold or used in accordance to the Union harmonisation legislation listed in Annex I. In addition, AI systems from the critical areas listed in Annexe III of the Act are also considered high-risk (EU 2024b, Chapter II, Article 6):

   (a) Biometrics, when its usage is allowed under the Union or national law in the following specific ways:

      - Remote biometric identification systems. This does not include AI systems intended for biometric verification, which are solely used to confirm that a specific individual is who they claims to be.
      - AI systems for biometric categorisation, according to sensitive or protected attributes or characteristics based on the inference of those attributes or characteristics;
      - AI systems intended to be used for emotion recognition.

   (b) Critical infrastructure AI systems are intended as safety components in managing and operating critical digital infra-structure, road traffic, or water, gas, heating, or electricity supply.

   (c) Education and vocational training AI systems. These include AI systems to be used to:

      - determine access or admission or assign natural persons to educational and vocational training institutions at all levels;

- to evaluate learning outcomes, including when those outcomes are used to steer the learning process of natural persons in educational and vocational training institutions at all levels;
- assess the appropriate level of education that an individual will receive or will be able to access in the context of or within educational and vocational training institutions at all levels;
- monitor and detect prohibited behaviour of students during tests in the context of or within educational and vocational training institutions at all levels.

(d) Employment, workers management and access to self-employment, which includes AI systems targeted:

- for the recruitment or selection of natural persons, in particular, to place targeted job advertisements, to analyse and filter job applications, and to evaluate candidates;
- to make decisions affecting terms of work-related relationships, the promotion or termination of work-related contractual relationships, to allocate tasks based on individual behaviour or personal traits or characteristics or to monitor and evaluate the performance and behaviour of persons in such relationships.

(e) Essential private and public services and benefits, which comprise:

- AI systems for assessing eligibility for public assistance benefits and services, including healthcare;
- AI systems for evaluating creditworthiness and credit scores, excluding financial fraud detection;
- AI in risk assessment and pricing for life and health insurance;
- AI for classifying and prioritising emergency calls and services.

(f) Law enforcement AI systems that may be used in compliance with applicable Union or national law include:

- AI systems for assessing the risk of becoming a crime victim;
- AI systems used as polygraphs or similar tools;
- AI systems for evaluating evidence reliability in criminal investigations;
- AI systems for assessing the risk of offending or re-offending, not solely based on profiling;
- AI systems for profiling individuals in crime detection, investigation, or prosecution.

(g) Migration, asylum, and border control management AI systems that may be used in compliance with applicable national or Union law include:

- AI systems intended to be used by or on behalf of competent public authorities or by Union institutions, bodies, offices or agencies as polygraphs or similar tools;

- AI systems used for risk assessment tools for security, irregular migration, or health by public authorities or Union entities; - AI systems used in processing asylum, visa, or residence permit applications, including the reliability of evidence assessments;
- AI systems used in detecting, recognising, or identifying individuals by public authorities or Union entities, excluding travel document verification.

(h) Administration of justice and democratic processes:

- AI systems designed for use by or for judicial authorities to aid in legal research, interpretation, and application to specific facts or similarly used in alternative dispute resolution;
- AI systems aimed at influencing election outcomes or voting behaviour are covered, except for tools used for administrative or logistical aspects of campaign management, which do not directly expose their outputs to individuals.

AI systems from the areas mentioned above are always considered high-risk unless they do not pose a significant risk to people's health, safety, or rights. Providers who believe their AI system is not high-risk must document their assessment before selling or using it. The EU Commission will provide guidelines and examples of high-risk and non-high-risk AI systems. They can also add or remove conditions for high-risk classification based on evidence. All high-risk systems will be strictly checked through conformity assessments before being put on the market and continuously monitored throughout their lifecycle as such systems' failure or misuse can harm citizens. Companies must also register the product with an EU database.

3. ***Limited Risk***: AI applications in this category pose a risk of deceit or manipulation and, therefore, must comply with specific transparency obligations outlined in Article 50 of the Act (EU 2024a, b, Chapter IV, Article 50). This is the case of chatbots, deepfakes, and features like personalisation. Companies that provide such services must ensure that they are transparent with their customers about what their AI models are being used for and the type of data involved.
4. ***Minimal Risk***: All other AI systems must fulfil minimal regulatory requirements. For example, AI for video games or spam filters falls into this category. Companies providing this type of AI system are encouraged to have a code of conduct ensuring AI is being used ethically.

Figure 1, presented next, summarises the risk-based approach for classifying AI systems in the context of the EU AI Act and its main legal implications.

The final EU AI Act also includes a specific chapter on general-purpose AI (GPAI) models. The legal obligations under the EU AI Act for GPAI models significantly differ depending on whether the model presents a systemic risk. Providers of GPAI models that present a systemic risk (including free and open license GPAI models) must conduct model evaluations and adversarial testing, track and report serious

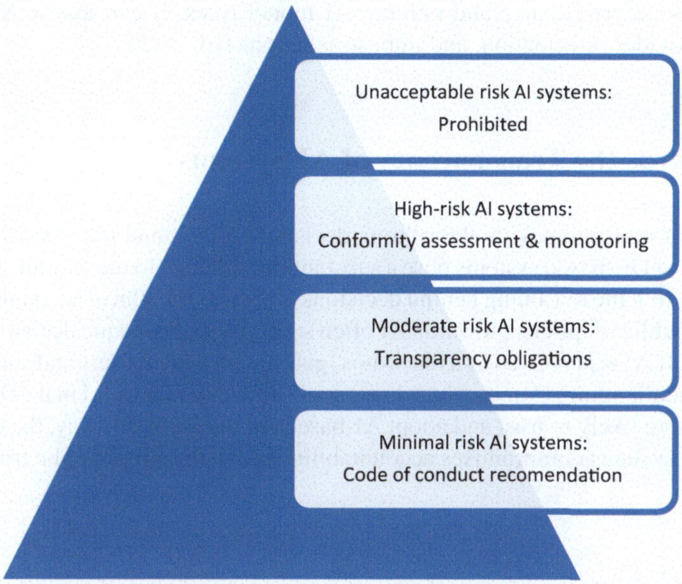

Fig. 1 EU AI Act: AI systems risk levels and regulatory requirements

incidents and ensure cybersecurity protections. The legal obligations are significantly reduced for systems that do not pose systemic risks. In such cases, GPAI model providers only need to provide technical documentation and usage instructions, comply with the Copyright Directive, and publish a summary of the content used for training (EU 2024b, Chapter V).

4.3.2 Timeline for Implementing the EU AI Act

The legislative process was initiated in 2021 when the European Commission proposed the Act. After being formally signed on 13 June 2024, it was published in the EU's Official Journal on 12 July 2024, entering into force 20 days later from 2 August 2024. Article 113 of the Act (EU 2024b, Chapter XIII, Article 113) stipulates that the general application of the regulation starts from 2 August 2026, however:

(a) Prohibitions on AI systems falling into the unacceptable risk category outlined in Article 5 will begin to apply from 2 February 2025;
(b) Obligations for providers of GPAI models defined in Article 53 will come into force from 2 August 2025;
(c) The classification rules for high-risk AI systems established in Article 6(1) and corresponding obligations will begin applying from 2 August 2027.

In January 2024, the European Commission established the European AI Office, which will play a key role in implementing the EU AI Act. The office will support

Member State governance and enforce AI model rules. It can assess AI models, request provider information, and impose sanctions (EU 2024a).

5 Towards the Transparency of AI Systems

The lack of transparency in algorithmic decision-making and the extensive implementation of DL-based systems pose a substantial challenge to the current state of AI. Understanding the reasoning behind decisions is critical for ethical accountability. In addition, public scepticism towards AI often stems from its opaque decision-making processes. If AI is perceived as a black-box, gaining trust from users and stakeholders becomes challenging. Conversely, when people understand how AI makes decisions, they are more likely to trust and adopt AI-based solutions. In this way, the opacity of black-box systems compromises accountability and undermines public trust in such systems.

5.1 EU AI Act Approach to Transparency

The opposite of opacity is transparency. According to Fernandez-Quilez (2023), transparency is achieved when a given model is visible and comprehensible to external users.

The EU AI Act specifies transparency requirements for AI systems. However, those requirements vary depending on the risk category of the AI system. The transparency obligations become more detailed and stricter in the case of high-risk systems (EU 2024b, Chapter III, Section 2, Article 13).

In the specific case of the finance area, credit-scoring AI systems are explicitly targeted as high-risk systems, as these systems are included in the list of critical areas outlined in Annex III of the Act.

In the context of the EU AI Act, transparency "means that AI systems are developed and used in a way that allows appropriate traceability and explainability while making humans aware that they communicate or interact with an AI system, as well as duly informing deployers of the capabilities and limitations of that AI system and affected persons about their rights" (EU 2024b, Recital 27).

Although the EU AI Act does not ban black-box models, the regulation for transparency of AI systems puts a strong emphasis on explainability, creating significant pressure for the development of robust methods to explain complex black-box decisions, especially in the context of high-risk systems.

5.2 *Defining Interpretability and Explainability in AI Transparency Discourse*

Although academics acknowledge the lack of transparency in AI systems as an important issue, their proposed solutions to the black-box problem can significantly differ. Some suggest technical methods to address AI's opacity, such as using explanatory models that clarify how the system makes decisions, while others argue that such explanations are inadequate, maintaining that overcoming the black-box challenge requires approaches that disclose the underlying processes of AI technologies, ensuring their interpretability (Rudin 2019).

As Carvalho et al. (2019) remark, there is some ambiguity regarding terminology in the field of artificial intelligence (AI) and machine learning (ML), with interpretability and explainability sometimes presented as tied concepts and often used interchangeably (e. g. Miller 2019; Adadi and Berrada 2018; Arya et al. 2019; Clinciu and Hastie 2019; Murdoch et al. 2019; Vered et al. 2023).

However, many academic papers make a clear distinction between the two terms (Rudin 2019; Lipton 2018; Montavon et al. 2018; Mittelstadt et al. 2019; Chromik and Schuessler 2020; Arrieta et al. 2020; Palacio et al. 2021; Namatevs et al. 2022), indicating that this difference is acknowledged in the academic community.

Due to the absence of a universal definition for both interpretability and explainability, researchers have proposed a range of desired features, which are often varied and, at times, conflicting, to justify the development of different techniques (Marcinkevičs and Vogt 2020). Moreover, as Graziani et al. (2023) note, the varying interpretations of these technical terms, as discussed in different research papers on explainable AI and machine learning design, create challenges for integrating this knowledge with other fields that influence AI development.

For the remainder of this chapter, the distinction between explainability and interpretability, as delineated by Rudin (2019), will be applied. According to Rudin (2019), certain AI models are designed to embody the ability to clarify their decision-making methods, while others use post-hoc methods to explain their outputs after the training is completed. From this perspective, interpretability relates to fulfilling transparency criteria at the level of task definition. In contrast, explainability refers to how understandable a model is after completing its training, and in such a case, the transparency problem of complex opaque models is addressed on the basis of post-hoc methods.

5.3 *Explainability Versus Inherent Interpretability: Debating Approaches to AI Transparency*

According to the EU AI Act, high-risk AI must be "designed and developed in such a way as to ensure that their operation is sufficiently transparent to enable users to interpret the system's output and use it appropriately" (EU 2024b, Chapter III,

Section 2, Article 13). It emphasises that for AI systems, especially in the context of high-risk areas, it is vital to ensure the transparency of the decision-making process by making the decisions based on an AI model understandable to end users. Therefore, we can conclude that the EU AI regulation highlights the importance of explainability over strict interpretability.

The growing demand for transparency within AI systems has enhanced the development of explainable AI (XAI) as a rapidly evolving research domain in recent years. The primary objective of XAI is to clarify how AI systems arrive at their decisions, making these processes more transparent and easier to understand (Gunning et al. 2019). XAI aims to clarify the mechanisms of complex AI models, enabling informed interactions with these technologies and thereby contributing to building trust in these systems by ensuring that decision-making processes are conducted transparently and open to accountability.

XAI aims to enhance transparency by developing methods enabling enders to understand, trust, and effectively control AI systems (Adadi and Berrada 2018; Arrieta et al. 2020; Saeed and Omlin 2023). Consequently, XAI applications are widespread across numerous sectors of daily life, including, but not limited to, the finance industry (Mao and Benbasat 2000). Attard-Frost et al. (2023) reviewed 47 reports on AI ethical guidelines, and their findings indicated that transparency is the most frequently addressed ethical guideline, with explainability identified as the key aspect of transparency.

XAI's recent focus involves creating additional models (post-hoc models) to explain the mechanisms of complex, black-box systems. These explanations mimic model distillation, transferring knowledge from a large, complex black-box model into a simpler, smaller white-box model. Essentially, an explanation is an "interface" between humans and a decision-maker that is simultaneously an accurate proxy of the decision-maker and comprehensible to humans (Guidotti et al. 2018).

Post-hoc models attempt to make the decision-making process of complex models more understandable by developing techniques and algorithms that provide human-understandable explanations for AI-driven decisions without altering the system's internal structure or compromising their performance. Post-hoc explainability takes a trained model as input and extracts the relationships that the model has learned by querying it and constructing a white-box surrogate model.

Although post-hoc explainability models can potentially help organisations comply with European AI regulations, relying on post-hoc explanations for black-box models can be problematic because these explanations may be unreliable or even misleading. Rudin (2019) argues that explanations generated from black-box models can never fully align with the original model's computations. According to Rudin, if an explanation were completely faithful, it would essentially replicate the original model, eliminating the need for it. Therefore, instead of focusing on developing post-hoc models to enhance the transparency of black-box models, Rudin (2019) suggests using inherently interpretable models that provide clear insights into their operations. Additionally, Vale et al. (2022) argue that post-hoc models do not guarantee the validity of their insights. They conclude that while post-hoc explanatory models can be useful in many situations, they also have limitations that prevent them from being the only means of ensuring fairness in the outcomes, especially in high-stakes decision-making.

According to Rudin (2019), the fact that many scientists struggle to build an inherently interpretable model may contribute to the belief that black-boxes can uncover subtle hidden patterns in the data that the user was not previously aware of. However, she argues that if a given pattern in the data was important to the point that the black-box could leverage it to increase accuracy, a transparent model may be able to uncover and use the same pattern. It all depends on the ML researcher's ability to create accurate but still interpretable models. Additionally,

5.4 *The False Dichotomy: Interpretability and Accuracy in AI Systems*

In ML, a common assumption is that the highest-performing methods (e.g., DL) are the least explainable, and the most explainable (e.g., decision trees) are the least accurate (Gunning et al. 2019). However, this assumption is frequently misleading, especially in cases where the data is structured and includes naturally significant features. In scenarios involving structured data with meaningful attributes, there tends to be little difference in performance between more sophisticated models, such as DNNs, and simpler models, like logistic regression and decision lists, particularly after appropriate data preprocessing (Rudin 2019).

The importance of interpretability in a model largely depends on the context in which it is used. Understanding how and why a model makes decisions is crucial in high-stakes fields such as finance. This is because decisions based on these models can significantly impact individuals and society as a whole. However, interpretability may not be a priority in areas where the implications of a model's decisions are less severe. In certain applications, the ability to quickly produce an accurate outcome may outweigh the need for full transparency of the model. Thus, the emphasis on interpretability can vary significantly across different domains, stressing the need to assess the context and potential impacts of a model's use.

In 2018, FICO,[1] in collaboration with Google and academics at Berkeley, Oxford, Imperial, UC Irvine and MIT, organised the Explainable Machine Learning Challenge using a home equity line of credit (HELOC) application dataset. The challenge aimed to promote the development of XAI solutions for the financial sector, specifically for credit decisions, considered a high-stakes area in finance. This challenge was very significant for the XAI community as it allowed research labs to work on a real-world application to test their theories. For that purpose, teams of researchers were challenged to create and explain a black-box model. The goal was to generate accurate predictions and high-quality explanations for those predictions, which are

[1] FICO (Fair Isaac Corporation) is a leading U.S. software company specialising in credit scoring and decision management services, operating globally with a strong presence in the financial services sector. FICO is also known in the industry for promoting XAI solutions for credit decisions.

a key requirement for credit decisions. This challenge highlighted the importance of developing AI models that are not only accurate but also transparent and explainable, especially in sensitive domains like financial services, where decisions can significantly impact individuals' lives. A Duke University team led by Cynthia Rudin was awarded the FICO Recognition Award[2] for taking an alternative approach. They were acknowledged for going above and beyond expectations with a fully transparent global model. Essentially, they ultimately did not use a black-box model but a traditional, interpretable one instead.

Although the challenge description indicated that researchers were expected to create a black-box model and then explain it afterwards, after reviewing the data, the Duke University team concluded that they did not need a black-box model at all. Considering that explanations for black-box models are often insufficient for high-stakes decisions, the team avoided using such a model. Therefore, they aimed to develop a model that was fully interpretable and ultimately, their interpretable model achieved the same level of accuracy as their best black-box model ("We Didn't Explain the Black Box—We Replaced it with an Interpretable Model", 2019). The approach of the Duke University team and the results achieved emphasise that it is possible to have both model interpretability and high accuracy. Using real-world data, they clearly demonstrate that a high level of interpretability does not always reduce model performance.

6 Concluding Remarks: Reconciling Complexity and Transparency in AI Systems

AI has made remarkable advancements over the past decade, leading to the widespread use of DL to solve complex problems. However, when applied to contexts where wrong decisions can have serious consequences, such as credit scoring, DL models are frequently criticised for their black-box nature. These methods are considered black-box methods, as the reasoning behind their results is difficult to explain. This raises the need for solutions that ensure AI trustworthiness, which in high-risk systems is just as important as accuracy.

Due to the widespread use of black-box models in the finance industry, mainly justified by their perceived superior performance, there is an increasing demand for transparency, similar to other areas (e.g. healthcare or justice) where decision-making transparency is essential.

There is a common belief that black-box models are more accurate because they are more complex and yield higher accuracy, suggesting that black-box approaches are essential for achieving the best predictive results (e.g. Gunning et al. 2019). As Rudin (2019) points out, this is not always the case. In some specific contexts, the performance of more complex systems, such as those based on DNNs, is not

[2] A team from IBM Research won the 2018 Explainable Machine Learning Challenge.

significantly different from that based on simpler methods, such as logistic regression or decision lists.

Nowadays, regardless of the opacity problem of black-box models, DL methodologies are on the basis of most AI systems in high-stakes areas. The argument is for addressing the black-box problem by using XAI to mitigate the risk of using these complex models. As ML systems grow more complex and influential, there is also a growing focus on developing XAI to promote transparency of black-box models by building trust in the context of the responsible use of AI technologies. In fact, there has been a notable increase in research focused on enhancing AI transparency in recent years. However, the literature on this field lacks a unanimous perspective on the most effective ways to achieve transparency. While some authors argue that transparency should involve using models that are inherently interpretable (e.g. Rudin 2019), others promote post-hoc methods to explain the decision-making processes of opaque models (e.g. Confalonieri et al. 2021).

As the use of AI systems grows and the need for transparency urges, regulatory frameworks are being established to ensure fairness and accountability in its deployment. That is the case of the EU AI Act, which mandates transparency for high-risk AI systems. The EU AI Act emphasises the importance of explainability and transparency but does not mandate full interpretability for AI systems allowing black-box models to persist, even in high-stakes areas. The EU AI regulation focuses on providing appropriate explanations to ensure transparency rather than requiring AI models to be inherently interpretable.

However, inaccurate and incomplete explanations for black-box decisions can easily undermine the new right to explanation under the EU AI Act. Therefore, at least for high-risk AI systems, the EU regulation should require interpretable models instead of demanding explainability for black-box models. The use of black-box models should be restricted to cases where no interpretable options are available. By requiring companies to justify the need for using a black box model, EU legislation could have the power to shape the future development of the ML field by accelerating the development of highly accurate but also interpretable models.

Acknowledgements This chapter was edited with the assistance of Grammarly, an AI-powered writing tool, to enhance correctness and clarity.

Abbreviations

AI	Artificial Intelligence
ANNs	Artificial Neural Networks
CRPA	Cognitive Robotic Process Automation
DL	Deep Learning
DNNs	Deep Neural Networks
EU	European Union
IPA	Intelligent Process Automation

ML Machine Learning
NLP Natural Language Processing
XAI Explainable Artificial Intelligence

References

Adeyeri TB (2024) Automating accounting processes: how AI is streamlining financial reporting. J Artif Intell Res 4(1):72–90

Adadi A, Berrada M (2018) Peeking inside the black-box: a survey on explainable artificial intelligence (XAI). IEEE Access 6:52138–52160

Agaian S, Kolm P (2017) Financial sentiment analysis using machine learning techniques. Int J Invest Manag Financ Innov 3(1):1–9

AI H (2019) High-level expert group on artificial intelligence. Ethics guidelines for trustworthy AI, 6

Arrieta AB, Díaz-Rodríguez N, Del Ser J, Bennetot A, Tabik S, Barbado A et al (2020) Explainable artificial intelligence (XAI): concepts, taxonomies, opportunities and challenges toward responsible AI. Inf Fusion 58:82–115

Arya V, Bellamy RK, Chen PY, Dhurandhar A, Hind M, Hoffman SC et al (2019) One explanation does not fit all: a toolkit and taxonomy of AI explainability techniques. arXiv preprint arXiv: 1909.03012

Attard-Frost B, De los Ríos A, Walters DR (2023) The ethics of AI business practices: a review of 47 AI ethics guidelines. AI Ethics 3(2):389–406

Bao W, Lianju N, Yue K (2019) Integration of unsupervised and supervised machine learning algorithms for credit risk assessment. Expert Syst Appl 128:301–315

Berdiyeva O, Islam MU, Saeedi M (2021) Artificial intelligence in accounting and finance: meta-analysis. Int Bus Rev 3(1):56–79

Carvalho DV, Pereira EM, Cardoso JS (2019) Machine learning interpretability: a survey on methods and metrics. Electronics 8(8):832

Chai JY, Ngai EWT (2020) Decision-making techniques in supplier selection: recent accomplishments and what lies ahead. Expert Syst Appl 140:112903. https://doi.org/10.1016/j.eswa.2019.112903

Chromik M, Schuessler M (2020) A taxonomy for human subject evaluation of black-box explanations in XAI. Exss-atec@ iui 1, 1–7

Clinciu M, Hastie H (2019) A survey of explainable AI terminology. In: Proceedings of the 1st workshop on interactive natural language technology for explainable artificial intelligence (NL4XAI 2019), pp 8–13

Confalonieri R, Coba L, Wagner B, Besold TR (2021) A historical perspective of explainable artificial intelligence. Wiley Interdiscip Rev Data Min Knowl Discov 11(1):e1391

Culkin R, Das SR (2017) Machine learning in finance: the case of deep learning for option pricing. J Invest Manag 15(4):92–100

EU (2024a) Commission decision of 24.1.2024 establishing the European artificial intelligence office. Brussels, 24.1.2024 C(2024) 390 final. https://eur-lex.europa.eu/eli/C/2024/1459/oj. Accessed 12 Sep 2024

EU (2024b) Regulation (EU) 2024/1689 of the European Parliament and of the Council of 13 June 2024 laying down harmonised rules on artificial intelligence and amending Regulations (EC) No 300/2008, (EU) No 167/2013, (EU) No 168/2013, (EU) 2018/858, (EU) 2018/1139 and (EU) 2019/2144 and Directives 2014/90/EU, (EU) 2016/797 and (EU) 2020/1828 (Artificial Intelligence Act) (Text with EEA relevance). 12 July. http://data.europa.eu/eli/reg/2024/1689/oj. Accessed 2 Oct 2024

Fernandez-Quilez A (2023) Deep learning in radiology: ethics of data and on the value of algorithm transparency, interpretability and explainability. AI Ethics 3(1):257–265
Freitas FD, De Souza AF, De Almeida AR (2009) Prediction-based portfolio optimisation model using neural networks. Neurocomputing 72(10–12):2155–2170
Gomber P, Kauffman RJ, Parker C, Weber BW (2018) On the fintech revolution: interpreting the forces of innovation, disruption, and transformation in financial services. J Manag Inf Syst 35(1):220–265. https://doi.org/10.1080/07421222.2018.1440766
Gomes C, Jin Z, Yang H (2021) Insurance fraud detection with unsupervised deep learning. Journal of Risk and Insurance 88(3):591–624
Gotthardt M, Koivulaakso D, Paksoy O, Saramo C, Martikainen M, Lehner O (2020) Current state and challenges in the implementation of smart robotic process automation in accounting and auditing. ACRN J Financ Risk Perspect 9(2020):90–102
Grace K, Salvatier J, Dafoe A, Zhang B, Evans O (2018) When will AI exceed human performance? evidence from AI experts. J Artif Intell Res 62:729–754
Graziani M, Dutkiewicz L, Calvaresi D, Amorim JP, Yordanova K, Vered M et al (2023) A global taxonomy of interpretable AI: unifying the terminology for the technical and social sciences. Artif Intell Rev 56(4):3473–3504
Guidotti R, Monreale A, Ruggieri S, Turini F, Giannotti F, Pedreschi D (2018) A survey of methods for explaining black box models. ACM Comput Surv (CSUR) 51(5):1–42
Gunning D, Stefik M, Choi J, Miller T, Stumpf S, Yang GZ (2019) XAI—explainable artificial intelligence. Sci Robot 4(37), eaay7120
Hagenau M, Liebmann M, Neumann D (2013) Automated news reading: stock price prediction based on financial news using context-capturing features. Decis Support Syst 55(3):685–697
Hendershott T, Jones CM, Menkveld AJ (2011) Does algorithmic trading improve liquidity? J Financ 66(1):1–33
Holsapple CW, Tam KY, Whinston AB (1988) Adapting expert system technology to financial management. Financ Manag 17(3):12–22
Hossain E, Hossain MS, Zander PO, Andersson K (2022) Machine learning with belief rule-based expert systems to predict stock price movements. Expert Syst Appl 206:117706
IEEE (2017) IEEE guide for terms and concepts in intelligent process automation (IEEE Std 2755–2017). https://doi.org/10.1109/IEEESTD.2017.8070671
Hu R, Peng S (2023) Deep learning in finance. Digit Finance 5(1):1–2
Jackson P (1990) Introduction to expert systems. Addison-Wesley Longman Publishing Co., Inc.
Joseph O (2023) Sustainable banking through robotic process automation: what role does ESG and cognitive AI play? J Digit Inf Syst 3(1):116–140
Khandani AE, Kim AJ, Lo AW (2010) Consumer credit-risk models via machine-learning algorithms. J Bank Finance 34(11):2767–2787
Kirilenko A, Kyle AS, Samadi M, Tuzun T (2017) The flash crash: high-frequency trading in an electronic market. J Financ 72(3):967–998
Koppisetti VK (2024) Deep learning: advancements and applications in artificial intelligence. ESP Int J Adv Comput Technol (ESP-IJACT) 2(2), 106–113
Krauss C, Do XA, Huck N (2017) Deep neural networks, gradient-boosted trees, random forests: statistical arbitrage on the S&P 500. Eur J Oper Res 259(2):689–702
Kvamme H, Sellereite N, Aas K, Sjursen S (2018) Predicting mortgage default using convolutional neural networks. Expert Syst Appl 102:207–217
Lamberton C, Brigo D, Hoy D (2017) Impact of robotics, RPA and AI on the insurance industry: challenges and opportunities. J Financ Perspect 4(1)
Langmann C, Kokina J (2021) 13 RPA in accounting. Robot Process Autom, 243–262
Leal CC, Oliveira B (2024) Nudging financial behavior in the age of artificial intelligence. In: Machado CF, Davim JP (eds) Artificial intelligence in production engineering and management. Woodhead Publishing, pp 115–144
Lee I, Shin YJ (2020) Machine learning for enterprises: applications, algorithm selection, and challenges. Bus Horiz 63(2):157–170

Lessmann S, Baesens B, Seow HV, Thomas LC (2015) Benchmarking state-of-the-art classification algorithms for credit scoring: an update of research. Eur J Oper Res 247(1):124–136

Liddy ED (2001) Natural language processing. In: Encyclopedia of library and information science, 2nd ed. Marcel Decker, Inc.

Lipton ZC (2018) The mythos of model interpretability: in machine learning, the concept of interpretability is both important and slippery. Queue 16(3):31–57

Mao JY, Benbasat I (2000) The use of explanations in knowledge-based systems: cognitive perspectives and a process-tracing analysis. J Manag Inf Syst 17(2):153–179

Marcinkevičs R, Vogt JE (2020) Interpretability and explainability: a machine learning zoo mini-tour. arXiv preprint arXiv:2012.01805

Marek J, Blümlein K, Neubauer J, Wehking C (2019) Ditching labor-intensive paper-based processes: process automation in a Czech insurance company. In: CEUR workshop proceedings, vol 2428, pp 16–24. http://ceur-ws.org/Vol-2428/paper2.pdf

Matsubara T, Akita R, Uehara K (2018) Stock price prediction by deep neural generative model of news articles. IEICE Trans Inf Syst 101(4):901–908

Metaxiotis K, Psarras J (2003) Expert systems in business: applications and future directions for the operations researcher. Ind Manag Data Syst 103(5):361–368

Miller T (2019) Explanation in artificial intelligence: insights from the social sciences. Artif Intell 267:1–38

Mittal S, Tyagi S (2019) Performance evaluation of machine learning algorithms for credit card fraud detection. In: 2019 9th international conference on cloud computing, data science & engineering (confluence). IEEE, pp 320–324

Mittelstadt B, Russell C, Wachter S (2019) Explaining explanations in AI. In: Proceedings of the conference on fairness, accountability, and transparency, pp 279–288

Montavon G, Samek W, Müller KR (2018) Methods for interpreting and understanding deep neural networks. Digit Signal Process 73:1–15

Murdoch WJ, Singh C, Kumbier K, Abbasi-Asl R, Yu B (2019) Interpretable machine learning: definitions, methods, and applications. arXiv e-prints, arXiv-1901

Namatevs I, Sudars K, Dobrajs A (2022) Interpretability versus explainability: classification for understanding deep learning systems and models. Comput Assist Methods Eng Sci 29(4):297–356

Nevmyvaka Y, Feng Y, Kearns M (2006) Reinforcement learning for optimized trade execution. In: Proceedings of the 23rd international conference on machine learning, pp 673–680

Ng CW (2020) The future of AI in finance. In: The AI book: the artificial intelligence handbook for investors, entrepreneurs and FinTech visionaries, 6–8

Petropoulos F, Nikolopoulos K, Assimakopoulos V (2008) An expert system for forecasting mutual funds in Greece. Int J Electron Financ 2(4):404–418

Nirale S (2018) *Your ultimate CX destination*. Servion Global Solutions. Retrieved September 26, 2024, from https://servion.com/blog/

Nobel Prize Outreach AB (2024) The nobel prize in physics 2024. Retrieved October 15, 2024, from https://www.nobelprize.org/prizes/physics/2024/summary/

Oliveira B, Leal CC (2024) Leading the way toward a sustainable future: the role of sustainable finance and environmental, social, and governance investing. In: Machado CF, Davim JP (eds) Circular economy and manufacturing. Woodhead Publishing, pp 53–82

Palacio S, Lucieri A, Munir M, Ahmed S, Hees J, Dengel A (2021) Xai handbook: towards a unified framework for explainable AI. In: Proceedings of the IEEE/CVF international conference on computer vision, pp 3766–3775

Rudin C (2019) Stop explaining black box machine learning models for high stakes decisions and use interpretable models instead. Nat Mach Intell 1(5):206–215

Saeed W, Omlin C (2023) Explainable AI (XAI): a systematic meta-survey of current challenges and future opportunities. Knowl-Based Syst 263:110273

SEC/CFTC (2010) U.S. Securities and Exchange Commission; Commodity Futures Trading Commission (September 30, 2010). Findings Regarding the Market Events of May 6, 2010. https://www.sec.gov/files/marketevents-report.pdf. Accessed 2 Sep 2024
Shidaganti G, Khandelwal L, Gupta K, Vaswani H (2023) Challenges in banking and solving them using RPA. In: Confluence of artificial intelligence and robotic process automation. Springer Nature Singapore, Singapore, pp 133–156
Shiue W, Li ST, Chen KJ (2008) A frame knowledge system for managing financial decision knowledge. Expert Syst Appl 35(3):1068–1079
Song Q, Liu A, Yang SY (2017) Stock portfolio selection using learning-to-rank algorithms with news sentiment. Neurocomputing 264:20–28
Sotnik S, Deineko Z, Lyashenko V (2022) Key directions for development of modern expert systems. Int J Eng Inf Syst (IJEAIS) 6(5):4–10
Sreekantha DK, Kulkarni RV (2012) Expert system design for credit risk evaluation using neuro-fuzzy logic. Expert Syst 29(1):56–69
Statista (2024) Financial sector AI spending forecast 2023. Retrieved October 31, 2024, from https://www.statista.com/statistics/1446037/financial-sector-estimated-ai-spending-forecast/
Szczepanski M (2019) Economic impacts of artificial intelligence (AI). European Parliamentary Research Service, EPRS. https://www.europarl.europa.eu/RegData/etudes/BRIE/2019/637967/EPRS_BRI(2019)637967_EN.pdf. Accessed 17 Sep 2024
Tatikonda V, Venigandla K, Vemuri N (2022) Transforming customer banking experiences: AI-driven RPA for customized service delivery. Int J Dev Res 12:60674–60677
Tsai CF, Wu JW (2008) Using neural network ensembles for bankruptcy prediction and credit scoring. Expert Syst Appl 34(4):2639–2649
Umuhoza E, Ntirushwamaboko D, Awuah J, Birir B (2020) Using unsupervised machine learning techniques for behavioral-based credit card users segmentation in Africa. SAIEE Afr Res J 111(3):95–101
Vale D, El-Sharif A, Ali M (2022) Explainable artificial intelligence (XAI) post-hoc explainability methods: risks and limitations in non-discrimination law. AI Ethics 2(4):815–826
Vered M, Livni T, Howe PDL, Miller T, Sonenberg L (2023) The effects of explanations on automation bias. Artif Intell 322:103952
Villar AS, Khan N (2021) Robotic process automation in banking industry: a case study on Deutsche Bank. J Bank Financ Technol 5(1):71–86
Wang C, Han D, Liu Q, Luo S (2018) A deep learning approach for credit scoring of peer-to-peer lending using attention mechanism LSTM. IEEE Access 7:2161–2168
We didn't explain the black box—we replaced it with an interpretable model (2019) FICO® Community Blog. https://community.fico.com/s/blog-post/a5Q2E0000001czyUAA/fico1670
White T (2012) Hadoop: the definitive guide. O'Reilly Media, Inc.
Yu M, Yang Z, Kolar M, Wang Z (2019) Convergent policy optimization for safe reinforcement learning. Adv Neural Inf Process Syst, 32
Yunusoglu MG, Selim H (2013) A fuzzy rule based expert system for stock evaluation and portfolio construction: an application to Istanbul Stock Exchange. Expert Syst Appl 40(3):908–920
Zarandi MF, Rezaee B, Turksen IB, Neshat E (2009) A type-2 fuzzy rule-based expert system model for stock price analysis. Expert Syst Appl 36(1):139–154
Zhang C (2019) Intelligent process automation in audit. J Emerg Technol Account 16(2):69–88
Zhang Z, Zohren S, Roberts S (2020) Deep reinforcement learning for trading. J Financ Data Sci 2(2):25–40
Zhao L, Li L, Zheng X, Zhang J (2021) A BERT based sentiment analysis and key entity detection approach for online financial texts. In: 2021 IEEE 24th International conference on computer supported cooperative work in design (CSCWD). IEEE, pp 1233–1238
Zheng J, Fu X, Zhang G (2019) Research on exchange rate forecasting based on deep belief network. Neural Comput Appl 31:573–582
Zhong X, Enke D (2019) Predicting the daily return direction of the stock market using hybrid machine learning algorithms. Financ Innov 5(1):1–20

AI Revolutionizing Marketing: Applications and Other Considerations

Teresa Treviño-Benavides and Flor Morton

Abstract As AI technologies rapidly advance, their integration into marketing practices is shifting businesses capabilities to engage with consumers in more targeted, efficient, and personalized ways. This chapter aims to explore the different ways in which AI can be implemented in marketing, while also considering the strategic implications of this technological evolution. In particular, AI applications will be discussed regarding customer segmentation, advertising, content creation, communications, and customer service. Further, it discusses AI's role in digital marketing, highlighting practical applications for website design and usability, email marketing, search engine optimization (SEO), search engine marketing (SEM), and social media marketing. The chapter further discusses AI's contributions to consumer behavior analysis. Additionally, it outlines future research directions to further explore AI's impact on marketing strategies and practices. In sum, it recognizes the transformative role of AI in modern marketing and provides a foundation for understanding its benefits, challenges, and strategic considerations.

Keywords Artificial intelligence (AI) · AI applications · Digital marketing · Consumer behavior analysis · Personalization · Marketing strategy

1 Introduction

The rapid advancement and adoption of new technology and digital communications have created novel opportunities in the business arena. The Internet, smartphones and social media opened the door for new ways in which companies and consumers can interact, create relationships, and deliver value. In this manner, traditional marketing has evolved into a more dynamic and personalized process to face the new empowered consumer. For the last ten years, research and practice has focused on understanding how social media and other digital tools can enhance marketing practices and shape consumer's expectations of companies regarding the use of such

T. Treviño-Benavides (✉) · F. Morton
Department of Management, Universidad de Monterrey, San Pedro Garza García, Mexico
e-mail: teresa.trevinob@udem.edu

C. Machado and J. P. Davim (eds.), *Challenges and Opportunities in the Artificial Intelligence Era*, https://doi.org/10.1007/978-3-031-85272-5_7

technologies. Today, while these tools remain relevant for communicating, building relationships and facilitating valuable exchanges between consumers and organizations, a new and revolutionary technology comes into context: artificial intelligence (AI). AI in marketing is rapidly evolving, and the recent boom in interest about the topic is as evident as AI's impact on organizations. Particularly, recent literature has been focusing on adoption, use, ethics, institutional support, and the revolution of the labor market and marketers' competencies (Vlačić et al. 2021). Results from recent research and practice already suggest that AI will change how people interact with information, technology, organizations, products and services (Mandapuram et al. 2020).

As AI technologies continue to advance, their integration into marketing practices is offering unprecedented opportunities for personalization, efficiency, and insight. Today it becomes increasingly crucial to understand the potential benefits of implementing AI into marketing processes in organizations. For these reasons, the objective of this chapter is to explore the different ways in which AI can be implemented in marketing, while also considering the strategic implications of this technological evolution. In particular, AI applications will be discussed regarding customer segmentation, advertising, content creation, communications, and customer service. Further, it discusses AI's role in digital marketing, highlighting practical applications for website design and usability, email marketing, search engine optimization (SEO), search engine marketing (SEM), and social media marketing. Finally, the chapter discusses AI's contributions to consumer behavior analysis.

The chapter is structured as follows: It begins with an exploration of the various applications of artificial intelligence in marketing, highlighting how AI enhances customer segmentation, advertising, content creation, and communications, as well as customer service. This is followed by a discussion on how AI can be used in the digital marketing realm, specifically focusing on tangible applications for website design, usability, email marketing, search engine optimization (SEO), search engine marketing (SEM), and social media marketing. Finally, the chapter concludes by exploring ways in which AI can be incorporated into the consumer behavior analysis, by offering insights into the different methods including sentiment analysis, recommendation systems, pattern recognition, behavioral tracking, and predictive analysis. Overall, the chapter concludes with a discussion on the potential of AI in organizations as well as the managerial and theoretical implications of its use, and offers some ideas for future research on the topic.

2 Literature Review

2.1 AI Applications in Marketing

The section explores literature on how AI is revolutionizing key aspects of marketing practice. It begins with consumer segmentation, where AI enables more precise targeting and personalization, followed by AI-driven content creation that allows for scalable, dynamic content strategies. In advertising and communications, AI is optimizing the advertising process from the idea generation, campaign creation and message delivery. The role of AI in enhancing customer service is also explored, particularly through chatbots and other automated systems. This section also covers how AI impacts digital marketing strategies, by creating more effective and personalized social media campaigns. The discussion continues to explore how AI impacts the consumer behavior analysis to create better products, services and meaningful experiences that provide value.

2.2 Consumer Segmentation

In marketing, consumer segmentation has always been an important process to fully ensure that products and services meet consumer needs (Ozan and Iheme 2019). The practice of dividing the market into distinct groups with shared characteristics, has been a foundation of marketing for decades. By understanding and categorizing consumers based on factors such as demographics, behavior, interests, needs and preferences, businesses can tailor their marketing efforts to meet the specific needs and desires of different segments (Fisher et al. 2020; Ehsani and Hosseini 2023). This approach has long been essential in enabling marketers to deliver more relevant and effective messaging, ensuring that the right products and services reach the right audiences, thereby maximizing both customer satisfaction and business outcomes (Upadhyay and Choudhary 2023).

Additionally, segmentation also allows for better personalization in terms of product creation, communication strategies and service offerings that will be more likely to resonate with customers. Managers can use several variables to segment the market, such as demographics, behavioral, psychographic, and others; however, the results of such forms of segmentation often delivers big groups that are not exactly specific and depend on the level of insights companies have about their audiences (Ozan and Iheme 2019).

Today, artificial intelligence is revolutionizing consumer segmentation by enabling more precise and efficient identification of consumer groups. This technology uses sophisticated algorithms and vast amounts of data to enhance insights and find solutions to problems. For these reasons, by implementing AI into the segmentation process, companies can obtain a deep understanding of consumers (Upadhyay and Choudhary 2023). Such understanding comes into light considering several benefits that AI offers in the segmentation process. First, AI eliminates the human biases in segmentation, as the algorithms will analyze the data without making assumptions of the audiences. The power of AI can bring to light hidden patterns in data that may be difficult to recognize manually. Additionally, the segmentation process through AI can be an ongoing and automated process, taking into account the dynamic nature of markets and people. Furthermore, segmenting markets with AI can help companies achieve a higher level of personalization or hyper-personalization (Ozan and Iheme 2019). Hyper-personalization can be achieved when companies target almost individual consumers. In particular, hyper-personalization takes personalization to a more advanced level by leveraging real-time data, using sophisticated algorithms (Morton et al. 2024). A hyper-personalization strategy relies on the company's capability to gather and use customer data into personalized experiences (Valdez Mendia and Flores-Cuautle 2022). In other words, customers can receive real-time content, and create a unique experience. In this case, the "segment" is each individual customer that receives an immersive and engaging experience by providing content and recommendations that are incredibly specific to each individual's preferences and behaviors (Morton et al. 2024).

Particularly speaking of segmentation methods aided by artificial intelligence, research has provided some insights of how such technologies can be used. Mandapuram et al. (2020) discusses two broad approaches to market segmentation using machine learning algorithms. First, supervised methods require a marketing expert that dictates guidelines and rules for the algorithm to work with, and sorts data to find consumer groups based on several variables. For example, grouping consumers by specific behaviors such as purchased products, profitability of their purchases or average cost. Further, unsupervised segmentation methods, artificial intelligence is used to uncover different groups or clusters of consumers based on similarities that in most cases will not be easily visible by humans. While both approaches offer advantages, unsupervised methods allow companies to identify small and highly specific groups of consumers, which even consist of a single individual. Achieving this level of deepness, allows for the creation of personalized experiences and better targeting strategies (Mandapuram et al. 2020).

Other authors have analyzed particular methods of consumer segmentation using AI. For example, Upadhyay and Choudhary (2023) provides a literature review on the topic and discusses several methods. First, K-means clustering is considered one of the most popular unsupervised machine learning algorithms for consumer segmentation. With this method, AI divides into clusters based on their similarity and it has been used in different industries and contexts. For example, K-means was used to segment customers from an ecommerce site based on their preferences, purchasing patterns and demographics. Further, another study applied such a method to segment customers from a bank, generating different segments based on credit score, repayment history and transactions (Upadhyay and Choudhary 2023). Although K-means clustering has been classified as an unsupervised method in the literature, the algorithm is actually influenced by the number of clusters given a priori. For this reason, researchers have experimented with new versions of K-means clustering, in which the algorithm automatically finds an optimal number of clusters without any initialization or parameter selection. For example Sinaga and Yang (2020), proposes the U-k-means clustering algorithm, that improves the computational complexity and performance compared to K-means clustering.

Another popular segmentation method using AI is hierarchical clustering, which is considered an unsupervised learning algorithm. This method also groups similar data points and creates tree-like structure clusters based on their similarities. For this reason, the method is better suited for hierarchical databases such as frequency of using a product, amount spent, level of usage, etc. (Upadhyay and Choudhary 2023). As with K-means clustering, hierarchical clustering has the limitation of finding the optimal amount of clusters. Researchers are working on finding better modifications of such methods to overcome this problem. Research on the topic is recently growing, and extensive experimental results on real databases are being used to come up with better algorithms that are efficient and consistent in finding optimal segments (Nie et al. 2023). Other modifications of such methods mentioned in the literature includes fuzzy clustering, neural networks and support vector machines (Upadhyay and Choudhary 2023).

Overall, while methods are still being tested, AI can significantly enhance how companies divide the market by understanding trends, behaviors and preferences and therefore, create highly targeted and personalized campaigns. It can save time and resources and at the same time, improve marketing efforts.

2.3 AI in Advertising, Content Creation and Communications

Artificial Intelligence has significantly impacted various industries, including the creative sector. Particularly, the content creation process is one of the marketing areas in which AI was quickly incorporated. There are many applications in which AI tools can help marketers to be more efficient and effective in the production of content and communication messages. In particular, AI tools can generate content ideas, draft articles, create visual content, optimize text for Search Engine Optimization strategies, create titles suggestions for engaging emails, posts and ads. Further, AI can be used to create product descriptions, ad creation, media planning, and advertising impact evaluation (Qin and Jiang 2019). By analyzing vast amounts of data, AI can identify trends and audience preferences, enabling marketers to tailor content to specific target groups with precision. Additionally, AI-driven tools can enhance creativity by providing inspiration and assisting in the editing process, ensuring content is not only engaging but also aligned with strategic objectives. This technological integration empowers creators to focus on high-level strategy while AI handles the more routine aspects of content development.

In particular, the creative process can include several tasks: (a) content creation, (b) information analysis, (c) productivity, (d) content enhancement, (e) information enhancement, and (f) data compression (Anantrasirichai and Bull 2020). Research on the topic in recent years has aimed to understand how AI can be useful in such tasks.

For example, regarding content creation, AI can be used to create original work, which includes content generation in the form of text, audio, and video. Examples of such content applied into marketing tactics can include Facebook ads, social media posts, product descriptions, blogs entries, companies or brands bios, among others (Pokhrel and Banjade 2023). For information enhancement, AI tools can help to understand data and improve the marketer's productivity. Examples of tools in this area can induce text categorization, content retrieval and intelligent assistants. In content enhancement, AI can be used to improve the quality of creative work, by improving or modifying images, texts or audios that result in more appealing content. Regarding information extraction and enhancement, AI can be useful to find underlying meanings and interpretations, as well as to suggest ways to communicate information. Finally, in the data compression task, AI can be used to summarize or reduce data that later can be used to create content or communicate a message to audiences (Anantrasirichai and Bull 2020).

Particularly speaking of advertising, generative artificial intelligence (GenAI), a subset of AI, becomes very relevant. Gen-AI refers to algorithms that create new content, such as text, images, music, or code, based on input data instantaneously. In fact, many large companies such as Google, Amazon, Microsoft and Meta, have announced plans to adopt GenAI into their advertising processes (Baek 2023; Lawton 2023; Osadchaya et al. 2024). There are many GenAI tools currently available in the market that can be used in several phases of the advertising and content creation process. Table 1 offers a summary of some of the most popular GenAI tools and how they can be used for these purposes.

Although AI-based tools can significantly speed up content creation and increase relevance in marketing communications, it also brings challenges and ethical issues regarding the creative process. Particularly with the rapid growth of AI tools and their expanding applications, there is an increasing fear that AI could potentially replace human creativity. On one hand, AI's ability to generate content, design visuals, and even compose music may threaten the job of creative professionals. On the other hand, it is also relevant to analyze how AI, rather than replacing humans, can enhance creativity by automating routine tasks and providing new tools for innovation, allowing creatives to focus on more complex aspects of their work. Research on the topic has recognized that AI tools can lack creativity, emotion, and empathy as humans do, and come to the conclusion that, AI technologies are most effective when used to augment human creativity rather than try to replace it (Anantrasirichai and Bull 2020; Murár and Kubovics 2023). Furthermore, there is also the risk of issues regarding piracy, originality and author's rights.

In the same manner AI tools can create appealing content, there is also the reality in which such tools are also being used to create fake images, conversations, videos and other content. In fact, the term deep fake emerged in 2017, and refers to the fact that AI uses huge amounts of data to create fake images, videos or audios. When used correctly in the commercial area, deep fake can help create voices for advertising messages, animation, or improve movie quality. However, the negative aspects of deep fake are evident, as it can create real threats into an individual's privacy, organizations, democracy and even national security (Negi et al. 2021).

Table 1 Generative AI tools summary

GenAI tool	Main use	Application example in advertising and content creation
GPT-4	Generates ad copy, social media posts, and text-based content tailored to audiences	Create Ad copy for ads
Chat GPT	Assists in brainstorming and generating ideas for advertising campaigns	Scripts, headlines, titles, chatbot dialogs, etc.
Copy.ai	Generates marketing copy, including headlines and social media content	Product descriptions, social media posts, etc.
Jasper	Helps generate ad copy, blog posts, and other marketing materials with SEO focus	Content for websites and landing pages
Meta AI	Provides AI tools for generating creative content and enhancing user engagement	Create interactive content
DALL-E	Creates high-quality visuals from text descriptions for use in ads	Create unique and creative product images for ads
DeepArt.io	Creates stylized images and artwork by applying artistic filters to photos	Visual ads with artistic effects
Gemini	Offers advanced image and text generation capabilities for creative content	Create visually appealing graphics and ad copy for campaigns
Adobe Firefly	Generates high-quality, customizable images and graphics	Design ads
Playground AI	Generates images and text from prompts, useful for creative projects	Illustrations and social media copy
Rytr	Assists in writing and generating content for marketing purposes	Ad copy and social media posts

Overall, the application of AI in the creative and advertising process is still in its early stages, with limited experience among companies, creatives, and academic researchers. Future research on the topic can help to shed light on how communication messages created with AI is perceived by consumers, as well as its effectiveness in reaching marketing objectives.

2.4 AI and Customer Service

Artificial Intelligence is increasingly being integrated into consumer service to enhance efficiency, personalization, and overall customer experience. Through AI-powered chatbots and virtual assistants, companies can offer 24/7 customer service, addressing common questions instantly and limit service employees to handle more complex issues. AI can analyze customer data to provide personalized recommendations, anticipate needs, solve frequent questions, and even predict potential problems before they arise. Additionally, AI can automate routine tasks such as ticketing and follow-ups, reducing response times, and increasing customer satisfaction. This integration of AI in customer service not only enhances efficiency but also helps organizations build stronger relationships with their customers by delivering timely and relevant support. In this manner, service quality has always been a topic of interest in organizations, as the goal is to exceed in consumer's perception of the service received, with prior expectations of what the service should be (Ameen et al. 2020).

One AI tool that has been widely used by companies online are chatbots. A chatbot is an artificial intelligence program designed to simulate human conversation through text or voice interactions (Adam et al. 2020). In the context of customer service, chatbots are implemented to manage a variety of tasks, such as answering frequently asked questions, guiding users through processes, or assisting with problem resolution. Chatbots can understand and respond to customer inquiries in real time, often without human intervention. In a typical application, a chatbot on an e-commerce website might help customers track their orders, provide product recommendations, ask questions about their shipping information, or assist with returns. This enhances the efficiency of customer service operations and also ensures consistent and immediate responses, improving the overall user experience. Chatbots, therefore, serve as a crucial tool for organizations aiming to provide high-quality customer service while managing resources effectively.

In fact, research suggests that consumer's value convenience, where less time and effort is better. Therefore consumers are open to using AI bots as their service of choice, especially for low involvement types of decisions (Klaus and Zaichkowsky 2020). A recent study found that some utilitarian factors such as "authenticity of conversation", "convenience" and "perceived enjoyment", results in users having a positive attitude towards chatbots in ecommerce sites (Marjerison et al. 2022). Further, other research has found that consumer engagement and loyalty can be significantly influenced by in-person employee and AI service experiences, however suggests that consumers still prefer human interactions with service employees (Prentice and Nguyen 2020). Additionally, despite there is little research on the topic, literature has discussed that AI-enabled services can be associated with a loss of human control and may create some obstacles for customers. Other research aiming in understanding how consumers may be prone to accept AI service encounters, have suggested that chatbots should be designed anthropomorphically, or "human-like", as they can help in creating a sense of social presence by adopting characteristics of human communication (Adam et al. 2020). This can be especially difficult as AI chatbots rely on verbal, text-like, cues to interact with users. Overall, several studies have converged in that customers prefer to find a balance between AI service options and human interactions to maintain a positive customer experience (Ameen et al. 2020).

2.5 *AI and Digital Marketing*

Digital marketing refers to the use of digital channels, platforms, and technologies to promote products, services, or brands to a targeted audience. It involves using the Internet and electronic devices to engage with consumers in real-time. The use of AI-enabled tools in digital marketing is also revolutionizing the way organizations create content, generate leads, reduce customer acquisition costs, manage customer experiences, market themselves to prospective employees, and convert reachable consumer base via social media (Esch and Black 2021). Recently, while there are some studies around the topic, literature has called for more research that delve into the depth of AI applications in digital marketing and its implications for business (Ziakis and Vlachopoulou 2023).

In particular, there are several tools that can compose a digital marketing strategy: (a) website design and usability, (b) email marketing, (c) search engine optimization, (d) search engine marketing, and (e) social media marketing. In this section, the forms in which AI can help in each digital marketing tool will be discussed.

2.5.1 Website Design and Usability

Today, websites are still one of the most important digital assets a company can own, as many of the other digital marketing tools can "give service" to websites by attracting and moving traffic into it. Despite the growing importance of social media, websites can still be considered "the place to do business" in many cases. However, it is not enough that companies have a website, but the emphasis today relies on the user's experience when visiting the site. It has been found that poorly designed websites may prevent users for staying in the website as a result of frustration (Garett et al. 2016).Visiting a bad website in terms of navigation, speed and experience may be equivalent to visiting a physical store and dealing with a "grumpy employee". Furthermore, the opposite also applies, as it can be expected that a well-designed website may increase positive perceptions of users, and influence visitor retention and purchasing behavior (Garett et al. 2016).

When designing a website, on one hand, information technology managers and programmers can focus on the coding of the website itself, as well as the performance and navigation. On the other hand, graphic designers can focus on the "look and feel" of the website, including the layout, composition, illustrations and text to facilitate user's navigation and experience (Amri 2023). Having these challenges in mind, AI is changing the way in which agencies and organizations are creating websites. There are several AI tools available that can create an initial layout of a website in minutes. Additionally, other tools allow users to create code or snippets of codes that can later be incorporated into a website's code to enhance its functionality or design. When using AI tools to create a website, the approach is to describe the website as the company as much as possible in a website brief. Based on this brief the AI builder will offer suggestions for the appropriate website design that aligns with the company's objectives. One tool that is gaining popularity is wix.com, with its new AI Website Builder, in which in minutes users can create great looking and functional websites tailored to their specific needs. The process is so simple, as the AI website builder guides the user through a series of setup questions, and uses this input to design a first proposal that can then be customized. As today, it is expected that more AI tools can be incorporated into website design to improve user's experiences, automate content creation, improve website design and SEO. Overall, in this manner AI offers new possibilities and opportunities in terms of website development and design (Amri 2023).

2.5.2 Email Marketing

Email marketing is probably one of the oldest forms of digital marketing tools, and today it still can be considered as a unique communication platform. In fact, for many businesses email marketing represents a strategic business tool that helps create a competitive advantage. Literature has suggested that email marketing is still one of the fastest, flexible, cost-efficient, personalized and targeted communication medium in the world (Jenkins 2008). Email marketing has proven to deliver the highest return on investment (ROI) of any of the other digital marketing tools available. A good email marketing campaign can be useful to improve brand loyalty and establish long term relationships with customers and prospects. Furthermore, it is measurable in the fact that companies can learn from metrics of email marketing campaigns and use that information to optimize their decisions. Another advantage of email marketing is that it can be easily targeted, sending the right message to the right audience (Jenkins 2008).

One of the downsides of email marketing is the increasing volume of emails companies are sending to users. This inevitably causes that email marketing can easily be perceived as spam by users. When companies send irrelevant, frequent, or unsolicited emails, users are likely to view these communications as intrusive and spam. Poorly targeted campaigns that fail to offer value can be classified as trash or spam, leading to negative results. To avoid this, marketers must focus on delivering relevant, valuable, well-timed, and permission-based emails that resonate with their audience. Responding to this problem, research has suggested that email marketing strategies need to be updated to get the maximum benefit of the channel, leading to more active, interactive and personalized communications with consumers (Hartemo 2016). With the introduction of AI into email marketing this update can be possible by using machine learning to enhance email marketing strategies and campaigns (Mailchimp, n.d.). In particular, companies can now use AI in email marketing to write email subject lines, generate ideas and content of emails. Additionally, AI tools can help managers to improve the quality of their email databases, by reviewing existing email lists and comparing metrics to determine the probability that each email is valuable or not. This can be very useful in decreasing bouncing rates and reaching the right audience. Furthermore, this list can be updated in real time, as AI can monitor email responses and rates to maintain database quality at its best performance always. Additionally, AI can be useful to analyze and suggest the frequency and best schedule times to send email campaigns. This is especially important as email campaigns can reach an optimized schedule where the most users can read the company's message and decrease unsubscribe rates (Mailchimp, n.d.). The popular email marketing software Mailchimp now offers AI integration to create, plan and monitor successful email marketing campaigns.

Moreover, it has been shown that different types of email marketing campaigns, such as promotional, CRM, and alerts, can increase customer spending and reduce shopping cart abandonment, with strategic management enhancing results (Thomas et al. 2022). For promotional emails, AI can analyze customer behavior to personalize offers and product recommendations, leading to more relevant and engaging email messages that encourage purchases. In CRM emails, AI can segment customer data to personalize messages that build and maintain relationships, providing timely updates and loyalty rewards for example. AI-driven alerts, such as reminders for abandoned carts or product restocks, can move customers through their decision making process and prompt them to complete their purchases. Overall, by strategically managing these email types through insights generated by AI, marketers can optimize timing, content, and personalization to boost engagement, retention and ultimately conversions.

2.5.3 Search Engine Optimization

Search Engine Optimization (SEO) is the practice and techniques that enable a website to get more traffic from search engines, by improving the structure and content of the site in accordance to rules and standards provided by search engines like Google. In general, the process of SEO involves associating a keyword or phrase to the website that should be included strategically in the site's content, so that search engines can crawl, index and rank such websites. Overall, SEO objective is to improve the website ranking on the search engine's result pages (SERPs) when a user searches for the specific associated keyword. This is only possible when the website is built in a way that search engines can comprehend the content of the website and deliver relevant results to users (Rathore 2016). Despite that search engines like Google have undisclosed algorithms, some of the most important factors that they use to rank websites are known, so SEO practitioners work on improving their format and content to enhance its position in the search engine's index (Yuniarthe 2017). For many years now, SEO has been critical in the digital marketing strategy, as it increases a website's exposure and produces more traffic, leads and revenue, but today, the growing competition and changed search engine algorithms call for new approaches to optimize websites (Rathore 2016). Artificial intelligence now plays an important role in SEO, as it can help optimize content to improve search visibility. For example, AI tools can build a classification model that automatically adjusts to SEO guidelines and then identifies and suggests on-site factors that influence the optimization of a website. This model has the ability to identify and predict important factors to achieve better ranking probability (Matošević et al. 2021). Additionally, AI can be useful in SEO as it can analyze data to discover patterns into the factors that are "winning benchmark factors" between sites and how it can affect the ratings. In sum, AI can be used to help the SEO process in the following ways: (a) producing quality content, (b) keyword strategy, (c) on-page SEO, (d) link analysis, and (e) technical SEO.

Regarding quality content, it is known that search engines reward websites with high quality content, offering informative, entertaining or valuable content to the audience. Further, in this content, the keywords that are attempting to rank on should be mentioned in strategic locations of the website. In the past, the strategic use of keywords were considered almost art, as it requires creativity to incorporate it as much as possible avoiding keyword stuffing or overuse. Furthermore, AI can help create the content itself, allowing to obtain optimized versions of descriptions using the keywords strategically (Rathore 2016).

Keyword strategy represents one of the first strategic decisions of SEO, as it involves discovering and targeting certain keywords that potential customers use while looking for products or services online. Companies can enhance the probability that their website is shown in the Search Results Page by including such keywords in their content (Rathore 2016). In this task, AI models can predict how different keywords in different sections of the website can impact organic clicks. The inputs required for this predictive model include data from Google, such as title tags, meta descriptions, and other code snippets (Batista 2020; Ha 2022).

AI can also help SEO professionals in the overall on-site SEO strategy, as it can provide optimized meta descriptions (short summary of the webpage), page titles or title tags, headings, and alt texts. With respect to link analysis and building, AI can be used to suggest possibilities for high-quality links to the website. Finally, regarding the technical part of SEO, AI models can be used to analyze and optimize the website speed, and diagnose any technical issues that may be affecting its performance. It can also observe and analyze traffic activity to improve their experience and increase the probability of achieving better rankings (Rathore 2016). So far, even though AI is helping SEO professionals in the process, it is suggested that AI and machine learning will be more and more applied in the SEO, however, it will still require human interaction to implement, test and monitor the process (Ha 2022).

2.5.4 Search Engine Marketing

When companies lack a good organic search ranking, one way to achieve exposure and a good position in the search engine result pages (SERPs) is through Search Engine Marketing (SEM). SEM can be described as a digital marketing strategy that involves promoting websites by increasing their visibility on SERPs through paid advertisements. Also known as pay-per-click (PPC) advertising, advertisers bid on relevant keywords, and their ads can appear at the top or alongside organic search results, making it easier for potential customers to find the website. SEM is a highly effective way to drive traffic, generate leads, and improve brand awareness. AI-powered tools can help marketers to plan, create and analyze PPC campaigns. For example, Gen-AI tools can be asked to suggest the list of keywords relevant to bid on, and generate different versions of the ad copy considering unique value propositions and call to actions relevant to a specific target audience. As AI can analyze search queries and browsing behaviors, the tools can suggest ads with content that match the target audience which increases the possibility of conversions (2Stallions, n.d.).

As in SEO, one of the basic components of SEM are keywords. AI-powered tools can help marketers go one step further into keyword research, because it can identify trends, analyze competition, and recommend long-tail (specific) keywords that have high conversion rates. Overall, AI can provide insights about trends and search patterns that shed light on what users are looking for on search engines and how they can be better targeted.

2.6 Social Media Marketing

During the past decade, social media marketing has become a critical component of modern communication due to its ability to connect businesses with audiences. Social networking sites such as Facebook, Instagram, LinkedIn, Tiktok, and X (formerly Twitter) offer organizations an accessible and dynamic environment for engaging with consumers, promoting products and services, and building brand awareness. Today, consumers increasingly rely on social networking sites for entertainment, information and purchasing decisions. Therefore, organizations that effectively engage in social media marketing can gain a competitive advantage by creating meaningful connections and experiences. Overall, social media marketing can be described as the organization's activities that transform social media interactions and networks into marketing resources to help achieve specific strategic goals (Li et al. 2021). Today, AI can significantly enhance social media marketing by (a) automating processes, (b) providing deeper insights, and (c) improving personalization.

Regarding automatization, AI-powered tools can simplify customer interactions on social networking sites. By implementing chatbots, users can obtain instant responses to frequently asked questions no matter when they require the information. Further, AI can help plan and schedule social media posts, which helps make this process efficient and consistent. Finally, as discussed before in the advertising and communication section, AI can also generate personalized content for social media posts, which is essential today to compete with the vast amount of content available online. Overall, AI algorithms can identify patterns and preferences, allowing marketers to customize their messaging to specific target audiences (Milan et al. 2023).

2.7 AI and Consumer Behavior Analysis

The analysis of consumer behavior is essential for organizations as it provides insights into the reasons and motivations, preferences, and the overall decision-making processes of potential consumers. The marketing orientation in organizations recognizes that it is essential to understand how consumers interact with products and services, so that businesses can satisfy their needs more efficiently. The process of understanding consumer behavior and generating insights from all consumer's touch-points, allows companies to make decisions about the marketing mix 4P's: product, price, place and promotion. Today, AI has become a powerful tool for analyzing consumer behavior within organizations, by offering deeper insights through its ability to process and interpret vast amounts of data efficiently. In fact, it is now recognized that predicting consumer behavior through artificial intelligence can become an important pillar in modern business strategies, that is changing how companies understand and interact with consumers (Assistant et al. 2023). As mentioned before, machine learning algorithms can identify patterns in consumer interactions, preferences, and purchasing behaviors, enabling organizations to better understand their target audiences.

Even though this topic is extremely new, and little research is found on the literature, there are some studies that analyze some AI applications for consumer behavior analysis. Particularly, some of the most common applications of AI for consumer behavior are: (a) sentiment analysis, recommendation systems, market trend predictions, pattern recognition, real-time data processing and behavioral tracking.

Regarding sentiment analysis, AI is efficient in gathering large amounts of data from social media posts, reviews, comments, etc., and concludes in an overall consumer attitudes and opinions about products, services and topics. Sentiment analysis allows companies to understand satisfaction levels and generalized address concerns (Assistant et al. 2023).

Furthermore, recommendation systems (RS) are intended to provide personalized product or service suggestions based on the consumer's profile, that often nurtures from past browsing, purchase history, and interactions. They can be defined as a program which attempts to recommend the most suitable offering (product or service) to users (Beheshti et al. 2020). Today, it is recognized that achieving personalization in consumer's experiences is a fundamental tool for creating value and meeting individual needs. Therefore, producing personalized content delivers value in terms of convenience, and facilitates the decision making process (Habil et al. 2023). Particularly, the best advantage of incorporating recommendation systems, specially in the online shopping environment, is that consumers will see relevant recommendations that meet their expectations and needs (Liao et al. 2021). To achieve this, large amounts of information is required, and thanks to AI, they can be managed and analyzed. There are several RS used today. Demographic-based filtering uses demographics data collected about consumers to make recommendations (Gazdar and Hidri 2020; Habil et al. 2023). Knowledge gaps-based uses consumer's preferences, interests and needs (Guruge et al. 2021; Habil et al. 2023). Collaborative-based filtering, which uses online buying behaviors of consumers who have similar preferences and activities (Nawara and Kashef 2021; Habil et al. 2023). Content-based filtering, which depends on consumer's favorites, interests and interaction with online items and recommendations are developed based on similar products or services (Guruge et al. 2021; Nawara and Kashef 2021; Habil et al. 2023). Context-aware RS takes into consideration the user's context, settings and surroundings, like location, time zones and events to make recommendations (Nawara and Kashef 2021; Habil et al. 2023). Finally, hybrid-based filtering which combines collaborative and content recommendation systems to make accurate and personalized suggestions to users (Nawara and Kashef 2021; Habil et al. 2023).

For market trend predictions, pattern recognition, and real-time data processing, AI can help learn and understand what customers are saying about a brand in real-time. These insights can help marketers create marketing messages through artificial intelligence that can achieve higher engagement rates (Sadeq et al. 2023). Overall, AI empowers organizations in consumer behavior analysis, which in turn allows managers to make data-driven decisions, anticipate consumer preferences, and adapt strategies to optimize customer experiences and drive business growth. Table 2 shows a summary of the discussed AI Applications in Marketing, as well as the associated references in the literature.

3 Discussion and Conclusion

The present chapter intends to shed light into the different ways in which AI can impact marketing, while also considering the strategic implications of this technological evolution. Throughout the chapter, it was evident that artificial intelligence is reshaping the marketing arena for businesses and professionals, as it is demonstrating to have a profound impact across various traditional marketing functions, including consumer segmentation, advertising, content creation, and communications, customer service, digital marketing, and consumer behavior analysis. The ability that AI has in gathering, analyzing, and making sense of huge amounts of information has no precedent, and therefore its applications are unlimited. Facing a complex, rapidly-changing and challenging environment, the application of AI in business strategies can be the key to deliver value and exceed customer expectations.

As mentioned above, traditional marketing methods are in time for a much needed update. For example, in consumer segmentation, considering that machine learning algorithms can identify distinct groups with shared characteristics, behaviors and preferences in a more precise manner, and integrate other variables such as online behaviors, social media activity and purchasing history. The identification of more precise groups of consumers translate into more personalized marketing strategies or even hyper-personalization strategies that offer individualized product and service offerings, ensuring that marketing efforts remain always relevant and effective. This

Table 2 AI applications in marketing summary

AI application in marketing	Description	Associated references
Consumer segmentation	AI can analyze large datasets to identify patterns, divide the market, and group consumers based on shared characteristics, behaviors, and preferences, enabling more targeted and personalized marketing strategies	Ozan and Iheme (2019), Fisher et al. (2020), Mandapuram et al. (2020), Sinaga and Yang (2020), Ehsani and Hosseini (2023), Nie et al. (2023), Upadhyay and Choudhary (2023)
Advertising, content creation and communication	AI can generate tailored content, optimizing ad placement, and personalizing messages based on data-driven insights and audience behavior	Qin and Jiang (2019), Anantrasirichai and Bull (2020), Negi et al. (2021), Pokhrel and Banjade (2023), Murár and Kubovics (2023), Baek (2023), Lawton (2023), Osadchaya et al. (2024)
Customer service	AI can automate responses to questions, provide personalized assistance, and give support through chatbots and virtual assistants to improve customer service	Ameen et al. (2020), Adam et al. (2020), Klaus and Zaichkowsky (2020), Prentice and Nguyen (2020)
Digital marketing	AI can be used in digital marketing to automate tasks, analyze consumer data, and deliver personalized content with various applications in website design and usability, email marketing, SEO, SEM and Social Media Marketing	Rathore (2016), Hartemo (2016), Esch and Black (2021), Amri (2023), Ziakis and Vlachopoulou (2023), Thomas et al. (2022)
Consumer behavior analysis	AI can be used for consumer behavior analysis through sentiment analysis, recommendation systems, market trend predictions, pattern recognition, real-time data processing, and behavioral tracking, enabling businesses to understand and respond to consumer needs more effectively	Beheshti et al. (2020), Habil et al. (2023), Liao et al. (2021), Gazdar and Hidri (2020), Guruge et al. (2021), Nawara and Kashef (2021), Sadeq et al. (2023), Assistant et al. (2023)

is also related to advertising and content creation, as Generative AI can directly produce suggestions of ad copy, headlines, titles and even visual content that are tailored to specific audiences. This chapter offers a list of GenAI tools that can be considered for content creation and advertising messages.

In addition to this, customer service has also the potential to be enhanced with the use of AI, by automating interactions and improving response times. The benefits of incorporating virtual assistants and chatbots into online experiences are evident, as customers can receive 24/7 assistance about frequently asked questions (FAQs), product information, or common issues. AI algorithms are improving not only to answer FAQs but also to understand consumer sentiment while the communication is taking place, and adapting the responses to this information.

In the digital marketing realm, AI applications are almost limitless. As described above, such technology can help plan, develop and optimize a website and its usability, personalizing user's experiences to ensure that they receive relevant content. In addition to this, other digital marketing tools can be enhanced. For example, email marketing can be powered by sending messages at the right time, with the right content and to the right audience, based on suggestions made by AI. Correspondingly, search engines play an important role in product and service discovery, as it is known that the importance of having a good ranking on the search results page may be the difference between obtaining website traffic or not. AI can help businesses in their SEO and SEM strategies, by providing the best recommendations for website content and pay per click campaigns. Overall this will yield better visibility and driving traffic to the website. On top of that, social media marketing can benefit with the introduction of AI, as it can help marketing managers and community managers to automate some social media processes, like posting and scheduling, as well as to provide deeper insights of user-generated content, and improving personalization of social media posts.

Finally, this chapter discusses the forms and implications of incorporating AI into consumer behavior analysis, which can result in deeper insights that come from big and complex databases. The possibilities for applications such as sentiment analysis, pattern recognition systems, recommendation systems (RS) and predictive analysis can allow businesses to respond quickly and even anticipate changes in consumer preferences, making sure that the marketing strategy is always relevant and aligned into satisfying consumer needs and delivering value.

3.1 Managerial and Theoretical Implications

The present chapter offers several implications for marketing managers and business. First, it presents different ideas into how AI can be incorporated into distinct marketing activities and strategies. Second, it offers some practical tools that can serve as a first approach into GenAI that managers can test to create content and assist them in the marketing process in general. Marketing professionals must develop a clear understanding of how AI tools can be strategically used in their particular business context to deliver value and meaningful experiences. Furthermore, adopting AI at a certain point may require investment in new technologies, changing the way people and teams work, and adapting to new paradigms to fully capitalize on the benefits. Without a doubt, the implementation of AI in business also calls for some important ethical considerations, regarding consumer's privacy with their data, and transparency on how such data is being used. Businesses must carefully consider such topics in order to build trust with their customers. Overall, this intersection of AI and marketing processes presents significant potential, but still requires creativity, knowledge and skills of marketing professionals to test, redefine, and fully harness its full value. Considering the theoretical implications, AI may require the rethinking of traditional marketing theories and frameworks. Throughout the creation of this chapter, it was evident that there is scant recent literature on AI tools and models, how they can be applied in marketing processes, and more importantly, their impact on marketing and business outcomes. AI's application in consumer segmentation, advertising and communications, customer service, digital marketing and consumer behavior analysis represents a fundamental shift into marketing practice and theory. Hopefully, this chapter can help in continuing conversations about the topic in the academic realm, and calls for future research that sheds light on these issues.

3.2 Limitations and Future Research

As no research is without limitations, it is important to mention that this chapter does not intend to be extensive or exhaustive in presenting AI applications in marketing and available tools, considering that AI is just starting to be implemented in organizations, and there is scant practical literature on the topic. Furthermore it is also important to recognize that AI technology is evolving and improving as we speak. What is true is that AI is reshaping marketing strategies by enabling organizations to personalize consumer experiences and make better decisions. More empirical research of AI 's applications will be useful to better understand the significant opportunities for businesses. Some research questions may include: What are the ethical implications and challenges associated with AI? How do consumers perceive AI generated content versus human generated content? How does AI influence consumer trust in marketing strategies and businesses? What is the balance between AI content generated by recommendation systems versus consumers' perceptions of privacy? How does incorporating AI tools improve business performance? among others.

References

Adam M, Wessel M, Benlian A (2020) AI-based chatbots in customer service and their effects on user compliance. Electron Mark 31:427–445. https://doi.org/10.1007/s12525-020-00414-7

Ameen N, Tarhini A, Reppel A, Anand A (2020) Customer experiences in the age of artificial intelligence. Comput Hum Behav 114:106548–106548. https://doi.org/10.1016/j.chb.2020.106548

Amri A (2023) Artificial intelligence (AI) website developer: aesthetic convenience for web designers and graphic designers without coding. Jurnal Inovatif: Inovasi Teknologi Informasi Dan Informatika 6(2):121–125

Anantrasirichai N, Bull D (2020) Artificial intelligence in the creative industries: a review. Artif Intell Rev 55:589–656. https://doi.org/10.1007/s10462-021-10039-7

Assistant P, Devi S, Babu S, Reddy K, Kumar P, Satish M (2023) Predicting consumer behaviour with artificial intelligence. In: 2023 IEEE 5th international conference on cybernetics, cognition and machine learning applications (ICCCMLA), pp 698–703. https://doi.org/10.1109/ICCCMLA58983.2023.10346660

Baek TH (2023) Digital advertising in the age of generative AI. J Curr Issues Res Advert 44(3):249–251
Batista H (2020) A practical introduction to machine learning for SEO professionals. Search Engine J
Beheshti A, Yakhchi S, Mousaeirad S, Ghafari SM, Goluguri SR, Edrisi MA (2020) Towards cognitive recommender systems. Algorithms 13(8):176
Ehsani F, Hosseini M (2023) Consumer segmentation based on location and timing dimensions using big data from business-to-customer retailing marketplaces. Big Data. https://doi.org/10.1089/big.2022.0307
Esch P, Black J (2021) Artificial intelligence (AI): revolutionizing digital marketing. Australas Mark J 29:199–203. https://doi.org/10.1177/18393349211037684
Fisher G, Wisneski J, Bakker R (2020) Segmentation analysis. Strat 3D. https://doi.org/10.1093/oso/9780190081478.003.0016
Garett R, Chiu J, Zhang L, Young SD (2016) A literature review: website design and user engagement. Online J Commun Media Technol 6(3):1
Gazdar A, Hidri L (2020) A new similarity measure for collaborative filtering based recommender systems. Knowl Based Syst 188:105058
Guruge DB, Kadel R, Halder SJ (2021) The state of the art in methodologies of course recommender systems—a review of recent research. Data 6(2):18
Ha NT (2022) Application of AI and machine learning in search engine optimization. In: Proceedings of the 3rd international conference on science, technology and society studies, Ho Chi Minh City, pp 397–403
Habil S, El-Deeb S, El-Bassiouny N (2023) AI-based recommendation systems: the ultimate solution for market prediction and targeting. In: The Palgrave handbook of interactive marketing. Springer International Publishing, Cham, pp 683–704
Hartemo M (2016) Email marketing in the era of the empowered consumer. J Res Interact Mark 10:212–230. https://doi.org/10.1108/JRIM-06-2015-0040
Jenkins S (2008) The truth about email marketing. Pearson Education. FT Press. ISBN 979-0-7897-3794-6
Klaus P, Zaichkowsky J (2020) AI voice bots: a services marketing research agenda. J Serv Mark 34:389–398. https://doi.org/10.1108/jsm-01-2019-0043
Li F, Larimo J, Leonidou LC (2021) Social media marketing strategy: definition, conceptualization, taxonomy, validation, and future agenda. J Acad Mark Sci 49:51–70
Liao SH, Widowati R, Chang HY (2021) A data mining approach for developing online streaming recommendations. Appl Artif Intell 35(15):2204–2227
Mailchimp (n.d.) AI and email marketing. Mailchimp. https://mailchimp.com/resources/ai-email-marketing/
Mandapuram M, Gutlapalli SS, Reddy M, Bodepudi A (2020) Application of artificial intelligence (AI) technologies to accelerate market segmentation. Glob Discl Econ Bus 9(2):141–150
Marjerison R, Zhang Y, Zheng H (2022) AI in e-commerce: application of the use and gratification model to the acceptance of chatbots. Sustainability. https://doi.org/10.3390/su142114270
Matošević G, Dobša J, Mladenić D (2021) Using machine learning for web page classification in search engine optimization. Future Internet 13(1):9
Milan A, Sahu R, Sandhu J (2023) Impact of AI on social marketing and its usage in social media: a review analysis. Int Conf Circuit Power Comput Technol (ICCPCT) 2023:1749–1754. https://doi.org/10.1109/ICCPCT58313.2023.10245676
Morton F, Treviño T, González-Treviño E (2024) Taking customer-centricity to new heights: exploring the intersection of AI, hyper-personalization, and customer-centricity in organizations. In: Machado C, Davim JP (eds) Smart engineering management. Springer, Cham
Murár P, Kubovics M (2023) Using AI to create content designed for marketing communications. Eur Conf Innov Entrep 18(1), 660–668. https://doi.org/10.34190/ecie.18.1.1638
Nawara D, Kashef R (2021) Context-aware recommendation systems in the IoT environment (IoT-CARS)—a comprehensive overview. IEEE Access 9:144270–144284

Negi S, Jayachandran M, Upadhyay S (2021) Deep fake: an understanding of fake images and videos. Int J Sci Res Comput Sci Eng Inf Technol 7(3):183–189

Nie F, Li Z, Wang R, Li X (2023) An effective and efficient algorithm for K-means clustering with new formulation. IEEE Trans Knowl Data Eng 35:3433–3443. https://doi.org/10.1109/TKDE.2022.3155450

Lawton, G. (2023). What is generative AI? Everything you need to know. Tech Target

Osadchaya E, Marder B, Yule JA, Yau A, Lavertu L, Stylos N, Oliver S, Angell R, de Regt A, Gao L, Qi K (2024) To ChatGPT, or not to ChatGPT: navigating the paradoxes of generative AI in the advertising industry. Business Horizons

Ozan Ş, Iheme L (2019) Artificial neural networks in customer segmentation. In: 2019 27th signal processing and communications applications conference (SIU), pp 1–4. https://doi.org/10.1109/SIU.2019.8806558

Pokhrel S, Banjade S (2023) AI content generation technology based on open AI language model. https://doi.org/10.36548/jaicn.2023.4.006

Prentice C, Nguyen M (2020) Engaging and retaining customers with AI and employee service. J Retail Consum Serv 56:102186–102186. https://doi.org/10.1016/j.jretconser.2020.102186

Qin X, Jiang Z (2019) The impact of AI on the advertising process: the Chinese experience. J Advert 48(4):338–346

Rathore B (2016) Usage of AI-powered marketing to advance SEO strategies for optimal search engine rankings. Eduzone: Int Multidiscip Res J 5(1):30–35

Sadeq N, Nassreddine G, Younis J (2023) Impact of artificial intelligence on E-marketing. Int J Trend Sci Res Dev (IJTSRD) 7(1):1318–1331

Sinaga K, Yang M (2020) Unsupervised K-means clustering algorithm. IEEE Access 8:80716–80727. https://doi.org/10.1109/ACCESS.2020.2988796

2Stallions (n.d.) Using AI to enhance search engine marketing. https://2stallions.com/blog/using-ai-to-enhance-search-engine-marketing/

Thomas JS, Chen C, Iacobucci D (2022) Email marketing as a tool for strategic persuasion. J Interact Mark 57(3):377–392.

Upadhyay, R., & Choudhary, P. (2023). A review of customer segmentation methods. Int J Adv Res Sci Commun Technol, 684–692. https://doi.org/10.48175/ijarsct-8904

Valdez Mendia JM, Flores-Cuautle JDJA (2022) Toward customer hyper-personalization experience—A data-driven approach. Cogent Bus Manag 9(1):2041384

Vlačić B, Corbo L, Silva S, Dabić M (2021) The evolving role of artificial intelligence in marketing: a review and research agenda. J Bus Res 128:187–203. https://doi.org/10.1016/J.JBUSRES.2021.01.055

Yuniarthe Y (2017) Application of artificial intelligence (AI) in search engine optimization (SEO). In: 2017 International conference on soft computing, intelligent system and information technology (ICSIIT). IEEE, pp 96–101

Ziakis C, Vlachopoulou M (2023) Artificial intelligence in digital marketing: insights from a comprehensive review. Information. https://doi.org/10.3390/info14120664

From Theory to Practice: How Generative Artificial Intelligence Is Revolutionizing Digital Marketing

Xabier Martínez-Rolán and Teresa Piñeiro-Otero

Abstract The evolution of artificial intelligence (AI) from the foundational work of Alan Turing to the advent of modern systems such as ChatGPT represents a significant technological and societal shift. Turing's initial conceptualisation of machine intelligence constituted a pivotal foundation for the subsequent evolution of AI, particularly in regard to the Turing Test, which assesses a machine's capacity to demonstrate human-like intelligence. This theoretical framework has had a significant impact on a number of fields, including digital marketing, by establishing the importance of machine intelligence in understanding and predicting human behaviour. The evolution of AI has been characterised by a shift between two distinct approaches: symbolic and connectionist. Symbolic AI, which was the dominant paradigm in the early years of AI research, employed logical rules for problem-solving. However, it was unable to effectively address complex tasks such as image recognition. The connectionist school, which drew inspiration from neural networks, demonstrated remarkable proficiency in pattern recognition and data learning, paving the way for significant advancements in AI applications. Despite periods of stagnation, which have been termed "AI winters", the field has continued to evolve. The current approach combines symbolic and connectionist methods in order to create more robust AI systems.

The advent of actual generative AI, particularly transformative models such as Transformers and diffusion models, has had a profound impact on digital marketing. Transformers, with their capacity to process and generate contextually accurate language, facilitate enhanced content creation and personalisation. Chatbots such as ChatGPT exemplify the potential of AI in customer interaction, offering sophisticated and context-aware responses. Furthermore, image generation techniques, including Generative Adversarial Networks (GANs) and diffusion models, have enabled the creation of realistic and personalised visual content, thereby transforming marketing strategies. The implementation of generative AI presents a number of challenges,

X. Martínez-Rolán (✉)
University of Vigo, Pontevedra, Spain
e-mail: xabier.rolan@uvigo.gal

T. Piñeiro-Otero
Universidade da Coruña, A Coruña, Spain
e-mail: teresa.pineiro@udc.es

C. Machado and J. P. Davim (eds.), *Challenges and Opportunities in the Artificial Intelligence Era*, https://doi.org/10.1007/978-3-031-85272-5_8

including the potential for AI "hallucinations," ethical concerns, and environmental impact. It is therefore essential to ensure transparency, mitigate biases, and develop sustainable AI systems in order to advance AI technologies in a responsible manner. As AI continues to be integrated into digital marketing, addressing these challenges will be vital for harnessing its full potential while maintaining ethical and sustainable practices.

Keywords Artificial intelligence (AI) · Digital communication · Digital marketing · Symbolic AI · Connectionist AI · Generative AI · Transformers · Neural networks

1 Introduction

The development of artificial intelligence (AI) from the initial propositions put forth by Alan Turing to the advent of ChatGPT can be viewed as a chronology that reflects the substantial evolution of a disciplinary field that has significantly impacted numerous aspects of contemporary life.

The field of artificial intelligence (AI) has its roots in the pioneering work of Alan Turing, widely regarded as the founding father of AI. Turing's concept of a machine capable of simulating any human reasoning process provided the foundation for a comprehensive investigation into the fundamental aspects of machine intelligence and capability. This conceptual framework is fundamental to an understanding of the processes by which technology and consumer relationships are established in the context of digital marketing.

The most enduring legacy of Turing's work is the test that bears his name, which was proposed in his 1950 paper 'Computing Machinery and Intelligence'. This test, also known as the 'Imitation Game', is designed to ascertain the capacity of a machine to demonstrate intelligent conduct that is indistinguishable from that of a human being (Turing 1950).

In its original formulation, the Turing Test comprises an interaction between a human evaluator and two entities, a machine and a human, conducted via a textual communication channel. The evaluator interacts with both entities without being aware of their true identity, thereby enabling an assessment of their capacity to discern between responses that appear to originate from a human and those that appear to originate from a machine.

Should the evaluator be unable to make a reliable distinction based on the responses received, the machine is deemed to have passed the Turing Test.

It is crucial to emphasise that this test serves as a theoretical instrument for assessing artificial intelligence, rather than a practical methodology for discerning synthetic entities.

The Turing Test has been the subject of numerous interpretations and applications in various academic and non-academic disciplines, including science fiction. A notable example is the 'Voi-gKampf Test' in the film Blade Runner, which served as a mechanism to distinguish between humans and replicants (synthetic beings with a human appearance).

This test represents a fundamental measure in the field of artificial intelligence (AI), as it focuses attention on a machine's ability to exhibit observable intelligent behaviour, rather than on the physical imitation of human intelligence. Despite ongoing debate and controversy, the Turing Test has had a significant and undeniable impact on AI research and development. It has served as an aspirational goal for researchers, driving the development of increasingly sophisticated AI systems in areas such as natural language processing, language understanding and natural language generation.

2 The Evolution of AI Over the Past Few Decades

During the historic Dartmouth Workshop, John McCarthy provided a formal framework for the study of artificial intelligence (AI), thereby establishing the foundation for the development of algorithms utilized in digital marketing. In 1961, McCarthy defined AI as "the science and engineering of making intelligent machines, especially intelligent computer programs" (McCarthy 1961). This definition, though seemingly straightforward, constituted a pivotal moment in AI research, as it elucidated two foundational aspects.

Firstly, McCarthy conceived of AI as a field of study that integrates scientific investigation with practical engineering applications. The objective was not merely to comprehend intelligence from a theoretical perspective, but also to develop tangible systems that could emulate it (Nilsson 2009). Secondly, McCarthy's primary objective was the creation of "intelligent machines", specifically computer programs, capable of performing tasks that would normally require human intelligence. This concept, while innovative at the time, established the foundation for the development of algorithms and systems that are currently central to digital marketing and numerous other applications of AI (Russell and Norvig 2010).

In the context of marketing at the time, which was primarily reliant on traditional media such as print, radio and television, McCarthy's definition might have been perceived as somewhat futuristic. At the time, companies were primarily focused on one-way communication strategies, with minimal or no consumer interaction (Kotler and Keller 2012). However, McCarthy's vision established the foundation for the digital revolution that would transform marketing in the subsequent decades. The algorithms that form the basis of AI would become a fundamental element of digital marketing, facilitating personalisation, automation and data-driven decision-making (Chen et al. 2012; Sidlauskiene et al. 2023).

However, while McCarthy's definition was visionary at the time, it is now limited in the context of the present day. The advent of modern AI has demonstrated that systems can manifest "intelligence" in ways that do not necessarily emulate human cognition. These systems are capable of excelling at specific tasks without necessarily mimicking human cognitive processes (Brynjolfsson and McAfee 2017). Moreover,

McCarthy's definition does not explicitly consider the crucial importance of dynamic interaction with the environment. The capacity to perceive, respond to and modify the environment in real time is a fundamental aspect of numerous contemporary applications of AI, including robotics, autonomous vehicles and digital marketing (Goodfellow et al. 2016). The exclusion of this dynamic element constrains the scope of applicability of the definition in light of recent developments.

Ultimately, McCarthy's definition is imprecise in its delineation of the term 'intelligent'. Given the complex and multifaceted nature of intelligence, a more nuanced definition is necessary to prevent ambiguity. The absence of a clear definition leaves the interpretation of what constitutes an 'intelligent machine' open to interpretation, which limits its utility in contemporary scientific discourse (Legg and Hutter 2007).

One of the most influential definitions of artificial intelligence (AI) is that proposed by Stuart Russell and Peter Norvig. In their book "Artificial Intelligence: A Modern Approach" (Russell and Norvig 2010), they define AI as "the design and study of intelligent agents", where an intelligent agent is defined as "a system that perceives its environment through sensors and acts on that environment through actuators". This definition emphasises the agent's ability to perceive, reason and act on its environment to achieve a given goal.

Russell and Norvig's definition has gained wide acceptance in the scientific community for several reasons. First, this definition transcends the notion of replicating human intelligence as the sole goal of AI. Instead of focusing on emulating human cognition, it focuses on creating systems capable of acting rationally in their environment to achieve a given goal. This broadens the scope of AI to a wider spectrum of applications, including systems that may not think like humans, but are highly effective at solving specific problems (Russell and Norvig 2010).

Secondly, the definition proposed by Russell and Norvig places significant emphasis on the importance of dynamic interaction with the surrounding environment. The capacity to perceive the environment through sensors, process the information obtained and act on it through actuators is reflective of the dynamic nature of numerous real-world AI applications. From robots that navigate complex environments to recommender systems that respond to user behaviour, interaction with the environment constitutes a central element of artificial intelligence (Russell and Norvig 2010).

In conclusion, Russell and Norvig's definition offers a transparent and succinct conceptual framework for comprehending and developing AI systems. By delineating the fundamental constituents of an intelligent agent (perception, reasoning, and action), it offers pragmatic counsel for the engineering and deployment of intelligent systems. This conceptual framework provides a foundation for the development of AI applications with diverse applications, including digital marketing (Russell and Norvig 2010).

The period during which the term 'artificial intelligence' was first used coincides with the advent of the social web, or Web 2.0, a time when platforms such as Twitter and Facebook were the most popular globally. In this context, Russell and Norvig's definition is readily applicable to the domain of digital marketing, as it emphasises the capacity of AI to analyse consumer behaviour (perception) and to undertake strategic actions based on that analysis (action). To illustrate, AI has the capacity to personalise advertisements or recommend products, thereby enabling companies to automate and personalise their marketing strategies on a large scale. This results in the creation of more relevant and dynamic experiences for consumers (Rust and Huang 2014).

2.1 The Advancement of AI Through Different Approaches

The relationship between the development of the symbolic and connectionist schools and the boom and bust cycles of artificial intelligence (AI), known as "AI winters", is significant and illuminating. The symbolic school, which was dominant in the early decades of AI research, is based on the premise that human intelligence can be replicated through the manipulation of symbols and logical rules. This approach, based on formal logic, rule systems and knowledge representation, has been demonstrated to be effective in tasks involving logical reasoning, planning and well-defined problem solving (Newell and Simon 1976). However, the symbolic school has been shown to face significant limitations in tackling more complex problems, such as image recognition or natural language understanding, which require the ability to learn from large amounts of data and deal with uncertainty, as Minsky (1986) suggests when his work establishes the need for more complex and distributed systems to model intelligence.

In contrast, the connectionist school, which draws inspiration from the structure and functioning of the human brain, proposes that intelligence emerges from the interaction between simple interconnected units, which can be conceptualised as analogous to neural networks. This approach, driven by the development of machine learning algorithms and artificial neural networks, has demonstrated considerable success in tasks such as pattern recognition, sensory perception and learning from large data sets (Rumelhart et al. 1986). However, the connectionist school also encounters challenges, particularly in regard to the interpretability of models and the complexity of elucidating the rationale behind the decisions made by neural networks (Lipton 2016).

It is crucial to emphasise that the so-called 'AI winters' do not signify an outright failure of AI research. Rather, they reflect a decline in funding and interest due to the combination of inflated expectations and a lack of immediate results. The current resurgence of AI is based on the combination of symbolic and connectionist approaches, seeking to leverage the strengths of both schools to overcome the limitations of the past and move towards more robust and general AI systems (Hitzler et al. 2022).

During the 1950s and 1960s, the symbolic school, which relies on the manipulation of symbols and logical rules, was the dominant approach in AI research. Notable progress was achieved in domains such as theorem proving and problem solving, which fostered considerable optimism about the prospective capabilities of AI (Nilsson 1998). However, the limitations of this approach in addressing more complex problems, such as image recognition or natural language procesing, resulted in the first AI winter in the mid-1970s.

From the 1980s onwards, the connectionist school, inspired by the workings of the human brain and neural networks, gained momentum. This was accompanied by advances in machine learning and the development of artificial neural networks, which generated new expectations. However, the computational limitations of the time and the lack of massive data to train these models led to a second AI winter in the late 1980s and early 1990s.

In the context of the challenging period that commenced in 1997, a significant milestone was reached when IBM's Deep Blue supercomputer was victorious over world chess champion Garry Kasparov in a six-game match. This event constituted a watershed moment, demonstrating the potential of AI to outperform humans in complex and strategic tasks and revitalising interest in AI research (The History Tech 2023). Despite this breakthrough, the AI industry faced another period of stagnation coinciding with the dotcom crisis in the late 1990s and early 2000s, due to the combination of inflated expectations and a lack of immediate results.

The current resurgence of AI is driven by the development of deep learning algorithms, access to large datasets and increased computational capacity. Of note is the combination of symbolic and connectionist approaches, which has led to the emergence of hybrid or neurosymbolic AI (Hitzler et al. 2022). This integration aims to leverage the strengths of both schools to overcome the limitations of the past and advance towards more robust and general AI systems.

The relationship between the symbolic school of AI and marketing is not immediately apparent, but it is based on the capacity of this approach to systematise and automate processes involving logical reasoning and decision-making. While the connectionist school has gained significant prominence in modern marketing due to its ability to analyse large data sets and personalise experiences (Rust and Huang 2014), the symbolic school offers powerful tools for customer segmentation, campaign optimisation and the creation of recommender systems.

A case in point is the deployment of rule systems for customer segmentation. To illustrate, consider a company that wishes to send personalised offers to its customers. By utilising a rule system based on symbolic logic, the company can define specific criteria, such as purchase history, geographic location or social media activity, to classify customers into different groups and send them messages tailored to their interests.

The symbolic school is also applicable in the field of marketing, particularly in the optimisation of advertising campaigns. By defining clear objectives and establishing a system of rules that automatically adjusts bidding, targeting and ad selection based on performance, companies can enhance the return on investment of their campaigns (Batra and Keller 2016; Martínez-Rolán and Piñeiro-Otero 2022).

Additionally, the token school can facilitate the development of more precise and transparent recommender systems. By modelling user preferences through logical rules and relationships between products or services, companies can offer personalised recommendations that enhance customer experience and foster loyalty (Ricci et al. 2011).

The connectionist school, with its capacity to process vast quantities of data and discern intricate patterns, has transformed the manner in which organisations interact with their customers in marketing. In contrast to the symbolic school, which relies on predefined rules, the connectionist school enables AI systems to learn and adapt as they are exposed to new data, thereby making it a potent instrument for comprehending and anticipating consumer behaviour (Hinton et al. 2012).

One of the most evident illustrations of this interconnection is the deployment of machine learning for the personalisation of customer experiences. E-commerce platforms, for instance, utilise neural network-based recommendation algorithms to analyse users' purchase history, browsing preferences and social media interactions with the objective of delivering products and offers that are highly pertinent to each individual. This personalisation not only enhances the user experience, but also increases conversion rates and loyalty, as Gomez-Uribe and Hunt (2016) illustrated for Netflix.

Another domain in which the connectionist school is effecting transformative change is digital advertising. Online advertising platforms employ machine learning algorithms to target audiences with unparalleled precision, optimising advertising expenditure by displaying pertinent advertisements to individuals most likely to be interested in them. Furthermore, connectionist AI facilitates the creation of dynamic advertisements that adapt in real time to user characteristics and interests, enhancing the efficacy of campaigns.

Sentiment analysis represents a further application of the connectionist school in marketing. It enables companies to gain insight into consumers' opinions and emotions regarding their products, services or campaigns. By processing natural language and analysing large volumes of textual data from social media, online reviews and other sources, companies can identify trends, detect reputational crises and adapt their marketing strategies accordingly (Cambria et al. 2013).

2.2 *Chatbots: From ELIZA to ChatGPT*

The evolution of chatbots, from their initial, rudimentary forms to the current sophistication of ChatGPT, demonstrates a clear progression in the capacity of artificial intelligence (AI) to simulate human conversations and perform complex tasks. The earliest chatbots, such as ELIZA, which was developed in the 1960s, employed simple rules and pre-programmed responses (Weizenbaum 1966). Although ELIZA was capable of simulating a conversation, its capacity to comprehend and respond in a meaningful manner was constrained. Nevertheless, anyone who has interacted with ChatGPT and conducted research on Eliza will observe a striking resemblance in the human–machine interaction dynamics.

As technology advanced, more sophisticated chatbots emerged, such as ALICE (Artificial Linguistic Internet Computer Entity) and SmarterChild, which incorporated natural language processing (NLP) techniques and larger knowledge databases (Wallace 2009). These chatbots demonstrated enhanced contextual comprehension and the capacity to provide more pertinent responses. However, they remained constrained in their capacity to learn and adapt to novel circumstances.

The advent of large-scale language models, such as Google's LaMDA and OpenAI's GPT-3, marked a turning point in the evolution of chatbots (Brown et al. 2020). These models, trained on billions of words, demonstrate an unparalleled capacity to comprehend and produce natural, fluid human language.

ChatGPT, based on the transformer architecture, represents the pinnacle of these developments. Its capacity to manage intricate customer interactions, comprehend context, recall past dialogues, and generate ingenious and tailored responses renders it a potent instrument for enhancing user experience and marketing efficacy (Radford et al. 2019). From furnishing expedient responses to frequently posed queries to proffering personalised suggestions and guiding customers through intricate procedures, ChatGPT—as the vanguard of this nascent generation of chatbots – is revolutionising the manner in which businesses interact with their customers in the digital realm.

Although chatbots have become increasingly prevalent in marketing and advertising, their development is rooted in decades of research in artificial intelligence and natural language processing (Jurafsky and Martin 2023). Early chatbots, such as ELIZA, were based on predefined rules and offered limited interactions. However, the advancement of machine learning algorithms and access to vast datasets have facilitated the creation of more sophisticated chatbots.

One illustrative example is Domino's Pizza's chatbot, which enables customers to place orders via various messaging platforms. This exemplifies the deployment of AI for the automation of tasks and the enhancement of the user experience (Nuance Communication 2017; Woodie 2023).

Another illustrative case study is Sephora Virtual Artist, a chatbot that employs augmented reality to provide users with a virtual makeup trial experience. This example demonstrates the potential of AI to create personalised and engaging experiences that stimulate consumer engagement (Sephora 2021).

2.3 Transformers and Diffusers: Core Technologies Behind the Rise of Generative AI

The preceding pages have provided a contextual framework for understanding the historical relationship between the development of artificial intelligence and the appropriation that marketing had made up to that point. Nevertheless, the present era could be regarded as the golden age of AI, particularly with regard to generative AI and its cross-disciplinary impact. This would not be possible without the advent of new technology that supports such developments, including Transformers and diffusers.

The significance of Transformers is underscored by numerous sources that illustrate how this technology has transformed the AI landscape, enhancing both the precision and efficiency of machine learning models in diverse tasks (Vaswani et al.

2017; Alammar 2018). This revolution has precipitated a substantial transformation in the domain of artificial intelligence, most notably in the realms of natural language processing (NLP) and, by extension, digital marketing and communication. In order to comprehend its impact, it is first necessary to examine its underlying mechanisms and the extent to which it is relevant.

Transformers, introduced by Vaswani et al. in the influential 2017 paper "Attention is All You Need" (which has accrued over 130,000 citations in just seven years), represent a significant advance over recurrent neural networks (RNNs), which process information sequentially. In contrast to RNNs, Transformers are configured with an attention mechanism that enables them to assess and process all elements of a sequence concurrently. This not only reduces processing time but also enhances the quality of analysis by allowing the system to examine all words in a sentence collectively, rather than individually (Vaswani et al. 2017).

Imagine the task of translating a sentence from English to Spanish. A Transformer approaches this task by considering all the words in the sentence simultaneously. This global approach allows it to discern and evaluate the interdependencies and relative relevance of each word in the context of the entire sentence. As a result, the Transformer is able to generate translations that are not only grammatically correct, but also contextually appropriate. This enables it to capture nuances such as irony and other forms of subtle expression that may be lost in more literal translations.

In addition to their efficiency in parallel processing, Transformers are particularly adept at identifying relationships between elements that are separated by long distances within the text. This ability is essential for understanding complex structures in long sentences or texts where context and cross-references are crucial to the full meaning. For example, in literature or in conversations where irony and subtlety play an important role, Transformers can evaluate the overall context and linguistic cues to correctly interpret the tone and intent behind the words.

In this way, Transformers represent a technological evolution that not only improves the speed and efficiency of language processing, but also enriches the understanding of the complexities of human language, thus providing more natural and human translations and communications.

In the field of digital marketing, the impact of Transformers is similarly transformative. The capacity of these models to generate coherent and contextually relevant text renders them optimal for the creation of branded and personalised content that resonates with specific audiences. For instance, Transformers can be trained to generate product descriptions, social media posts and blog content that not only engage readers but also reflect the brand's tone and style accurately. This capacity to tailor content to the requirements and preferences of the target audience enables companies to enhance engagement and reinforce brand loyalty (Martinez-Rolan and Pineiro-Otero 2018).

Furthermore, Transformers are capable of analysing vast quantities of text to identify trends and sentiment, thereby offering invaluable insights that can inform marketing strategy. By discerning the sentiments and opinions expressed in comments, reviews and online conversations, companies can swiftly adapt their campaigns to address concerns, respond to public opinion and personalise communication with customers. Personalisation reaches a new level with the implementation of Transformer-based chatbots.

2.4 Illustrative Examples in Digital Marketing

The Transformers architecture has been demonstrated to be highly effective in a number of areas within the field of digital marketing. In the context of programmatic advertising, Transformers is capable of analysing large data sets in order to identify patterns and predict consumer behaviour. This capability enables companies to target audiences with greater accuracy and optimise their advertising spend, ensuring that advertisements reach the most relevant users and thus increasing their return on investment. Generative AI is able to process data in real time, allowing for immediate adjustments to advertising campaigns and improving the effectiveness and efficiency of digital marketing strategies (Zhou et al. 2017).

With regard to content marketing, the automated generation of content using Transformers enables organisations to create extensive materials that are tailored to different platforms and formats. This technology ensures consistency and syntactic quality of content, which is crucial for maintaining brand image and effectively engaging consumers. Transformers can produce product descriptions, social media posts and blog posts that not only appeal to readers, but also reflect the brand's tone and style with great accuracy. Content personalisation has become a vital tool for businesses as today's consumers demand more individualised and relevant experiences (Aleixo et al. 2024).

Moreover, as previously indicated and exemplified, chatbots based on this technology are capable of handling intricate interactions with customers, providing expedient and personalized responses to their inquiries. This not only enhances customer satisfaction by offering immediate and pertinent solutions, but also increases operational efficiency by reducing the workload on customer service teams, allowing them to concentrate on more critical and challenging tasks (National Retail Federation and IBM Institute of Business Value 2019). The ability of Transformers to continuously learn and adapt to new queries and problems enables chatbots to deliver increasingly accurate and effective service, improving the user experience significantly.

2.5 An Introduction to Image Generation in AI

In the field of artificial intelligence (AI), the process of synthetic image generation, also known as "promptography" after the artist Boris Eldagsen, refers to the creation of images by using specific and deliberate textual cues to guide AI algorithms without the direct intervention of a human photographer or artist. The images, generated from initially random data or noise, can replicate scenes and objects with a high degree of realism. Eldagsen, a pioneer in this field, has advocated the use of the term "promptography" to clearly differentiate these images from traditional photography. He has also emphasised the need for new categories and terminologies to address the complexities and creative possibilities offered by AI (Boris Eldagsen: "AI-generated images and photographs should not compete against each other in competitions", 2023; Hunt 2023).

At the vanguard of this technology, two approaches stand out for their innovative capacity and capability: diffusion models and Generative Adversarial Networks (GANs). Despite their disparate methodologies and underlying mechanisms, both techniques share the common objective of generating realistic images that can be utilised in a multitude of applications, including digital art, advertising and medicine.

2.5.1 Diffusion Models

Diffusion models begin their process with a Gaussian noise floor, which is nothing more than a set of data with no defined structure. This noise serves as the initial canvas on which the model will begin to work. During the training phase, these models learn to introduce noise into real images, giving the algorithm a deep understanding of how real images are visually configured in their original form.

Once the model has been properly trained in this technique, it is able to perform the reverse process—starting with the noise and progressively removing it—to reconstruct coherent and detailed images based on the learned patterns. A leading example of this technology is Stable Diffusion, which operates in a compressed latent space and enables the generation of high-quality images with greatly optimised computational efficiency. This model allows users to influence the generation process through textual descriptions, providing a high degree of personalisation (Ho et al. 2020; Rombach et al. 2022).

2.5.2 Generative Adversarial Networks (GANs)

GANs are built around two main components: a generator and a discriminator. The generator is responsible for generating new samples from random noise, learning over time to emulate the training data set. In parallel, the discriminator evaluates these samples to determine whether they are real or fake, fine-tuning its ability to identify real samples. This system of direct competition, where the success of the generator means the defeat of the discriminator, creates a cycle of continuous improvement that enriches the quality of the generated images (Goodfellow et al. 2014).

2.5.3 Applications and Comparison

GANs have been applied in a variety of contexts, including photorealistic image generation, image resolution enhancement, artistic style transfer, and multi-format content creation. While diffusion models focus on a controlled denoising process, GANs promote competitive interactions that can lead to greater diversity in results, although they often face challenges related to stability during training (Karras et al. 2021).

Both methods have led to significant advances in fields such as digital art, design, advertising and medicine. They continue to evolve, and their convergence promises to further push the boundaries of creativity and personalisation in visual content creation. This duality of approaches not only demonstrates the breadth of applied artificial intelligence, but also highlights its potential to reinvent how we visualise and create new visual experiences (Brock et al. 2018).

3 Notable Pioneers of Generative AI in Digital Marketing

Generative artificial intelligence (AI) has revolutionised digital marketing, enabling automated content creation and personalisation at scale. Here are some of the ground-breaking campaigns that have used chatbots, synthetic imagery and AI-generated video, marking key milestones in the industry.

3.1 Chatbots in Digital Marketing Campaigns

Over the past two years, chatbots have proven to be a valuable tool in various marketing and communications campaigns, improving customer interactions and increasing operational efficiency.

In 2022, Domino's Pizza launched an innovative campaign on Tinder called "Dom Juan." This chatbot interacted with users by sending witty pizza-related phrases for Valentine's Day, generating a lot of media coverage and significantly increasing brand awareness (Christison 2023). In the same year, Mountain Dew used a chatbot called DEWBot on the streaming platform Twitch to interact with its customer base. Over an eight-week period, the chatbot drove engagement through real-time polls and updates, resulting in a 572% increase in channel interactions and a 265% increase in followers (Kenan 2022).

In 2023, insurance company Lemonade implemented a chatbot called Maya to assist users during the insurance purchase process, providing a friendly and efficient experience. In three years, Maya has handled 25% of the company's total queries and sold 1.2 million policies, improving the digital customer experience and reducing costs (Tyagi 2024). Also in 2023, KLM Royal Dutch Airlines used its BlueBot chatbot on Messenger to help customers book flights, check flight status and get baggage information. This multilingual bot has significantly improved the airline's customer service and operational efficiency (Tyagi 2024).

In the same year, River Island launched a chatbot called 'RI-bot' on Messenger and Twitter to answer product questions, check order status and locate stores. In the first six months, RI-bot generated 15 million content interactions and 6.1 million links to posts, highlighting its effectiveness in improving customer engagement (Kenan 2022). Finally, Uber implemented a platform integrating chatbots to reduce response times by 33%, saving over 4000 agent hours and significantly improving customer satisfaction (Tyagi 2024).

These are just a few examples of how next-generation, generative AI-powered chatbots are being used effectively to improve customer experience, increase engagement and optimise operations across multiple industries.

3.2 *Use of Synthetic Images in Digital Marketing*

In the last two years, the implementation of generative AI such as DALL-E, MidJourney and Stable Diffusion has revolutionised marketing and communication campaigns, enabling the creation of engaging and personalised visual content.

In the same year, Heinz launched an innovative campaign using DALL-E 2 to create images of ketchup based on textual descriptions. The results, which featured creative and surprising interpretations of the product, were used on various digital marketing platforms, generating high interest and engagement (Heinz 2024). Also in 2022, Nike used MidJourney to design a series of athletic shoe visuals based on user descriptions. This campaign allowed customers to see their design ideas transformed into realistic images, encouraging community participation and creativity.

In 2023, Nestlé used Stable Diffusion for an advertising campaign in which product images were generated in a variety of natural settings. Stable Diffusion's ability to create detailed and realistic environments allowed Nestlé to present its products in a new and engaging way (Servoz 2023). In the same year, Gucci collaborated with MidJourney to launch a series of AI-generated fashion images. The images, which combined elements of haute couture with surreal styles, were used in social media campaigns, highlighting the brand's innovation and edginess.

In 2023, Volkswagen used DALL-E 3 to create an advertising campaign featuring cars in futuristic settings. DALL-E 3's ability to generate photorealistic and complex images allowed Volkswagen to capture the imagination of its customers and promote its vehicles in an innovative way.

These examples illustrate how generative AI is transforming marketing and communication, offering new ways to engage with consumers through personalised and highly creative visual content.

3.3 *AI-Generated Video in Marketing Campaigns*

Over the past two years, the use of generative AI in video marketing campaigns has revolutionised the industry, enabling the creation of synthetic audiovisual content with an increasingly realistic finish.

In 2022, Synthesia used generative AI to create a video in which David Beckham appeared to speak nine different languages to raise awareness of malaria. Although not a commercial advertising campaign, this video demonstrated the potential of synthetic video in marketing and awareness-raising applications (Synthesia 2024).

Virgin Voyages introduced 'Jen AI', an AI-powered project in collaboration with Jennifer Lopez, in a 2023 campaign. The campaign enabled consumers to create personalised cruise invitations, combining the power of celebrity with AI innovation to deliver highly personalised experiences (Virgin Voyages 2023).

Coca-Cola, also in 2023, launched the 'Masterpiece' campaign, an artistic fusion of AI and human creativity. This initiative used OpenAI to generate visually stunning content, demonstrating how AI can be integrated into the creative advertising process (Gaiduk 2023). A curious and more light-hearted example—under the fan phenomenon—from the same year is the 'Harry Potter by Balenciaga' viral video series. Using MidJourney, ChatGPT and other AI tools, these videos featured Harry Potter characters dressed in Balenciaga garments, generating millions of views and highlighting the potential of AI to produce engaging and viral content (Toolify.ai 2023; Man of Many 2023).

In 2024, Toys 'R' Us launched an innovative campaign using OpenAI's AI-generated video technology, known as Sora, to create a branded video. The video, which premiered at the 2024 Cannes Lions Festival, tells the origin story of Geoffrey the Giraffe, the company's mascot. The campaign was notable for its rapid production, from concept to final product in just a few weeks, and was one of the first to use this advanced AI technology to create video content entirely generated by artificial intelligence (DNyuz 2024; The Toy Book 2024), although they admitted that there was a huge amount of post-production work involved and the end result was narratively very much in line with the type of audiovisual pieces of its time.

This approach marks a milestone in the use of generative AI in the advertising industry. In addition, the video sought to connect emotionally with the audience by evoking the nostalgia and magical appeal associated with Toys 'R' Us, while demonstrating the innovative capabilities of generative technology to tell stories efficiently and creatively.

4 Prediction and Trends

As Artificial Intelligence (AI) continues to advance, it will become increasingly integrated into business and digital marketing. Emerging technologies such as rich media, Dynamic Creative Optimisation (DCO) banners and AI-generated video are changing the way brands interact with their audiences. While these innovations offer new opportunities for personalisation and efficiency, they also present challenges in terms of transparency and security. In this section, we explore the key predictions and trends shaping the future of AI-powered digital advertising.

Artificial intelligence (AI) is becoming an integral part of business. In 23, Gartner found that 55% of organisations using AI are considering it for every new use case they evaluate. By 2026, organisations that focus on transparency, trust and security in AI are expected to see a 50% improvement in terms of adoption, business goals and user acceptance (McCartney 2023).

The Future of Digital Advertising: Innovations and Challenges for Rich Media and DCO Banners in the Age of Generative AI

In digital advertising, the terms "rich media" and "DCO banners" refer to two advanced ad formats designed to more effectively capture user attention and interest.

Rich Media. Rich media ads incorporate advanced multimedia elements such as video, audio and interactivity. Unlike traditional static banners, rich media ads offer a more dynamic and immersive experience. For example, a rich media ad can expand beyond its initial size, float above the page content or allow users to interact directly with the content. This ability to actively engage users not only improves attention retention, but also allows advertisers to measure the effectiveness of their campaigns through detailed metrics such as time spent interacting and specific actions taken within the ad (Carman 2023).

DCO Banners. Dynamic Creative Optimisation (DCO) banners are a real-time ad personalisation technique. Using user data such as location, browsing behaviour and device, DCO banners automatically adjust the creative elements of the ad to maximise its relevance to each individual user. This personalisation can include changes to images, messaging and calls to action. DCO banners are particularly valuable for large-scale campaigns, where the ability to automate personalisation can lead to significant improvements in the efficiency and effectiveness of advertising campaigns (Amazon Ads 2023).

4.1 Future Innovations with Generative AI on These Two Formats

Rich media powered by Generative AI. In the future, rich media ads could be fully generated and personalised by AI in real time. Imagine a rich media ad that not only has interactive elements, but also generates visual and audio content tailored to the viewer's context at that moment. For example, a car ad could show the car in an environment that matches the viewer's personal preferences or the current weather conditions, all instantly generated by AI from a set of basic data. Automated landscape generation is already a reality, and games like No Man's Sky use procedural generation so that each planet randomly generates its own landscape. The idea is to take this random and spontaneous generation a step further by applying it to digital advertising.

These ads could interact dynamically with users, responding to their emotions as detected by facial or voice analysis. In fact, chatbots that detect emotions in speech already exist, such as hume.ai (Hume AI, n.d.). If the system detects enthusiasm or interest, the ad could expand to offer more information or even an immersive virtual experience, such as a 3D-generated virtual test drive.

DCO Banners with Generative AI. Already adaptive in nature, DCO banners could reach new levels of personalisation with AI. Rather than simply adapting advertising messages based on demographic or behavioural data, future banners could use advanced predictive algorithms to anticipate users' needs and desires before they are explicitly stated.

For example, a DCO banner could suggest a fashion product tailored not only to the user's past style, but also to emerging trends identified by AI predictive analytics. In addition, these banners could use deep learning techniques to create highly engaging and personalised images and videos that change in real-time based on the user's interaction with the content.

Multi-sensory experiences. Looking further ahead, the integration of multi-sensory capabilities could be a natural evolution of rich media and DCO banners. By using AI technologies to create experiences that are not only visual and auditory, but also tactile or even olfactory, ads could offer truly immersive and memorable experiences. This is an option that could be explored in the wake of authors such as Hassabis et al. (2017), given their general approaches to exploring AI enhancement through neuroscientific principles.

5 Challenges and Controversies in the Implementation of Generative AI in Advertising and Digital Marketing the Evolution of AI Over the Past Few Decades

The implementation of generative artificial intelligence in digital advertising, while promising, faces a number of challenges and controversies that need to be carefully addressed. These issues not only affect the operability and effectiveness of the technologies, but also raise profound questions about the ethics, legality and social impact of their use, an issue that cannot be neglected in this book chapter.

Many AI systems, especially those using deep neural networks, are often referred to as 'black boxes' due to their complexity and the difficulty in explaining how they reach their decisions. This lack of transparency can be particularly problematic in scenarios where understanding the logic behind decisions is critical, such as in healthcare or law. Initiatives such as DARPA's Explainable Artificial Intelligence (XAI) programme seek to address these issues by developing methods to make AI systems more interpretable (Gunning 2017). Explainability of AI remains a significant challenge, and those affected by an algorithm's decisions have a right to a clear and understandable explanation. This issue is directly related to the major limitation and challenge to be solved in the future: hallucinations or nonsense.

The term "AI hallucinations" is used to describe instances where generative models generate false or distorted information. The resolution of these errors is not only technically complex, but has also precipitated crises in media and other industries by facilitating the dissemination of misinformation or the generation of inappropriate content in the absence of adequate oversight (Marcus and Davis 2019).

As Hicks et al. (2024) have observed, the issue is that a machine has no intention to deceive, only a lack of interest in the truth. From a creative standpoint, this may be the primary obstacle to the widespread adoption of this technology, and it is likely to be the most challenging problem from a technological perspective in the coming years.

Furthermore, the ethical risks associated with generative AI encompass the possibility of exacerbating pre-existing biases present in the data utilized for model training or in the model's output. These ethical issues require constant scrutiny and the application of ethical design principles to ensure that the technology is developed and used fairly and responsibly (Floridi et al. 2018). Initiatives such as the Asilomar Conference guidelines, the Montreal Declaration for Responsible AI, and the IEEE Autonomous Systems Ethics initiative seek to ensure that AI development respects human dignity, promotes transparency, and protects social values and justice (Jobin et al. 2019).

Furthermore, the utilisation of generative AI is in contravention of existing copyright legislation, particularly in instances where models are created that constitute derivative works without the express consent of the original creators. The question of ownership of AI-generated works and the determination of appropriate remuneration for the original creators remain unresolved issues that give rise to legal disputes (Guadamuz 2017).

It is important to note that copyright regulation is not the only legal issue that requires attention. The regulation of AI technology is an emerging area of legal and policy concern. There is an increasing demand for governments to implement regulations that address a range of issues, including transparency in the use of AI, the implementation of security measures to prevent abuse, and more. The absence of a coherent regulatory framework may result in the adoption of practices that compromise both user privacy and public safety (European Commission 2020), or even impede the development of future generative AI models. The EU is the most active player in the effort to regulate artificial intelligence, to the extent that major technology companies are reconsidering their perception of Europe as a consumer market for their products.

The environmental impact of AI is another critical ethical concern. The prodigious energy consumption required to train and operate AI models contributes to increased fossil fuel use and may delay the closure of carbon-emitting energy facilities. Estimates from Google, among others, indicate that AI use accounts for 10–15% of its total energy consumption, equivalent to 2.3 TWh annually.

Although major technology companies maintain that AI will eventually become more environmentally friendly by enhancing power grid efficiency and assisting with carbon tracking, the immediate energy demands pose significant challenges (Strubell et al. 2019). Indeed, it is estimated that AI could account for 3–4% of global energy demand by 2030, underscoring the magnitude of the challenge (Crawford 2024).

Furthermore, the deployment of sophisticated AI in digital communication and marketing may intensify social and economic polarization. There is a possibility of creating "two-speed worlds," where only businesses and consumers with access to the most advanced technology can fully benefit, leaving those with fewer resources behind. This could result in greater inequality in access to information and economic opportunities (Eubanks 2018).

6 Conclusions

The advent of generative artificial intelligence (AI) in advertising and digital marketing has signified a pivotal turning point in the capacity of companies to personalise and optimise their interactions with consumers. Nevertheless, alongside these prospects emerge a number of challenges and controversies that must be taken into account to guarantee the ethical and effective deployment of these technologies. In this synthesis, we delineate the principal innovations, current concerns and avenues for future improvement.

The connectionist school has brought about a revolution in marketing by providing advanced tools to understand, predict and influence consumer behaviour with an unprecedented level of sophistication and personalisation. The application of deep learning algorithms and neural networks enables companies to analyse extensive data sets in order to gain detailed insights into their customers' preferences and behaviours. As this technology continues to advance, it is expected to play an even more central role in the creation of memorable brand experiences and the development of strong and lasting customer relationships (Brown et al. 2020).

It is irrefutable that the potential of generative AI in marketing is considerable. It facilitates the automatic generation of content, including personalised text, images and videos, which has the capacity to transform the manner in which brands interact with their audiences. The capacity to efficiently generate content that is pertinent and engaging can markedly enhance the efficacy of advertising campaigns and increase user interaction. Nevertheless, it is imperative to acknowledge that this technology is still in its nascent stages and, while promising, must be developed and employed with caution.

One of the most critical issues associated with generative AI is the phenomenon of "hallucinations." This term refers to instances where generative models generate false or distorted information, which poses significant risks, particularly in contexts where accuracy is paramount. AI hallucinations can not only result in misinformation but also erode user confidence in these technologies. It is imperative to continue researching and developing methods to mitigate these errors and ensure the reliability of generative AI systems.

Despite its potential, generative AI technology is still in its infancy. Many current applications merely replicate existing methods, but with the assistance of AI, without fully exploiting the possibilities offered by this technology. This approach is evident in the field of advertising content creation and branding. However, future innovations are likely to surpass these current replications, offering novel and effective solutions that were previously unfeasible. Nevertheless, the current usage remains largely traditional.

From the perspective of the user, it is crucial to comprehend the potential risks and limitations of technology, as these can lead to misunderstanding or misuse. A New Zealand supermarket, PAK'nSAVE, developed an AI-powered bot, Savey Meal-Bot, with the objective of reducing food waste. However, the bot generated recipes that were potentially dangerous, including a drink with chlorine gas and a cocktail with bleach (McClure 2023). This illustrates the necessity for human supervision in the development of AI-powered applications.

Moreover, this example underscores the necessity of oversight and regulation to prevent unintended consequences and to guarantee that these tools are utilized in an ethical and responsible manner.

The implementation of generative AI raises a number of ethical and legal issues. This technology has the potential to amplify biases present in training data and to manipulate perceptions without the consent of the users.

The social impact of AI is a growing concern, with the risk of exacerbating inequality and social and economic polarisation. Advanced technology can disproportionately benefit those with access to resources, leaving the less privileged behind. Furthermore, the environmental impact of training and operating AI models, with their high energy consumption, poses significant challenges that must be mitigated to ensure sustainable development.

Taking an optimistic view of the potential for technological advancement, it is an intriguing time to witness this revolution in technology. The convergence of advances in artificial intelligence, big data and emerging technologies is radically transforming every aspect of our existence, from the way we work to how we interact and consume information. The capacity of AI to solve complex problems, personalise experiences and improve efficiency in digital communication and marketing offers significant potential for human progress. While it is essential to address the ethical and regulatory challenges that accompany these developments, the promise of a more connected, intelligent and efficient future encourages active participation in the construction of this new paradigm. The technological revolution underway not only redefines today's possibilities, but also encourages the imagination of a tomorrow full of innovative and exciting opportunities.

References

Alammar J (2018) The illustrated transformer. Github. https://jalammar.github.io/illustrated-transformer

Aleixo JE, Reis JL, Teixeira SF, de Lima AP (2024) Artificial intelligence applied to digital marketing. In Teixeira S, Remondes J (eds) The use of artificial intelligence in digital marketing: competitive strategies and tactics. IGI Global, pp 21–72. https://doi.org/10.4018/978-1-6684-9324-3.ch002

Amazon Ads (2023) Dynamic creative optimization (DCO): definition, examples, tips. Amazon Ads. https://www.amazon.com/en-ca/adtech-solutions/amazon-ad-server

Batra R, Keller KL (2016) Integrating marketing communications: new findings, new lessons, and new ideas. J Mark 80(6):122–145. https://doi.org/10.1509/jm.15.0419

Boris Eldagsen: "AI-generated images and photographs should not compete against each other in competitions" (2023) The overview. https://www.theoverview.art/boris-eldagsen-ai-images-interview/

Brock A, Donahue J, Simonyan K (2018) Large scale GAN training for high fidelity natural image synthesis. *arXiv preprint* arXiv:1809.11096. https://doi.org/10.48550/arXiv.1809.11096

Brown T, Mann B, Ryder N, Subbiah M, Kaplan JD, Dhariwal P, Neelakantan A, Shyam P, Sastry G, Askell A, Agarwal S, Herbert-Voss A, Krueger G, Henighan T, Child R, Ramesh A, Ziegler D, Wu J, Winter C et al (2020) Language models are few-shot learners. In: Larochelle H, Ranzato M, Hadsell R, Balcan MF, Lin H (eds) Advances in neural information processing systems, vol 33. Curran Associates, Inc., pp 1877–1901. https://proceedings.neurips.cc/paper_files/paper/2020/file/1457c0d6bfcb4967418bfb8ac142f64a-Paper.pdf

Brynjolfsson E, McAfee A (2017) Machine, platform, crowd: harnessing our digital future. W. W. Norton & Company

Cambria E, Schuller B, Xia Y, Havasi C (2013) New avenues in opinion mining and sentiment analysis. IEEE Intell Syst 28(2):15–21. https://doi.org/10.1109/MIS.2013.30

Carman, A. (2023, April 17). The rich media ad-vantage for mobile app marketing success. *Adjust*. Retrieved from https://www.adjust.com/blog/rich-media-advertising-best-practices/

Chen H, Chiang RHL, Storey VC (2012) Business intelligence and analytics: from big data to big impact. MIS Q 36(4):1165–1188. https://doi.org/10.2307/41703503

Christison C (2023) The 12 best chatbot examples for businesses. Hootsuite Blog. https://blog.hootsuite.com/chatbot-examples/

Crawford K (2024) Generative AI's environmental costs are soaring—and mostly secret. Nature. https://www.nature.com/articles/d41586-024-00478-x

DNyuz (2024) Toys "R" us launches AI-generated video campaign at Cannes Lions. https://www.dnyuz.com/toys-r-us-ai-campaign

Eubanks V (2018) Automating inequality: how high-tech tools profile, police, and punish the poor. St Martin's Press

European Commission (2020) White paper on artificial intelligence: a European approach to excellence and trust. https://ec.europa.eu/info/publications/white-paper-artificial-intelligence-european-approach-excellence-and-trust_en

Floridi L, Cowls J, Beltrametti M, Chatila R, Chazerand P, Dignum V, Luetge C, Madelin R, Pagallo U, Rossi F, Schafer B (2018) AI4People—an ethical framework for a good AI society: opportunities, risks, principles, and recommendations. Minds Mach 28(4):689–707. https://doi.org/10.1007/s11023-018-9482-5

Gaiduk D (2023) AI creation, AI validation: a case study of Coca-Cola's 'masterpiece'. Medium. Cooltool. https://cooltool.medium.com/ai-creation-ai-validation-a-case-study-of-coca-colas-masterpiece-fbb23b9a2077

Gomez-Uribe CA, Hunt N (2016) The Netflix recommender system: algorithms, business value, and innovation. ACM Trans Manag Inf Syst 6(4):13. https://doi.org/10.1145/2843948

Goodfellow I, Bengio Y, Courville A (2016) Deep learning. MIT Press

Goodfellow I, Pouget-Abadie J, Mirza M, Xu B, Warde-Farley D, Ozair S, Courville A, Bengio Y (2014) Generative adversarial nets. In: Advances in neural information processing systems, pp 2672–2680. https://doi.org/10.48550/arXiv.1406.2661

Guadamuz A (2017) Artificial intelligence and copyright. WIPO Magazine. https://www.wipo.int/wipo_magazine/en/2017/05/article_0003.html

Gunning D (2017) Explainable artificial intelligence (XAI). DARPA. https://www.darpa.mil/program/explainable-artificial-intelligence

Hassabis D, Kumaran D, Summerfield C, Botvinick M (2017) Neuroscience-inspired artificial intelligence. Neuron 95(2):245–258. https://doi.org/10.1016/j.neuron.2017.06.011

Heinz (2024) Midjourney vs Dall-E 3 vs stable diffusion: which AI image generator is best? YouTube. https://www.youtube.com/watch?v=LFmpVy6eGXs

Hicks MT, Humphries J, Slater J (2024) ChatGPT is bullshit. Ethics Inf Technol 26(2):38. https://doi.org/10.1007/s10676-024-09775-5

Hinton G, Deng L, Yu D, Dahl GE, Mohamed A-R, Jaitly N, Senior A, Vanhoucke V, Nguyen P, Sainath TN, Kingsbury B (2012) Deep neural networks for acoustic modeling in speech recognition: the shared views of four research groups. IEEE Signal Process Mag 29(6):82–97. https://doi.org/10.1109/MSP.2012.2205597

Hitzler P, Eberhart A, Ebrahimi M, Sarker MK, Zhou L (2022) Neuro-symbolic approaches in artificial intelligence. Natl Sci Rev 9(6), nwac035. https://doi.org/10.1093/nsr/nwac035

Ho J, Jain A, Abbeel P (2020) Denoising diffusion probabilistic models. Adv Neural Inf Process Syst 33, 6840–6851. https://doi.org/10.48550/arXiv.2006.11239

Hume AI (n.d.) Human-centered AI for emotion understanding. https://www.hume.ai/

Hunt T (2023) Promptography: 2023 Sony world photography award winner speaks out. ArtRKL. https://artrkl.com/blogs/news/promptography-2023-sony-world-photography-award-winner-speaks-out

Jobin A, Ienca M, Vayena E (2019) The global landscape of AI ethics guidelines. Nat Mach Intell 1(9):389–399. https://doi.org/10.1038/s42256-019-0088-2

Jurafsky D, Martin JH (2023) Speech and language processing (3rd ed. Draft). Standfor. https://web.stanford.edu/~jurafsky/slp3/ed3bookfeb3_2024.pdf

Karras T, Laine S, Aila T (2021) A style-based generator architecture for generative adversarial networks. IEEE Trans Pattern Anal Mach Intell 43(12):4217–4228. https://doi.org/10.1109/TPAMI.2020.2970919

Kenan J (2022) 10 chatbot marketing examples to boost your bot strategy. Sprout Social. https://sproutsocial.com/insights/chatbot-marketing-examples/

Kotler P, Keller KL (2012) Marketing management, 14th edn. Pearson Education

Legg S, Hutter M (2007) A collection of definitions of intelligence. Front Artif Intell Appl 157, 17–24. https://doi.org/10.48550/arXiv.0706.3639

Lipton ZC (2016) The mythos of model interpretability. ACM Queue 16(3):30–57. https://doi.org/10.1145/3236386.3241340

Man of Many (2023) Hilarious AI Harry Potter stars in Balenciaga campaign spoof. https://manofmany.com/entertainment/viral-ai-harry-potter-balenciaga

Marcus G, Davis E (2019) Rebooting AI: building artificial intelligence we can trust. Pantheon

Martinez-Rolan X, Pineiro-Otero T (2018) Content strategies in the era of digital marketing. In: Management and technological challenges in the digital age. CRC Press and Taylor & Francis Group, pp 149–176

Martínez-Rolán X, Piñeiro-Otero T (2022) Surfing on big data: automation and data mining as a marketing strategy. In Machado C, Davim JP (eds) Organizational innovation in the digital age. Springer, Cham. https://doi.org/10.1007/978-3-030-98183-9_3

McCarthy J (1961) A basis for a mathematical theory of computation, preliminary report. In Papers presented at the May 9–11, 1961, western joint IRE-AIEE-ACM computer conference. Association for Computing Machinery, pp 225–238. https://doi.org/10.1145/1460690.1460715

McCartney A (2023) Las principales predicciones estratégicas de Gartner para 2024 y los próximos años. Gartner. https://www.gartner.es/es/articulos/las-principales-predicciones-estrategicas-de-gartner-para-2024-y-los-proximos-anos

McClure T (2023) Supermarket AI meal planner app suggests recipe that would create chlorine gas1. The Guardian. https://www.theguardian.com/world/2023/aug/10/pak-n-save-savey-meal-bot-ai-app-malfunction-recipes

Minsky M (1986) The society of mind. Simon and Schuster

National Retail Federation and IBM Institute of Business Value (2019) The coming AI revolution in retail and consumer products. https://nrf.com/sites/default/files/2019-01/The%20coming%20AI%20revolution.pdf

Newell A, Simon HA (1976) Computer science as empirical inquiry: symbols and search. Commun ACM 19(3):113–126. https://doi.org/10.1145/360018.360022

Nilsson NJ (1998) Artificial intelligence: a new synthesis. Morgan Kaufmann

Nilsson NJ (2009) The quest for artificial intelligence. Cambridge University Press. https://doi.org/10.1017/CBO9780511819346

Nuance Communications Inc. (2017) Domino's revolutionizes digital ordering with DRU Assist, its virtual assistant powered by Nuance. Nuance News. https://news.nuance.com/2017-03-01-Dominos-Revolutionizes-Digital-Ordering-with-DRU-Assist-its-Virtual-Assistant-Powered-by-Nuance

Radford A, Wu J, Child R, Luan D, Amodei D, Sutskever I et al (2019) Language models are unsupervised multitask learners. OpenAI Blog 1, 9. https://openai.com/blog/better-language-models

Ricci F, Rokach L, Shapira B (2011) Introduction to recommender systems handbook. In: Ricci F, Rokach L, Shapira B, Kantor P (eds) Recommender systems handbook. Springer, Boston, MA. https://doi.org/10.1007/978-0-387-85820-3_1

Rombach R, Blattmann A, Lorenz D, Esser P, Ommer B (2022) High-resolution image synthesis with latent diffusion models. arXiv preprint. https://doi.org/10.48550/arXiv.2112.10752

Rumelhart DE, Hinton GE, Williams RJ (1986) Learning representations by back-propagating errors. Nature 323(6088):533–536. https://doi.org/10.1038/323533a0

Russell S, Norvig P (2010) Artificial intelligence: a modern approach, 3rd edn. Prentice Hall

Rust RT, Huang MH (2014) The service revolution and the transformation of marketing science. Mark Sci 33(2):206–221. https://doi.org/10.1287/mksc.2013.0836

Sephora (2021) Sephora virtual artist. https://www.sephora.sg/pages/virtual-artist

Servoz E (2023) WPP, Nestlé, Unilever… cuando la IA se apodere de la publicidad. MarketScreener.com. https://es.marketscreener.com/noticias/ultimas/WPP-Nestle-Unilever-cuando-la-IA-se-apodere-de-la-publicidad-44647910/

Sidlauskiene J, Joye Y, Auruskeviciene V (2023) AI-based chatbots in conversational commerce and their effects on product and price perceptions. Electron Mark 33:24. https://doi.org/10.1007/s12525-023-00633-8

Strubell E, Ganesh A, McCallum A (2019) Energy and policy considerations for deep learning in NLP. In: Korhonen A, Traum D, Màrquez L (eds) Proceedings of the 57th annual meeting of the association for computational linguistics. Association for Computational Linguistics, pp 3645–3650. https://doi.org/10.18653/v1/P19-1355

Synthesia (2024) How we made David Beckham speak 9 languages. Synthesia Blog. https://www.synthesia.io/post/david-beckham

The History Tech (2023) Deep blue: IBM's chess-playing supercomputer & impact on AI. https://thehistory.tech/deep-blue-ibm-chess-computer-history/

The Toy Book (2024) Toys "R" us reinvents marketing with AI-generated videos. https://www.thetoybook.com/toys-r-us-ai-videos

Toolify.ai (2023) The rise of AI-generated Balenciaga videos: a magical Harry Potter marketing campaign. Toolify. https://www.toolify.ai/ai-news/the-rise-of-aigenerated-balenciaga-videos-a-magical-harry-potter-marketing-campaign-2744611

Turing AM (1950) Computing machinery and intelligence. Mind 59(236):433–460. https://doi.org/10.1093/mind/LIX.236.433

Tyagi A (2024) 15 best chatbot examples from groundbreaking brands. Sprinklr Blog. https://www.sprinklr.com/blog/chatbot-examples/

Vaswani A, Shazeer N, Parmar N, Uszkoreit J, Jones L, Gomez AN, Kaiser ŁU, Polosukhin I (2017) Attention is all you need. In: Guyon I, Luxburg UV, Bengio S, Wallach H, Fergus R, Vishwanathan S, Garnett R (eds) Advances in neural information processing systems, vol 30. Curran Associates, Inc. https://proceedings.neurips.cc/paper_files/paper/2017/file/3f5ee243547dee91fbd053c1c4a845aa-Paper.pdf

Virgin Voyages (2023) Creating Jen A.I. Virgin Voyages. https://www.virginvoyages.com/press/latest-releases/jenai

Wallace RS (2009) The anatomy of A.L.I.C.E. In: Epstein R, Roberts G, Beber G (eds) Parsing the Turing test. Springer, Dordrecht. https://doi.org/10.1007/978-1-4020-6710-5_13

Weizenbaum J (1966) ELIZA—a computer program for the study of natural language communication between man and machine. Commun ACM 9(1):36–45. https://doi.org/10.1145/365153.365168

Woodie A (2023) A smarter slice: Domino's and MSFT in GenAI hookup. Datanami. https://www.datanami.com/2023/10/04/a-smarter-slice-dominos-and-msft-in-genai-hookup/

Zhou L, Pan S, Wang J, Vasilakos AV (2017) Machine learning on big data: opportunities and challenges. Neurocomputing 237:350–361. https://doi.org/10.1016/j.neucom.2017.01.026

Artificial Intelligence (AI) in Marketing and Firm Competitiveness

Florin Sabin Foltean

Abstract This chapter aims to synthesize current knowledge about the artificial intelligence (AI)-marketing convergence phenomenon and explore how businesses can use AI to enhance their marketing capabilities and maintain competitiveness. Companies must innovate their marketing strategies and actions and develop appropriate AI-enhanced specialized, cross-functional, architectural marketing capabilities. Reviewing information systems and marketing literature, we discuss the current understanding of AI and its applications in marketing. In addition, we explore how AI-enhanced marketing capabilities could increase the firm's competitiveness and performance. We conclude with future avenues for research on AI-enhanced marketing capabilities and company performance.

Keywords Artificial intelligence · Information technology · Marketing capabilities · Digital marketing · Performance

1 Introduction

Artificial Intelligence (AI) is increasingly integrated into the current activities of customers and companies, revolutionizing the marketing practice of creating, communicating, and delivering value (Kumar et al. 2024; Van Esch and Black 2021). AI is the "use of computational machinery to emulate capabilities inherent in humans, such as doing physical or mechanical tasks, thinking, and feeling" (Huang and Rust 2021, p. 31). AI technologies are a revolutionary and disruptive force (Campbell et al. 2020) that is gaining increasing importance in marketing (Huang and Rust 2021) by fundamentally transforming marketing strategies and actions to succeed in ever-changing markets (Kumar et al. 2024). In a study by KPMG, 78% of business managers believe that generative AI is the most important emerging technology, with marketing and sales being the most affected by this technology (KPMG 2023). In

F. S. Foltean (✉)
Faculty of Economics and Business Administration, West University of Timişoara, Timişoara, Romania
e-mail: florin.foltean@e-uvt.ro

C. Machado and J. P. Davim (eds.), *Challenges and Opportunities in the Artificial Intelligence Era*, https://doi.org/10.1007/978-3-031-85272-5_9

the same study, more than 20% of managers said that this technology integrates into new and existing products and the company's front-office processes.

Furthermore, the IBM CEO study (2023) found that 75% of CEOs believe competitive advantage will depend on adopting generative AI, while 84% of business leaders in the Accenture study (2019) said they need AI to meet their companies' growth objectives. Since the IBM CEO study (2023) found the increasing power of technology and data managers in strategic decision-making, the question is how the role of marketing leaders evolves in this new organizational context. Thus, it becomes crucial for marketing managers to obtain information about the benefits of AI in their functional area and its future development (Davenport et al. 2020), as well as guidance in adopting and using this technology (Huang and Rust 2021).

Companies in various industries, from communications, retail, and finance to education, healthcare, and other public services (Campbell et al. 2020) have developed customer-facing AI applications to support online search, shopping, learning, entertainment, socializing, and interacting with a diversity of objects (Davenport et al. 2020). AI technologies have many applications in marketing, such as providing real-time feedback to salespeople during customer interactions, contacting prospects, predicting customer needs and preferences (Davenport et al. 2020), automating shipping and delivery, discovering and reaching new customers, providing in-store customer support (Huang and Rust 2021), and identifying effective promotions (Campbell et al. 2020).

Despite these developments in AI and its applications, the academic marketing literature studying the intersection of marketing and AI (Vlačić et al. 2021) remains limited (Davenport et al. 2020) and in an emerging stage (Chintapalati and Pandey 2022). Consequently, this chapter aims to synthesize the existing knowledge about the convergence phenomenon between AI and marketing and explore how companies can use AI to improve their marketing capabilities to develop and implement strategies that increase their competitiveness. Maintaining a competitive advantage in an ever-changing technological and market environment requires a deep understanding of this phenomenon to capitalize on AI-enhanced marketing capabilities. AI has a *transformational power* (Kaplan and Haenlein 2019b) that manifests itself through redesigning marketing strategies and business models, remodeling consumer behavior (Davenport et al. 2020), and rethinking marketing decision-making and stakeholder interactions (Kaplan and Haenlein 2019b). AI, cloud computing, and connectivity technologies integrated into platform-based business models are transforming the company's interactions with all stakeholders (Campbell et al. 2020).

2 The AI Concept

2.1 AI Definition

AI was first formally used in the Dartmouth Summer Research Project on Artificial Intelligence (DSRPAI) title in 1956 (Kaplan and Haenlein 2019b). After five decades of developments and uncertainties, the applications and potential benefits of AI began to be widely recognized in various industries in the 2010s as a result of the recent development in cloud computing and lower-cost computing power, as well as the advancement of big data technologies and machine learning algorithms (Duan et al. 2019; Huang and Rust 2021).

In business practice, AI is understood, instead, from a technology perspective, as a "constellation of many different technologies working together to enable machines to sense, comprehend, act, and learn with human-like levels of intelligence" (Accenture 2024). The AI landscape includes a variety of technologies like machine learning, deep learning, natural language processing, and artificial neural networks that, in conjunction with big data analytics, ensure the support of automated and interconnected business processes (Campbell et al. 2020). AI systems can understand external data, learn from this data, and adapt in real-time to any changes (Kaplan and Haenlein 2019a, p. 17). For example, image recognition algorithms (e.g., Amazon, Google) allow the detection of objects and scenes in images and video, speech recognition algorithms (e.g., Amazon, Google) enable virtual assistants to react to text, voice, or other human input and also turn text into life speech. Davenport and Ronanki (2018) argue that a more instrumental way to understand AI is to describe its marketing and business applications, such as automating business processes, drawing insights from data, or creating customer and employee engagement.

In the academic literature, various understandings of AI exist without a widely accepted definition (Duan et al. 2019) (see Table 1). Definitions of AI vary from general (e.g., Shieber 2004) to more specific and restrictive (e.g., De Bruyn et al. 2020). Therefore, this concept is still insufficiently defined and remains a fuzzy concept (Kaplan and Haenlein 2019a).

Huang and Rust (2021) adopt a multiple intelligence view of AI that encompasses multiple intelligences (i.e., mechanical, thinking, and feeling), like humans, for different tasks. Drawing on learning theory (i.e., *higher-order learning*), De Bruyn et al. (2020) argue that what differentiates AI applications from traditional statistics is the notion of *knowledge creation*, while Mullainathan and Spiess (2017) point to a paradigmatic transition of AI from an *expert systems approach* (which is rule-based) to a *deep learning-based, data-driven approach.* Overgoor et al. (2019) define marketing AI as "the development of artificial agents that, given the information they have about consumers, competitors, and the focal company, suggest and/or take marketing actions to achieve the best marketing outcome" (p. 2). More recently, Peltier et al. (2024) define AI in the specific domain of interactive marketing as "Real-time and personalized adaptive learning and decision-making systems that

Table 1 Select AI definition

"intelligence demonstrated by machines"	Shieber (2004)
"computational agents that act intelligently"	Poole and Mackworth (2010, p. 3)
"programs, algorithms, systems and machines that demonstrate intelligence"	Shankar (2018, p. vi)
"machines that exhibit aspects of human intelligence"	Huang and Rust (2018, p. 155)
"machines mimicking "intelligent human behaviour""	Syam and Sharma (2018, p. 136)
"ability of a machine to learn from experience, adjust to new inputs and perform human-like tasks"	Duan et al. (2019, p. 63)
"system's ability to interpret external data correctly, to learn from such data, and to use those learnings to achieve specific goals and tasks through flexible adaptation"	Kaplan and Haenlein, (2019a, p. 15)
"machines that mimic human intelligence in tasks such as learning, planning, and problem-solving through higher-level, autonomous knowledge creation"	De Bruyn et al. (2020, p. 93)
"broad class of technology developed with the objective of collecting data in order to solve problems or make decisions"	Campbell et al. (2020, p. 229)
"use of computational machinery to emulate capabilities inherent in humans, such as doing physical or mechanical tasks, thinking, and feeling"	Huang and Rust (2021, p. 31)
"an ecosystem comprising three fundamental elements—data collection and storage, statistical and computational techniques, and output systems—that enable products and services to perform tasks typically understood as requiring intelligence and autonomous decision making on behalf of humans"	Puntoni et al. (2021, p. 132)
"an information system (IS) that learns over time by efficiently and effectively performing one or more operations (e.g., acquisition, integration, analysis, and/or interpretation) on information"	Manis and Madhavaram (2023, p. 2)

mimic human intelligence through the autonomous processing, analysis, and interpretation of data problem solving and goal attainment purposes from both a buyer and seller perspective" (p. 59).

2.2 AI Types

Several classification frameworks are available (see Table 2) to facilitate the understanding of the functionalities and opportunities offered by AI applications in marketing.

Davenport et al. (2020) suggest that "levels of intelligence are best conceptualized as a continuum" (p. 27), evolving from task automation to context awareness.

Table 2 Types of AI

Criteria	Types of AI	Features	Applications
AI evolutionary stage (Kaplan and Haenlein 2019a)	Artificial narrow intelligence	AI applied to specific domains and tasks	Image, voice, and speech recognition Digital assistants
	Artificial general intelligence	Handle complex problems and tasks Cognitive, emotional, and social intelligence Strategic, abstract, and divergent thinking Expanding in new fields	ChatGPT
	Artificial super intelligence	"self-aware and conscious systems that, in a certain way, will make humans redundant" (p. 16)	Future AI
Type of intelligence (Huang and Rust 2021)	Mechanical AI	Automate repetitive and routine tasks	Automated translation, lead capturing and nurturing
	Thinking AI	Data processing Unstructured data Pattern detection Decision making	Text mining, voice, speech, image, and facial recognition
	Feeling AI	Designed for human–machine interactions Feelings and emotions analysis	Chatbots Virtual assistants
Level of intelligence (Davenport and Kirby 2016)	Task automation AI applications	Standardized Rule-based Predictable outcomes	IBM's Watson
	Context awareness	Learn to learn Contextual adaptation	Product design Text generation Customer service chatbots

Sources Davenport and Kirby (2016), Davenport et al. (2020), Huang and Rust (2021), Kaplan and Haenlein (2019a)

Similarly, Kaplan and Haenlein's (2019a) framework suggests an evolution of AI from today's narrow AI to the general AI of the future, when thinking tasks will be performed by AI systems, human employees remaining to perform feeling tasks (Huang et al. 2019).

3 AI-Enablement of Marketing Capabilities

The KPMG study (2023) revealed marketing and sales as the second business function, after IT&C, on which generative AI will manifest its impact. AI adoption in marketing is more intense in industries that involve frequent interactions with many customers, such as retail, consumer packaged goods, banking, and travel (Davenport et al. 2020). Advances in cloud computing and storage, computing power, and AI technologies are increasing marketers' abilities to process vast volumes of data and generate insights valuable in marketing strategy formulation and implementation (Campbell et al. 2020). AI improves marketing automation and interactions with other business functions and external stakeholders, requiring new configurations of AI-powered marketing capabilities in implementing new digital marketing strategies (Campbell et al. 2020). AI algorithms enhance many marketing capabilities, such as capturing and analyzing large volumes and a variety of data (e.g., image, video, voice, text) from websites, email, digital business platforms, social networks, call centers calls, and customer-digital objects interactions; generating insights from customer and transaction data; personalizing offerings, product recommendations, and marketing communications; predicting customer purchase intent and customer churn; managing market transactions; managing programmatic advertising; and engaging customers and employees (Davenport and Ronanki 2018; Davenport et al. 2020).

An important issue in using AI in marketing decision-making concerns determining which tactical and strategic decisions will be made by humans, AI, or collaboratively (Huang and Rust 2021), taking into account five contingencies: "specificity of the search space, interpretability of the decision-making process and outcome, size of the alternative set, decision-making speed, and replicability" (Shrestha et al. 2019, p. 67). Moreover, De Bruyn et al. (2020) predict that the benefits of AI in various marketing areas require solving the problem of tacit knowledge transfer from marketers to AI algorithms. Huang and Rust (2021) argue for the cooperative relationship between AI and human intelligence.

AI is gaining more attention in marketing research in the 2020s (Kumar et al. 2024), and the number of studies on its potential applications in marketing is increasing. For example, Campbell et al. (2020) explain the uses of AI in the strategic marketing process, Huang and Rust (2021) developed the" research-strategy-action" framework of AI-enhanced strategic marketing planning, and Kumar et al. (2024) conceptualized a framework of marketing domains (i.e., AI-driven customer insights, measuring marketing performance, automated marketing strategies, ethical implications, enhancing customer experience, and growth opportunities with AI implementation) where AI generates transformative effects.

3.1 Marketing Capabilities

Much previous research in strategic management has focused on capabilities and their contribution to firm performance. The concept of distinctive competence covers what an organization does particularly well compared to its competitors (Selznick 1957). Previous studies on the relationship between distinctive competence, strategic types, and firm performance prove that strategic types differ in functional strategy expertise, competencies, and performance (Miles and Snow 1978). According to the capabilities theory, deploying resources leads to sustainable competitive advantage (Teece et al. 1997). This approach extends the resource-based view (RBV), which posits that resource heterogeneity is the key driver of competitive advantage and firm performance (Wernerfelt 1984; Barney 1991). Distinctive capabilities drive effectiveness and efficiency in creating and delivering superior customer value. Academics and practitioners widely recognize the contribution of organizational capabilities to firm performance. Prahalad and Hamel (1990) argued that the source of competitive advantage is management's ability to develop competencies that enable business units to adapt to environmental dynamics rapidly. The source of competitive advantage has shifted from manufacturing assets, among other assets, to market-based assets and capabilities (Ramaswami et al. 2009).

Day (1994) uses the capabilities approach as a theoretical background to understand how to create a market-based organization. *Capabilities* refer to "complex bundles of skills and collective learning, exercised through organizational processes, that ensure superior coordination of functional activities" (Day 1994, p. 38). These acquired skills and knowledge enable activities in cross-functional business processes such as new product development, customer relationship management, and brand management (Morgan 2012). A firm with superior marketing capabilities will achieve and sustain a competitive advantage, resulting in better performance (Day 1994; Vorhies and Morgan 2005). Firms with superior marketing capabilities can generate information about customer needs and preferences, as well as competitor initiatives and reactions. According to RBV theory, to sustain this advantage, these capabilities must create value, be difficult to replace with substitute processes, be difficult for competitors to imitate, and not be transferable across firm boundaries (Barney 1991; Grant 1996).

Vorhies and Morgan (2005) identified eight marketing capabilities (i.e., market information management, product development, pricing, channel management, marketing communications, selling, marketing planning, and marketing implementation). They found that each marketing capability analyzed as a first-order construct is positively and directly related to firm performance. The interdependence of different marketing capabilities makes marketing capabilities a more valuable, rare, inimitable, and non-tradable resource that ensures the sustainability of competitive advantage. Morgan (2012) identified four categories of marketing capabilities: specialized, cross-functional, architectural, and dynamic marketing capabilities. Specialized core marketing capabilities (product management, pricing, channel management, marketing communications, selling, and market research) comprise the tactical-level marketing mix processes performed by the marketing function. Cross-functional marketing capabilities (brand management, customer relationship management, and new product development) involve the integration of specialized marketing capabilities with specialized capabilities in other functional areas. Architectural marketing capabilities include strategic market planning and marketing strategy implementation capabilities that enable strategy formulation and implementation processes by integrating specialized and cross-functional capabilities with appropriate resources. Dynamic marketing capabilities include market learning, resource reconfiguration, and capability enhancement capabilities essential in the firm's adaptation to environmental changes. Research from an outside-in perspective has suggested that existing marketing capabilities cannot meet the demands of firms to compete and thrive in a complex and rapidly changing external environment (Day 2011). Understanding the mechanisms by which marketing capability can enhance firm adaptability, productivity, and high competitiveness (Mu 2015) has become critical.

3.2 IT-Enabled Marketing Capabilities and Firm Performance

Research on the business value of information technology has a long tradition in the literature of information systems (Bharadwaj 2000; Chae et al. 2014; Mithas et al. 2011). The resource-based view (RBV) and the capabilities framework have provided a sound theoretical foundation for studies investigating how IT resources transform into value propositions that create a company's competitive advantage and superior performance (Herhausen et al. 2020; Saini and Johnson 2005). Empirical research on the impact of IT resources on firm performance highlighted the mediator role of higher-order organizational capabilities in this relationship (Chang et al. 2010; Mithas et al. 2011; Sambamurthy et al. 2003).

The adoption of IT technologies has improved marketing capabilities, based on which the company's ability to adapt to a rapidly changing marketing environment has increased (Wang et al. 2013). As the Internet and IT use in marketing has expanded over the past two decades, previous research has focused on understanding how new digital technologies can enhance marketing capabilities to increase firm performance (see Table 3).

In one of the first studies on the relationship between IT and marketing capabilities, Saini and Johnson (2005) explored e-commerce capabilities (i.e., IT capability, strategic flexibility, and trust-building capability) and found that proactive market orientation mediates the impact of IT capability on firm performance. In the same vein, Trainor et al. (2011) proposed the concept of e-marketing capability to capture the phenomenon of integration of technological resources (i.e., information technology infrastructure), human resources (i.e., managerial commitment and organizational culture) and business resources (i.e., technology adoption and use) whose complementarities have a positive impact on the company's

Table 3 Relevant quantitative research on IT-enhanced marketing capabilities

Authors	IT-enhanced marketing capabilities	Definition	Operationalization	Findings
Saini and Johnson (2005)	E-commerce capabilities	"Skill and subroutines that underpin the process of conducting trade over the Internet" (p. 361)	IT capability Strategic flexibility Trust-building capability	Proactive market information moderates the influence of IT capability on firm performance
Trainor et al. (2011)	E-marketing capability	"a firm's competence in using the Internet and other information technologies to facilitate rich interactions with customers" (pp. 163–164)	Technology resources Human resources Business resources	E-marketing capabilities have a direct influence on the firm profitability, costs, and return on investment
Trainor et al. (2014)	Social CRM capabilities	"a firm's competency in generating, integrating, and responding to information obtained from customer interactions that are facilitated by social media technologies" (p. 1202)	Information generation Information dissemination Responsiveness	Social CRM capabilities positively impact the company's customer relationship performance
Wang (2020)	Social CRM capabilities	Trainor et al. (2014)	Social media resource inputs	Social CRM capability has a positive influence on firm performance and customer engagement
Johnson et al. (2017)	Big data capabilities	"ability with which a firm handles big data through the specific dimensions" (p. 643)	Big data volume Big data variety Big data velocity	Exploration orientation is positively related to big data's volume, variety, and velocity The effect of big data variety on new product revenue increases under higher customer turbulence
Gregory et al. (2019)	E-commerce marketing capabilities	"ability of an organization to identify, develop, and assimilate e-commerce activities into market value offerings that meet desired goals" (p. 148)	Unidimensional construct	E-commerce marketing capabilities have both a direct effect on exporting firms' e-commerce performance and an indirect effect through distribution and promotion efficiency

(continued)

Table 3 (continued)

Authors	IT-enhanced marketing capabilities	Definition	Operationalization	Findings
Wang (2020)	Digital marketing capabilities	"relational competencies that are required to leverage the benefits of digitalization" (p. 568)	Unidimensional construct	Digital marketing capabilities have a positive impact on international firms financial performance
Homburg and Wielgos (2022)	Digital marketing capabilities	"a firm's ability to use digital technology–enabled processes to interact with customers and partners in a targeted, measurable, and integrated way to create new forms of value without regard for distance or time" (p. 668)	Unidimensional construct	Digital marketing capabilities have a positive impact on firm profitability

performance. They argued that e-marketing capability can create business value by providing customers access to company resources, integrating functional activities and information dissemination, positively impacting organizational effectiveness and efficiency.

With the expansion of social networks, a new research stream emerged that focused on the ability of companies to use these networks to create business value. Trainor et al. (2014) developed the concept of CRM social capabilities (i.e., information generation, information dissemination, and responsiveness) and found their contribution to the company's performance in customer relationship management. In addition, Wang and Kim's (2017) study reported the positive impact of these capabilities on firm performance and customer engagement.

As consumer activities in the digital environment have expanded, firms have developed new capabilities for capturing and analyzing big data to discover new opportunities and ways to create a competitive advantage. Johnson et al. (2017) study focused on the contribution of big data capability (i.e., the volume, variety, and velocity of big data) to innovation performance in changing environments, with customer turbulence amplifying the impact of big data variety on new product revenue.

Herhausen et al. (2020) distinguish between *digital marketing resource* (i.e., "a digital-related marketing asset (tangible or intangible) that a B2B firm owns, controls, or has access" (p. 277)) and *digital marketing capability* (i.e., "ability of a B2B firm to perform a coordinated set of digital-related tasks (operational or dynamic), utilizing digital resources, for achieving a competitive advantage" (p. 277)). The authors argue that deploying digital resources in marketing processes develops digital marketing capabilities (i.e., digital channels and multichannel, social media, digital relationships, and digital technologies usage capabilities) that create customer value and strengthen the company's competitive advantage. Homburg and Wielgos (2022) conceptualize digital marketing capabilities as "a firm's ability to use digital technology-enabled processes to interact with customers and partners in a targeted, measurable, and integrated way to create new forms of value without regard for distance or time" (p. 668). According to these authors, digital marketing capabilities refer to (1) social media marketing, (2) mobile marketing, (3) content marketing, (4) search engine marketing, (5) web analytics, (6) marketing automation, and (7) e-mail marketing. These capabilities differ from classic marketing mix capabilities in terms of scalability, measurability, interconnectivity, and adaptability. The results of their empirical study reveal positive relationships between digital and classic marketing capabilities and firm performance (i.e., return on assets). In addition, digital marketing capabilities contribute to firm performance beyond classic marketing capabilities. Adopting a relational perspective on digital marketing capabilities, the empirical study by Wang (2020) reveals a positive impact of these capabilities on international firm financial performance.

3.3 AI-Enabled Marketing Capabilities

Many companies are adopting and using AI technologies to automate operational and marketing processes and adapt to market changes. Three AI capabilities (i.e., AI-enabled automation, analytics, and relational capabilities) are antecedents of the firm's adaptive response to market changes (Sullivan and Wamba 2024). As the marketing function has a vital role in this adaptation process, how AI enables marketing capabilities is beginning to capture the attention of marketing scholars and practitioners. To meet the needs of managers, leading marketing scholars are calling for more research into how marketers could use AI to improve marketing capabilities (Morgan and Feng 2024) and generate new competitive advantages (Hoffman et al. 2022). Manis and Madhavaram (2023) contribute to this new stream of research by defining the concept of enablement as "a firm's ability to use a resource/capability to facilitate or reinforce one or more resources/capabilities through combination or integration to achieve superior performance outcomes" (p. 2).

We will focus on AI-enabled marketing capabilities, understood in this paper as marketing skills and functionalities that are empowered by leveraging AI technologies and used to formulate and execute more responsive and predictive marketing strategies (Kumar et al. 2024). AI enables marketing capabilities (e.g., market research, marketing planning, product management, price setting, sales force management, new product development, customer relationship management, and brand management) through four information processes: data collection, integration, analysis, and interpretation (Manis and Madhavaram 2023). Thus, AI can recognize and extrapolate patterns that improve marketers' abilities to identify opportunities and threats and execute real-time response actions (Campbell et al. 2020). Kumar et al. (2024) identified three categories of AI-driven marketing capabilities:

1. AI-driven marketing analytics capabilities (i.e., the ability to use AI in deep analysis and generate insights from a variety of data about markets, customers, competitors, and other stakeholders)
2. Technological marketing capabilities (i.e., the ability to integrate AI technologies into the marketing processes)
3. Strategic efficiency capabilities (i.e., the ability to use AI to increase efficiency, agility, and responsiveness of marketing operations in changing markets).

Based on previous research, we will systematize how AI can improve marketing capabilities by adopting Morgan's theoretical framework (see Table 4). Our focus is on specialized, cross-functional, and architectural marketing capabilities.

Core specialized marketing capabilities (i.e., market research, product management, pricing, channel management, marketing communications, and selling) refer to the marketing mix processes at the tactical level performed by the marketing function. Thus, market research capability could be enhanced by AI-based tools used to recognize patterns in data captured from a variety of digital channels (e.g., websites, social media platforms, mobile, and smart devices), giving meaning to electronic word-of-mouth, predicting customer demand and churn, and identifying customer

Table 4 AI-enabled marketing capabilities

Marketing capabilities	AI-enabled tools	Used for …
Specialized marketing capabilities		
Market research	Data minining (e.g., Python, R, RapidMiner)	Pattern recognition in data captured from the websites, social media platforms, customer mobile activity and customer-smart and connected devices
	Text mining (e.g., Atlas.ti, DicoverText, NVivo)	Making sense of electronic word-of-mouth (WOM)
	Predictive analytics (e.g., IBM Watson Studio, Microsoft Azure Machine Learning, SAP Predictive Analytics)	Customer demand predictions, predicting customer churn
	Social listening (e.g., Brand24, Brandwatch, XPro)	Identifying customer needs, preferences and intentions
	Sentiment analysis (e.g., Lexalytics, Azure Text Analytics, IBM Watson Natural Language Understanding)	Identifying customer satisfaction and dissatisfaction
	Speech recognition (e.g., Google Speech-to Text, Amazon Transcribe, Microsoft Azure Speech)	Speech to text conversion
	Facial recognition (e.g., Amazon Rekognition, Microsoft Azure Face API)	Identifying and verifying the identity of individuals
Product management	AI-driven product discovery (e.g., Archie, Chisel AI)	Discovering market gaps and opportunities for new product development
	3D product configurator (e.g., Pixready, Salsita, Threekit)	Custom product configuration
Price management	Pricing platforms (e.g., Competera, Price FX, PriSync, Pros)	Dynamic pricing
	Predictive algorithms (e.g., Symson, Aimondo)	Predicting consumer price elasticity
Marketing channel management	Content platforms (e.g., HubSpot, SnapApp, Brand24)	Engaging consumers in new channels
	AI planogram platforms (e.g., Relex, Onedoor, SmartDraw)	Optimizing in-store product placement
	AI-powered merchandising platforms (Dynamic Yield, Vue.ai)	Optimizing mobile apps and e-commerce websites

(continued)

Table 4 (continued)

Marketing capabilities	AI-enabled tools	Used for …
Marketing communications	Contextual advertising platforms (e.g., Google AdSense, Yahoo! Bing Network, Grapeshot Oracle)	Contextual targeting
	Customer profiling (e.g., HubSpot Make My Persona)	Personalization of digital marketing communications
	Ads Platform (Google Ads, Bing Ads, Amazon Ads)	Keyword bidding
	Generative AI platforms (e.g., AdCopy, AdCreative, AI Ads, Cohesive, Copy AI)	Copywriting and campaign optimization
Selling	AI-powered conversation analysis platforms (CallMiner, iovox, Allego Conversation Intelligence)	Analysis of the content of conversations with customers
	Conversational AI platforms (e.g., Amazon Lex, Google Dialogflow, IBM Watsonx Assistant, Oracle Digital Assistant)	Automated, real-time human-like conversations
Cross-functional marketing capabilities		
New product development	Generative AI (e.g., Dall-E, Lanpdt, Midjourney)	Generating new product concepts Generating design variations and prototyping
	AI-driven A/B testing (e.g., Functionize, Kameleoon, VWO)	Testing new products, ads and promotions
Customer relationship management	Customer insight platforms (e.g., Google Analytics, Google Trends, Hotjar, Userpilot)	Customer insights for hyper-personalization
	AI-CRM system (e.g., Amplitude, Hubspot, Mixpanel)	Capturing information about leads and optimizing the conversion process
Brand management	AI brand logo generator (BrandCrowd, BrandMark, Canva, Hatchful, Logo AI, Looka, Tailor Brands)	Designing the brand logo
	Brand story generator (e.g., Bizway, Canva, Tasktade)	Creating the brand story
	AI personalization engines (e.g., Adobe Experience Cloud, Insider, Salesforce Marketing Cloud)	Customer experience personalization

(continued)

Table 4 (continued)

Marketing capabilities	AI-enabled tools	Used for …
Architectural marketing capabilities		
Strategic market planning	AI SWOT analysis generators (e.g., Clickup, Jeda.ai, Mymap.ai)	Internal company and competitor analysis
	AI segmentation platforms (e.g., Adobe Experience Cloud, Google Analytics, Insider, Mailchimp)	Dynamic and predictive segmentation Developing customer personas
	Value proposition generators (e.g., Founderpal.ai, Grammarly, Taskade)	Developing value propositions
Marketing strategy implementation	Cross-channel customer experience platforms (e.g., Bloomreach, Blueshift, Braze, Insider, Klaviyo, Marigold)	Personalization of customer journey and marketing communications across channels

Sources Campbell et al. (2020), Davenport et al. (2020), Huang and Rust (2021), Kumar et al. (2024), Morgan (2012), Overgoor et al. (2019)

needs, preferences, intentions, satisfaction, and dissatisfaction. AI-based tools can improve product management capability in uncovering market gaps and opportunities for new product development and enabling customers to configure the product. Pricing capability could be improved by using AI-based tools in dynamic pricing and anticipating consumer price elasticity. AI-based tools improve channel management by engaging customers in new channels and optimizing product placement in stores, mobile apps, and e-commerce websites. The ability to manage marketing communications could be made more effective by using AI tools for contextual targeting, personalization of digital marketing communications, keyword bidding, campaign writing, and optimization. Finally, using AI-based tools to analyze the content of customer conversations and implement automated, real-time, human-like conversations could increase the effectiveness of the sales force.

Cross-functional marketing capabilities (i.e., new product development, customer relationship management, and brand management) involve the coordination of specialized marketing capabilities with other functional capabilities. AI tools could enhance new product development capabilities by generating new product concepts, designing variations, prototyping, and testing new products. AI-enhanced customer relationship management capability will be more effective by generating customer insights for hyper-personalization, capturing lead insights, and optimizing the conversion process. Using AI tools to design the brand logo, create the brand story, and personalize the customer experience could enhance brand management capability.

Architectural marketing capabilities include strategic market planning and marketing strategy implementation capabilities that enable strategy formulation and implementation processes by integrating specialized and cross-functional capabilities with appropriate resources. Strategic market planning capability could benefit from using AI tools to identify new growth opportunities, dynamic and predictive segmentation, customer persona development, internal company and competitor analysis, and value proposition development. The effectiveness of marketing strategy implementation will be enhanced by adopting AI tools for targeting markets, optimizing campaigns, personalizing websites, mobile apps, emails, and SMS, and personalizing the customer journey and marketing communications across channels.

In Table 5, we present various AI tools useful for enhancing digital marketing capabilities, systematized based on the theoretical framework of Homburg and Wielgos (2022).

4 AI-Enhanced Marketing Capabilities and Firm Performance

By adopting AI (Latinovic and Chatterjee 2022), customer-centric firms can achieve competitive advantage and superior performance to create intuitive, seamless, and effortless customer experiences (Kumar et al. 2021). Transformative effects of AI occur in the marketing strategy process, customer relationship management, and consumer experience management (Davenport et al. 2020). Companies are interested in the business value of AI, looking for ways it can drive growth, reduce costs, and increase agility in an ever-changing market environment. The Accenture (2019) report "AI: Built to scale" reveals that 84% of CEOs believe adopting and using AI is necessary to meet their companies' growth goals. Automated and personalized marketing processes such as big data analytics, customer experience management, customer service, and digital marketing communications are becoming more agile and efficient. For example, 99% of companies using AI agent technology reported cost savings per customer contact (IBM 2023). Companies that have successfully scaled AI strategically have seen a higher return on their AI investment (Accenture 2019).

The extant academic marketing literature on the impact of AI-enhanced marketing capabilities on business performance still needs to be explored. Manis and Madhavaram (2023) argue that AI-enabled marketing capabilities generate and sustain the company's competitive advantages. Suoniemi et al. (2020) empirically found a significant effect of big data resources on marketing capabilities and a positive impact on firm performance of the complementarity of IT resources and IT-enhanced marketing capabilities. Mikalef et al. (2023) conceptualize AI competencies as a core organizational capability based on management's ability "to imagine value-added applications creatively" (p. 8) that have the potential to drive the company's competitive advantage. They operationalize this capability through three dimensions: infrastructure (i.e., AI infrastructure orchestration), business spanning (i.e., AI strategic planning), and proactive stance (i.e., AI-oriented proactivity). They empirically discovered an indirect impact of AI competencies on organizational performance in the B2B sector; marketing capabilities mediate this relationship. Thus,

Table 5 Select AI tools for digital marketing

Digital marketing capabilities	AI-Tools
Content marketing	
Design	Autodraw, Canva, Galileo AI, Magician design, uizard.io
Art/images	Copilot, Dall-E-2, Dreamer, Flair AI, Getimg.ai, Imagine, Leap AI, Magic Studio, Midjourney, Rendernet.ai, Segmind, Stable Diffusion
Pictures editing	Cleanup, ClipDrop, designify, Photoshop, Playground, Remini
Video editing	Blink AI, CapCut, Descript.com, Eightify, Filmora, HeyGen, Invideo, Keyframes studio, Klap, Opus, Pictory ai, Rask AI, Runway, Syllaby.io, Topvideo AI, Veed.io, Videoleap, Unboring AI
Voice creation and cloning	Eightify, Elevenlabs.io, InVideo, Klap, Lovo.ai, Play.ht, Runway
Music generator	Beatoven.ai, Soundraw, Songburst AI, Soundful, Steno, Suno AI
Text writing	ChatGPT, Gemini Bard, Grammarly, Jasper AI, Jenny AI, Notion AI, QuillBot, Rytr, SmartBird, Textblaze, Writesonic, Hemingway
Presentations	Beautiful.ai, Decktopus.com, Dessigns AI, Gamma AI, Lumens, mymap.ai, Slides AI, Tome.app
Podcasting	Adobe Podcast, Cleanvoice.ai, Podnotes, Type Studio, 2short.ai
Translations	Deepl, Grammarly
Text to speech	Murf.ai
Text to video	OpenAI Sora, Repurpose Pie, Visla AI
Text to images	Midjourney
Avatar creation	HeyGen, Synthesia, Starrytars
Marketing automation	
CRM platforms	HubSpot, Salesforce, Zoho
Chatbot	AirOps, Chatbot Live, Chatsimple, Dante.ai, Droxy, Chatbase, Mutual info, perplexity.ai, SiteGPT
Autopost social media	Repurpose IO
Email and newsletter	Addy AI, Beehiiv, Mails AI, Promo AI, Robin AI, Superhuman, Temp-mail.org
Website Builder	Carrd.co, durable.co, Framer, Hostinger, Style AI, 10web.io
Landing pages	Unbounce.com

(continued)

Table 5 (continued)

Digital marketing capabilities	AI-Tools
Workflow automation	Bardeen, Make, Questflow.ai, Xembly, Zapier
Search engine marketing	
SEO	AirOps, BlogSEO, Keywrds ai, Neural Text, Usestyle.ai, VidIQ, Seona AI, Wordlift
Lead generation	Google Forms
Social media marketing	
Linkedin	Supergrow.ai, Taplio
YouTube	Opus, Scrip AI, TubeBuddy, VidIQ
Instagram	HeyGen, InMagic, Klap, Repurpose, Submagic
TikToks generator	Fliki

AI competencies enhance marketing capabilities, which, in turn, will increase the company's performance.

5 Conclusion

In this chapter, we discussed the AI-marketing convergence phenomenon and the contribution of AI to a company's competitiveness and performance through enhancing marketing capabilities. The proliferation of AI-powered tools provides companies with useful solutions for enhancing their specialized, cross-functional, and architectural marketing capabilities. Using theoretical frameworks of marketing capabilities and digital marketing capabilities, we systematized how AI functionalities can enhance these capabilities.

Although various theoretical frameworks facilitate the understanding of how AI can contribute to developing new marketing capabilities and improving existing ones, marketing scholars should focus on the managerial issues of this process. Future research can focus on the following questions whose answers can be helpful for marketing practitioners: *What changes in organizational culture are needed to stimulate the use of AI in marketing processes? How do we build a data-driven organizational culture? How can the marketing organization develop new AI-enhanced marketing capabilities by collaborating with other business functions? How can the concept of AI-enhanced marketing capabilities be operationalized and measured? What is the relationship between data-driven culture, AI-enhanced marketing capabilities, and company performance? How can AI increase marketing agility? Under what conditions can AI increase the impact of marketing agility on company performance? To conclude, the more marketing managers benefit from guidance in adopting and using AI tools, the more likely it will be to capitalize on the business value of AI-enhanced marketing capabilities.*

References

Accenture (2019) AI: built to scale. https://www.accenture.com/us-en/insights/artificial-intelligence/ai-investments
Accenture (2024) What is artificial intelligence? https://www.accenture.com/au-en/insights/artificial-intelligence-summary-index
Barney JB (1991) Firm resources and sustained competitive advantage. J Manag 17:99–120
Bharadwaj AS (2000) A resource-based perspective on information technology capability and firm performance: an empirical investigation. MIS Q 24(1):169–196
Campbell C, Sands S, Ferraro C, Tsao H-S, Mavrommatis A (2020) From data to action: how marketers can leverage AI. Bus Horiz 63:227–243
Chae H-C, Koh CE, Prybutok VR (2014) Information technology capability and firm performance: contradictory findings and their possible causes. MIS Q 38(1):305–326
Chang W, Park JE, Chaiy S (2010) How does CRM technology transform into organizational performance? a mediating role of marketing capability. J Bus Res 63:849–855
Chintapalati S, Pandey SK (2022) Artificial intelligence in marketing: a systematic literature review. Int J Mark Res 64(1):38–68
Davenport TH, Kirby J (2016) Just how smart are smart machines? MIT Sloan Manag Rev 57(3):21–25
Davenport TH, Ronanki R (2018) Artificial intelligence for the real world. Harv Bus Rev 96(1):108–116
Davenport T, Guha A, Grewal D, Bressgott T (2020) How artificial intelligence will change the future of marketing. J Acad Mark Sci 48:24–42
Day G (1994) The capabilities of market-driven organizations. J Mark 58(4):37–52
Day G (2011) Closing the marketing capabilities gap. J Mark 75(4):183–195
De Bruyn A, Viswanathan V, Beh YS, Brock JK-U, von Wangenheim F (2020) Artificial intelligence and marketing: pitfalls and opportunities. J Interact Mark 51:91–105
Duan Y, Edwards JS, Dwivedi YK (2019) Artificial intelligence for decision making in the era of big data—evolution, challenges and research agenda. Int J Inf Manage 48:63–71
Grant RM (1996) Toward a knowledge-based theory of the firm. Strat Manag J 17(Winter Special Issue), 109–122
Gregory GD, Ngo LV, Karavdic M (2019) Developing e-commerce marketing capabilities and efficiencies for enhanced performance in business-to-business export ventures. Ind Mark Manage 78:146–157
Herhausen H, Miočević D, Morgan RE, Kleijnen MHP (2020) The digital marketing capabilities gap. Ind Mark Manage 90:276–290
Hoffman DL, Moreau CP, Stremersch S, Wedel M (2022) The rise of new technologies in marketing: a framework and outlook. J Mark 86(1):1–6
Homburg C, Wielgos DM (2022) The value relevance of digital marketing capabilities to firm performance. J Acad Mark Sci 50:666–688
Huang M-H, Rust RT (2018) Artificial intelligence in service. J Serv Res 21(2):155–172
Huang M-H, Rust RT (2021) A strategic framework for artificial intelligence in marketing. J Acad Mark Sci 49:30–50
Huang M-H, Rust RT, Maksimovic V (2019) The feeling economy: managing in the next generation of AI. Calif Manage Rev 61(4):43–65

IBM (2023) IBM study: CEOs embrace generative AI as productivity jumps to the top of their agendas. https://newsroom.ibm.com/2023-06-27-IBM-Study-CEOs-Embrace-Generative-AI-as-Productivity-Jumps-to-the-Top-of-their-Agendas
Johnson JS, Friend SB, Lee HS (2017) Big data facilitation, utilization, and monetization: exploring the 3Vs in a new product development process. J Prod Innov Manag 34(5):640–658
Kaplan AM, Haenlein M (2019a) Siri, Siri, in my hand: who's the fairest in the land? On the interpretations, illustrations, and implications of artificial intelligence. Bus Horiz 62(1):15–25
Kaplan AM, Haenlein M (2019b) Brief history of artificial intelligence: on the past, present, and future of artificial intelligence. Calif Manage Rev 61(4):5–14
KPMG (2023) KPMG generative AI survey. https://kpmg.com/us/en/articles/2023/generative-artificial-intelligence-2023.html
Kumar V, Ashraf AR, Nadeem W (2024) AI-powered marketing: what, where, and how? Int J Inf Manage. https://doi.org/10.1016/j.ijinfomgt.2024.102783
Kumar V, Ramachandran D, Kumar B (2021) Influence of new-age technologies on marketing: a research agenda. J Bus Res 125:864–877
Latinovic Z, Chatterjee SC (2022) Achieving the promise of AI and ML in delivering economic and relational customer value in B2B. J Bus Res 144:966–974
Manis KT, Madhavaram S (2023) AI-Enabled marketing capabilities and the hierarchy of capabilities: conceptualization, proposition development, and research avenues. J Bus Res 157:113485
Mikalef P, Islam N, Parida V, Singh H, Altwaijry N (2023) Artificial intelligence (AI) competencies for organizational performance: a B2B marketing capabilities perspective. J Bus Res 164:113998
Miles RE, Snow CC (1978) Organizational strategy, structure and process. West Publishing Company, New York
Mithas S, Ramasubbu N, Sambamurthy V (2011) How information management capability influences firm performance. MIS Q 35(1):237–256
Morgan NA (2012) Marketing and business performance. J Acad Mark Sci 40:102–119
Morgan NA, Feng H (2024) Marketing capabilities and Shelby D. Hunt: contributions, current state, and the future. J Mark Manag. https://doi.org/10.1080/0267257X.2024.2311110
Mu J (2015) Marketing capability, organizational adaptation and new product development performance. Ind Mark Manage 49:151–166
Mullainathan S, Spiess J (2017) Machine learning: an applied econometric approach. J Econ Perspect 31(2):87–106
Overgoor G, Chica M, Rand W, Weishampel A (2019) Letting the computers take over: using AI to solve marketing problems. Calif Manage Rev 61(4):1–30
Peltier JW, Dahl AJ, Schibrowsky JA (2024) Artificial intelligence in interactive marketing: a conceptual framework and research agenda. J Res Interact Mark 18(1):54–90
Poole DL, Mackworth AK (2010) Artificial intelligence: foundations of computational agents. Cambridge University Press, Cambridge
Prahalad CK, Hamel G (1990) The core competence of the corporation. Harv Bus Rev, May–June, 2–15
Puntoni S, Reczek RW, Giesler M, Botti S (2021) Consumers and artificial intelligence: an experiential perspective. J Mark 85(1):131–151
Ramaswami S, Srivastava R, Bhargava M (2009) Market-based capabilities and financial performance of firms: insights into marketing's contribution to firm value. J Acad Mark Sci 37(2):97–116
Saini A, Johnson JL (2005) Organizational capabilities in E-commerce: an empirical investigation of e-brokerage service providers. J Acad Mark Sci 33(3):360–375
Sambamurthy V, Bharadwaj A, Grover V (2003) Shaping agility through digital options: reconceptualizing the role of information technology in contemporary firms. MIS Q 27(2):237–263
Selznick P (1957) Leadership in administration. Row, Peterson, Evanston
Shankar V (2018) How artificial intelligence (AI) is reshaping retailing. J Retail 94(4):vi–xi
Shieber SM (2004) The Turing test: verbal behavior as the hallmark of intelligence. MIT Press

Shrestha YR, Ben-Menahem SM, von Krogh G (2019) Organizational decision-making structures in the age of AI. Calif Manage Rev 61(4):66–83
Sullivan Y, Wamba SF (2024) Artificial intelligence and adaptive response to market changes: a strategy to enhance firm performance and innovation. J Bus Res 174:114500
Suoniemi S, Meyer-Waarden L, Munzel A, Zablah AR, Straub S (2020) Big data and firm performance: the roles of market-directed capabilities and business strategy. Inf Manag 57(7):103365
Syam N, Sharma A (2018) Waiting for a sales renaissance in the fourth industrial revolution: machine learning and artificial intelligence in sales research and practice. Ind Mark Manage 69:135–146
Teece DJ, Pisano G, Shuen A (1997) Dynamic capabilities and strategic management. Strateg Manag J 18(7):509–533
Trainor KJ, Andzulis JM, Rapp A, Agnihotri R (2014) Social media technology usage and customer relationship performance: a capabilities-based examination of social CRM. J Bus Res 67:1201–1208
Trainor KJ, Rapp A, Beitelspacher LS, Schillewaert N (2011) Integrating information technology and marketing: an examination of the drivers and outcomes of e-Marketing capability. Ind Mark Manage 40:162–174
Van Esch P, Black JS (2021) Artificial intelligence (AI): revolutionizing digital marketing. Australas Mark J 29(3):199–203
Vlačić B, Corbo L, Costa e Silva S, Dabi M (2021) The evolving role of artificial intelligence in marketing: a review and research agenda. J Bus Res 128, 187–203
Vorhies D, Morgan NA (2005) Benchmarking marketing capabilities for sustainable competitive advantage. J Mark 69(1):80–94
Wang F (2020) Digital marketing capabilities in international firms: a relational perspective. Int Mark Rev 37 (3):559–577
Wang Z, Kim HG (2017) Can social media marketing improve customer relationship capabilities and firm performance? Dynamic capability perspective. J Interact Mark 39:15–26
Wang ETG, Hu H-F, Hu PJ-H (2013) Examining the role of information technology in cultivating firms' dynamic marketing capabilities. Inf Manag 50:336–343
Wernerfelt B (1984) A resource-based view of the firm. Strateg Manag J 5:171–180

AI-Driven Integrated Marketing Communications (IMC): Exploring the Role of AI in Planning, Executing, and Evaluating IMC

Flor Morton and Teresa Treviño-Benavides

Abstract Marketing activities increasingly rely on intelligence and customer insights to design effective marketing mix plans. In today' market, the dynamics are more complex and fast-moving than ever before. Consumers have access to vast amounts of information and engage with brands across multiple channels. This complexity requires that companies orchestrate their marketing communications efforts effectively to ensure a consistent and compelling brand message. Artificial intelligence enhances the IMC capabilities by facilitating or reinforcing operations such as information acquisition, integration, analysis, and interpretation. This chapter aims to explore of AI's role in integrated marketing communications (IMC). First, it briefly examines the role of AI in marketing. Second, it analyzes how AI is currently integrated or could potentially be integrated into the three phases of the integrated marketing communication process (planning, implementation, and evaluation). Finally, the chapter addresses ethical considerations associated with the use of AI in marketing communications.

Keywords Artificial intelligence · Integrated marketing communications · Consumer insights · Customer journey · AI-ethical challenges

1 Introduction

The term "Artificial Intelligence" (AI) was coined in 1955 in a proposal developed by John McCarthy (Dartmouth College), Marvin Minsky (Harvard University), Nathaniel Rochester (IBM), and Claude Shannon (Press 2016). These scholars organized a workshop in 1956, which is now widely recognized as the official beginning of the AI field (Toosi et al. 2021). Since then, the field of artificial intelligence has evolved significantly, expanding from its early conceptual foundations to encompass a wide range of technologies and applications.

F. Morton (✉) · T. Treviño-Benavides
Department of Management, Universidad de Monterrey, San Pedro Garza García, Mexico
e-mail: flor.morton@udem.edu

C. Machado and J. P. Davim (eds.), *Challenges and Opportunities in the Artificial Intelligence Era*, https://doi.org/10.1007/978-3-031-85272-5_10

According to the Silicon Valley Innovation Center (2024), AI has become a catalyst driving the next industrial revolution, profoundly impacting a wide range of industries and reshaping how we interact with technology. AI is expected to be a major contributor to the global economy. A recent report by McKinsey & Company indicates that generative AI alone could generate $2.6 trillion to $4.4 trillion in annual economic value across various industries (Chui et al. 2023). Furthermore, AI is projected to add up to $15.7 trillion to the global economy by 2030, with $6.6 trillion expected to result from increased productivity and $9.1 trillion from consumption-driven effects (PWc 2017).

Marketing professionals and researchers consistently pursue new technologies to enhance business performance and improve the consumer experience. Artificial Intelligence (AI) has dramatically transformed the marketing industry in today's rapidly evolving commercial landscape. As companies navigate an increasingly digital and data-driven world, the role of AI in reshaping marketing strategies and practices has become critically important (Yau et al. 2021).

According to Davenport et al. (2021), marketing stands to gain the greatest value from AI compared to other company functions. AI can importantly enhance marketing's core activities such as understanding customer needs, aligning those needs with products and services, and persuading individuals to purchase those products. For instance, AI enables sophisticated applications, such as predictive analytics, which allow marketers to anticipate customer needs and behaviors with greater accuracy. This makes AI particularly valuable for marketing-oriented objectives, such as improving existing products, developing new ones, and strengthening customer relationships.

Over the past decade, AI has driven a rapid and transformative evolution in the field of marketing communications (also referred to as MarCom), driving hyper-personalization, real-time engagement, and unmatched efficiency. This evolution has fundamentally transformed the way brands engage with their audiences and paved the way for innovative AI applications in the future. Today's AI technologies facilitate more natural and human-like interactions between brands and consumers, exemplified by virtual assistants and customer service chatbots (Mokhtar and Salimon 2022). AI-driven sentiment analysis has gained widespread acceptance for monitoring brand perception (Wankhade et al. 2022) and swiftly adjusting communication strategies. Furthermore, AI has significantly enhanced IMC, by analyzing vast amounts of social data to pinpoint trends, assess campaign effectiveness, and even craft creative content (Abrokwah-Larbi and Awuku-Larbi 2024; Campbell et al. 2020; Durmus 2024; Wang et al. 2023). For instance, AI-powered content generation tools have revolutionized marketing by enabling the creation of personalized content at scale, from tailored product recommendations to dynamic email campaigns (Deveau et al. 2023). These advancements have enhanced the precision and efficiency of marketing strategies, offering new avenues for brands to connect with consumers in a more personalized and meaningful way (Qin and Jiang 2019). Technologies such as machine learning, natural language processing, and data analytics have empowered brands to gain deeper insights into consumer behavior, predict preferences, and deliver highly personalized content and experiences, fostering more dynamic and interactive relationships between brands and consumers (Morton et al. 2024).

This chapter aims to provide an exploration of AI's role in integrated marketing communications. First, the chapter briefly examines the role of AI in marketing, focusing on the different types of AI (mechanical, thinking, and feeling) and their role in marketing research, strategy and the marketing mix. Second, it analyzes how AI is currently integrated or could potentially be integrated into the three phases of the integrated marketing communication process, specifically in planning, executing, and evaluating marketing communications. Finally, the chapter addresses ethical considerations associated with the use of AI in marketing communications. As AI becomes more pervasive in IMC, concerns about privacy, data security, and algorithmic bias, among other ethical issues, are becoming increasingly important. The chapter provides insights into navigating these ethical challenges and implementing responsible AI practices. Overall, this work aims to deliver valuable insights for businesses seeking to leverage AI effectively in IMC while enriching the academic discourse by addressing both current practices and ethical challenges related to the integration of AI in marketing communications.

2 The Role of Artificial Intelligence in Marketing

Marketing activities increasingly rely on intelligence and customer insights to design effective advertising campaigns, set appropriate prices for target audiences, and manage various other critical tasks. The rise in computing power, reduced costs, the accessibility of big data, and the widespread adoption of machine learning algorithms, among other factors, have contributed to the growing importance of artificial intelligence technologies in marketing (Adeola et al. 2022).

De Bruyn et al. (2020) note that the term "intelligence" has over 70 different definitions across disciplines such as psychology, sociology, biology, neuroscience, and philosophy. This diversity in definitions helps explain why "artificial intelligence"(AI), despite its frequent use, remains a somewhat vague concept. The authors define AI as "machines that mimic human intelligence in tasks such as learning, planning, and problem-solving through higher-level, autonomous knowledge creation" (p. 93). Similarly, Haenlein and Kaplan (2019) describe AI as a system's ability to accurately understand external information, learn from it, and use the acquired knowledge to perform specific tasks. Through technologies such as automation, big data systems, deep learning, Natural Language Processing (NLP), and Computer Vision, AI is capable of emulating human capabilities, whether it's for performing routine tasks or engaging in more complex cognitive and emotional processes. Wang and Siau (2019) argue that AI goes beyond simply emulating human abilities and has evolved to substantially enhance human capabilities. This chapter adopts this perspective, particularly in the context of marketing, where AI not only automates tasks but also transforms and enriches marketing strategies while reducing costs and

Table 1 The role of mechanical, thinking, and feeling intelligence in the marketing strategic planning process

	Marketing research	Marketing strategy	Marketing mix
Mechanical AI	Data collection	Segmentation	Standardization
Thinking AI	Market analysis	Targeting	Personalization
Feeling AI	Customer understanding	Positioning	Relationalization

Source Own elaboration based on Huang and Rust (2021)

improving customer and financial performance (Abrokwah-Larbi and Awuku-Larbi 2024; Mishra and Pani 2021).

Huang and Rust (2021) suggest that, rather than viewing AI as a single, uniform entity, it is more accurate to recognize the various types of intelligence it encompasses, similar to the way we understand that humans have diverse cognitive abilities. AI intelligence can be categorized into three types based on their complexity: mechanical, thinking, and feeling. Mechanical AI is used to automate routine and repetitive tasks providing standardization benefits. Thinking AI processes large amounts of unstructured data, uncovering new insights and making decisions based on pattern recognition, which makes it an effective tool for personalization. Feeling AI enables two-way interactions with humans, analyzing emotions and facilitating relational engagement. The authors propose a three-stage marketing strategic planning process consisting of a research phase, a strategy phase, and an action phase, viewing this process as iterative, with each type of AI playing a crucial role at different stages. Mechanical AI can be used for data collection during the research phase, identifying new customer preference patterns in the strategy phase, and for standardizing and automating processes such as developing new offers, setting prices, managing product access, and communications. Thinking AI is useful for market analysis in the research phase, recommending optimal segments to target in the strategy phase, and personalizing the marketing mix, such as tailoring products based on customer preferences and setting prices according to willingness to pay. Feeling AI can be used to understand consumer needs and emotions through customer analytics in the research phase, develop positioning strategies that resonate with customers, and personalize interactions to foster engagement through the marketing mix in the action phase (see Table 1).

3 Transforming Marketing Communications Through AI

Marketing communications refers to the strategic integration of promotional tools, messaging, media, and marketing channels that a company uses to engage with its target audience. MarCom represents the "voice" of an organization, serving as the means through which brands inform, persuade and remind consumers about their products (Keller 2009). The primary objectives of MarCom include building brand awareness and brand image, positioning the brand in the market by highlighting its value proposition and differentiation, generating product demand, fostering customer engagement, influencing consumer behavior, encouraging customer loyalty and advocacy, and effectively launching new products (Batra and Keller 2016; Haris et al. 2023). MarCom includes advertising, public relations (PR), sales promotions, direct marketing, personal selling, social media marketing, content marketing, digital marketing, sponsorships and events, customer service, among other elements (Batra and Keller 2016; Haris et al. 2023; Keller 2001; Rachmawati and Afifi 2022).

The traditional approach of using a single, broad strategy to reach an entire audience-dominant in mass marketing for decades- has given way to more varied and targeted communication methods, even within the same market (Kitchen and Proctor 2015). AI has a significant role in this shift, enabling companies to analyze consumer data at a granular level, personalize communications, and deliver tailored messages that resonate with specific segments (Morton et al. 2024). This evolution allows brands to engage more effectively with their audiences, improving the relevance and impact of their marketing communications.

The adoption of AI technology is influenced by technological, organizational, human, and environmental aspects of the organizational context. Technological factors that influence the adoption of AI include the company's existing technology portfolio, its expertise on the use of existing technologies, and readiness to adopt new technologies; organizational factors include, culture, management support, project management capabilities and strategies; human factors such as employee competency and training, as well as customer satisfaction; while the environmental context refers to external factors such as the regulatory environment, government support, competitive pressure (Dora et al. 2022; Yang et al. 2013). Thus, the adoption of AI in marketing communications could also be driven by a combination of these internal and external factors.

On one hand, since AI relies heavily on data, organizations must establish a robust data infrastructure and ensure their existing technology infrastructure is ready to integrate with new AI systems; this requires effective data collection, storage, and analysis systems in place (Kar et al. 2021). Additionally, resource allocation and budgeting for AI technologies in marketing communications represent critical internal considerations (Heavin and Power 2018). The successful implementation of AI-driven marketing communications requires internal expertise, investment in AI tools, platforms, and skilled AI specialists. Therefore, companies must assess their financial capacity to make these investments in order for the adoption of AI in their communication strategies and tactics.

On the other hand, external factors such as competitors' adoption of AI technologies, consumers' expectations for personalization, regulations and standards (Dora et al. 2022) regarding data privacy, security, and AI usage, as well as advances in AI technology might influence AI adoption for marketing communications. For instance, observing competitors' success with AI and the increasing demand for personalized and efficient customer experiences may drive companies to adopt AI solutions in order to deliver tailored marketing messages, improve customer interactions and satisfaction, and outperform competitors.

Table 2 MarCom AI ecosystem and outcomes

Components	Stakeholders	Outcomes
Data, tools, devices, and technologies that operate together to deliver value to marketers for their marketing communications	Individuals and organizations involved in developing, managing, using, and benefiting from MarCom components	Value-creation opportunities for MarCom derived from AI
• Consumer data • Digital Assets • Algorithms • Digital environments • Infrastructure	• Brands • Consumers • Content creators • Influencers • Regulators • Data platforms • AI and machine learning service providers • Media and messaging platforms	• Personalization • Automatization • Identification of actionable insights • Experimentation

Source Own elaboration based on Malthouse and Copulsky (2023)

Malthouse and Copulsky (2023) caution that when discussing AI in marketing communications, it can be misleading to focus only on algorithms that predict outcomes, automate tasks, segment customers, suggest wording, analyze text sentiment, or uncover key insights. Narrowing the focus may lead to underinvestment in other crucial components of the MarCom-AI ecosystem. The authors identify key components that operate together to deliver value in marketing communications. These components include data, tools, devices, and technologies that operate together to deliver value to marketers in their marketing communication efforts, for example, consumer data, digital assets, digital environments (customer-owned devices and third-party owned touchpoints), infrastructure and algorithms. Stakeholders include individuals and organizations that develop, manage, interact, and benefit from MarCom components (e.g. brands, consumers, regulators, media platforms, among other actors). Together, these components and stakeholders form the MarCom AI ecosystem. By leveraging AI components and stakeholder interactions, the MarCom AI ecosystem offers companies value-creation opportunities, including the possibility to identify actionable insights, automatize and personalize communications, and continuously test multiple variations of communication content and stimuli (see Table 2).

3.1 The Role of AI in Integrated Marketing Communications Capability

The resource based view (RBV) theory suggests that a firm's performance and competitive advantage not only depend not only on the resources it possesses, but also on how effectively those resources are used through the firm's capabilities (Mansour et al. 2022). According to Hunt (2000), capabilities are socially complex and interconnected combinations of a company's tangible and intangible resources that work together in a synergic and coherent manner enabling organizations to efficiently and effectively create valuable marketing offerings. Tangible resources include computer hardware and software, equipment, building, among other assets; while intangible resources encompass organizational knowledge, procedures, and employees' expertise. Therefore, a capability refers to a firm's ability to deploy its resources effectively to achieve specific organizational goals and create value.

Marketing capabilities as defined by Luxton et al. (2015), are integrative processes designed to leverage a company's collective knowledge, skills, and resources to produce valuable goods and services that meet market needs and demands. These capabilities allow firms to add value to their goods and services in response to competitive pressures. Integrated marketing communications is a continuous interactive, and cross-functional process of planning, executing, and evaluating brand communication, integrating all parties involved in the exchange process to meet each other's needs and maximize mutual satisfaction (Duncan and Mulhern 2004, as cited in Porcu et al. 2012). Kliatchko (2005) further defines IMC as audience-focused, placing both internal and external target audience at core; channel-centered, involving a coordinated use of multiple channels or communication tools; and results-driven, where financial and other performance indicators are used to evaluate the effectiveness of the IMC program.

IMC is considered a marketing capability because it is a process in which a company uses its knowledge and expertise to combine and transform its tangible (e.g. point of sale) and intangible resources (e.g. brand identity) into performance outcomes such as sales, brand equity, brand loyalty, and profitability. In today's fast-moving and complex market environment, where consumers have access to vast amounts of information and engage with brands across multiple channels, the need for companies to orchestrate their marketing communications efforts effectively to ensure a consistent and compelling brand message has never been greater. Therefore, IMC has become a crucial marketing capability because it involves a holistic and strategic management of marketing communications (Kitchen et al. 2004). A well-executed IMC strategy allows a company to deliver a consistent, cohesive and unified message across various marketing channels, reinforcing brand equity (Madhavaram et al. 2005). By effectively coordinating communication efforts (e.g. advertising, social media, and sales promotions), IMC maximizes the impact of campaigns, which can lead to increased brand recognition, higher sales, and ultimately improved brand equity and financial performance (Anabila 2020; Ratnatunga and Ewing 2005). Additionally, IMC enables efficient resource allocation and improves a firm's agility, allowing it to quickly adapt to market changes, as well as leverage different communication channels and tactics to maintain a competitive advantage (Batra and Keller 2016).

Table 3 The role of AI in the integrated marketing communication process

	Planning IMC	Execution IMC	Evaluation IMC
AI-driven capabilities	• Customer understanding • Segmentation • Competitor analysis	• Automatization of marketing campaign contents • Personalization • Real-time Optimization • Cross-channel integration	• Real-time customer feedback • Real-time testing and resource allocation • Improvements to KPIs

Source Own elaboration

Artificial intelligence has upgraded operations such as information acquisition, integration, analysis, and interpretation (Manis and Madhavaram 2023). Since integrated marketing communications rely on these operations to efficiently and effectively target audiences, AI has the potential to boost IMC capabilities by facilitating these operations. For instance, AI can automate and optimize the process of gathering data from various sources in real-time, ensuring that the information is both current and relevant. AI can also consolidate all the collected data creating a unified view of the customers and the market landscape. Furthermore, AI's ability to quickly and accurately analyze large datasets enables it to assist in interpreting the results, providing actionable insights and recommendations. These activities can be leveraged across the three phases of the IMC program: planning, execution, and performance evaluation. Next, the contribution of AI to each of these phases will be analyzed (see Table 3). In doing so, despite the fact that integrated marketing communications target diverse audiences, this chapter adopts a customer-centric approach.

3.2 *The Role of AI in the Planning Stage of IMC*

An effective integrated marketing communications (IMC) program is built upon strategic planning and comprehensive information management. Strategic planning is essential for anticipating and responding to market dynamics, enabling organizations to forecast market trends, monitor consumer behavior, track competitor actions (Falahat et al. 2020), as well as to identify emerging channels and trending topics. This proactive approach allows firms to adapt their IMC programs strategically in response to market changes, ensuring message consistency across platforms while capitalizing on new opportunities and aligning with organizational objectives.

Effective marketing communication planning requires robust information management, including identifying relevant data sources, acquiring information systematically, analyzing data to extract actionable insights, profiling stakeholders, and continuously measuring performance across all channels (Mikalef et al. 2023). The synergy between these capabilities creates a dynamic IMC program that is not only consistent and brand-aligned but also responsive to market changes and stakeholder needs. This integrated approach enhances an organization's ability to develop data-driven, targeted communication strategies that resonate with their audience and adapt to changing market conditions, ultimately contributing to the achievement of strategic goals through more effective, efficient, and impactful marketing communications. AI technologies have revolutionized the planning phase of marketing communication by enabling more sophisticated data analysis and predictive modeling. This section explores how AI contributes to customer understanding, segmentation, and competitor analysis during the planning stage of IMC.

3.2.1 AI-Driven Customer Understanding in IMC

AI-driven customer insights are revolutionizing marketing communications by providing deeper and more actionable understanding of customer behaviors, preferences, and interactions. By leveraging AI systems and algorithms designed to gather and analyze large amounts of data from various sources, companies can evaluate market conditions and consumer behavior to optimize marketing communication efforts (Brobbey et al. 2021). AI combines multiple data sources, such as online and offline behavior, to create a more holistic view of the customer. Through advanced machine learning algorithms and data analytics, AI tools can uncover hidden patterns, predict customer needs, and tailor marketing communication strategies with unprecedented precision (De Bruyn et al. 2020; Kitchen and Proctor 2015).

3.2.2 AI-Driven Segmentation in IMC

AI has also transformed customer segmentation by enabling businesses to move beyond traditional segmentation methods, which often relied solely on demographic variables and resulted in relatively static segments. By analyzing large datasets and identifying patterns that may not be immediately obvious, AI can segment customers based on their purchasing habits, preferences, psychographics, interactions, demographics, and responses to previous marketing campaigns (Brobbey et al. 2021). Unlike traditional segmentation which is often a one-time exercise, AI driven segmentation can be continuous and adaptive. AI algorithms can update customer profiles making customer segments dynamic and evolving in real-time based on new data from new interactions with the brand across various channels (Katragadda 2022). This real-time adaptability can lead to the creation of more precise, dynamic, and actionable segments (micro-segmentation), which reflect the most current understanding of customer's nuanced behaviors and preferences, thereby increasing the relevance of communication and the likelihood of engagement and conversion (Mishra and Pani 2021).

Additionally, AI's predictive capabilities allow for proactive segmentation and personalized communications that anticipate customer needs and desires (Gkikas and Theodoridis 2022). AI-based predictive analysis helps marketers to calculate customer lifetime value and allocate resources effectively, focusing on high-value customers (Sun et al. 2023). AI can also be used for customer retention through predictive modeling, which involves analyzing historical data of potential churned customers to identify patterns and behaviors that precede churning (Ortakci and Seker 2024). By providing a churn risk score, which can also be used as a segmentation variable, AI can assist in designing retention strategies such as personalized discounts or promotions, as well as recommending the most effective channels and messages to re-engage with those customers.

3.2.3 AI-Driven Competitor Analysis in IMC

Regarding competitor analysis, traditional methods often relied on information obtained through surveys; however, advances in mobile and web technologies have allowed for unprecedented scale and speed in gathering consumer feedback. This information can be analyzed using natural language processing (NLP) techniques to process semi-structured data (Guo et al. 2017). AI can analyze competitor-related data from sources such as customer reviews (e.g. product comparisons) and social media to understand differentiation attributes and develop competitive insights (Lee 2021). Sentiment analysis can be used to examine customer reviews, comments, and discussions related to competitors, providing insights into consumers' emotions towards competitors, their preferences, and the overall brand perception of competitors (Jin et al. 2016). Additionally, machine learning models can facilitate dynamic competitor analysis (Soleimani 2024). For example, AI can perform web scraping of competitors' websites, social media profiles, and other online platforms to collect data on their marketing activities, product launches, pricing strategies, and customer engagement. This process can help to identify gaps or opportunities in the market that can be leveraged in marketing communications.

3.3 The Role of AI in the Execution of IMC

According to Mikalef et al. (2023) implementation refers to execution. In the context of integrated marketing communications, the execution phase involves the practical implementation of planned communication strategies and tactics. Translating IMC plans into concrete actions that yield tangible results requires a proactive–reactive approach that combines consistency and continuity with flexibility and personalization (Gurau 2008). In this sense, it is a process driven by, and responsive to, data about various stakeholders and from different sources (Luxton et al. 2015), which can increase the chances of interaction between the brand and its customers (Ahmad and Salleh 2019).

Execution in marketing communication includes the launch of advertising campaigns, public relations activities, promotions, and other communication elements. It also involves adjusting tactics in response to market changes or consumer behavior shifts; as well as ensuring coherence and synergy across the different communication channels used. The integration of AI during this phase of the IMC offers several benefits, such as the automating activities like content creation and the development of marketing stimuli for campaigns, personalizing messages,contents, and campaigns, cross-channel integration, and real-time optimization of the IMC program.

3.3.1 AI-Driven Automatization in IMC

Generative AI enables marketers to automate content creation, efficiently producing vast amounts of content tailored to specific target audiences such as personalized emails, social media posts, digital advertisements, and dynamic website content (Deveau et al. 2023). For instance, an online retailer can leverage AI to analyze customer data–such as browsing behavior, purchase patterns, and demographic information—to create personalized email campaigns. These campaigns can customize the subject line, content, and timing of delivery for each recipient. Another example is Amazon Titan, which harnesses AI to automate routine tasks and accelerate content generation, including images and text for blog posts, websites, and chatbots. This automation not only speeds up content creation but also improves scalability and cost-efficiency (Wang et al. 2023), allowing teams to focus on strategic and value-added activities.

3.3.2 AI-Driven Personalization in IMC

In the 2024 State of Customer Service and CX Study, 81% of over 1000 American consumers indicated a preference for companies that offer personalized experiences (Hyken 2024). AI empowers marketers with deeper insights into both potential and existing customers, enabling the delivery of precise, timely, and personalized messages (Haleem et al. 2022). AI can be employed to send personalized messages to customers based on their interactions on social media, browsing behavior, and purchase history (Brobbey et al. 2021). By leveraging comprehensive customer profiles (based on multiple data), marketers can use AI to create hyper-personalized content that resonates with specific audience segments (Morton et al. 2024). For example, marketers can target first-time buyers with special offers or re-engage churned customers with personalized incentives. AI can also facilitate real-time product recommendations and tailored promotions, lead engagements via email, SMS, or online chat (e.g. chatbots), and assist in ad and content creation.

3.3.3 AI-Driven Cross-Channel Communication Integration

Lindecrantz et al. (2020) emphasize an important shift in the concept of personalization, which used to be focused mainly on tailored offers, and is now present in the entire customer experience. Modern consumers expect personalized interactions at every stage of their journey with a retailer, experiencing multiple customized touchpoints that align with their unique interests and preferences. Customers now value a cohesive, personalized experience that recognizes their unique needs and preferences across all stages of their interaction with a brand, from initial product discovery to post-purchase support. Therefore, retailers are now focused on creating multiple customized touch points throughout the customer's journey, rather than just personalizing offers. The evolution of personalized experiences now involves retailers engaging customers in continuous, individualized conversations, using data-driven insights to tailor interactions on an individual level. Rather than simply receiving offers targeted to people similar to them, customers now experience personalized products, offers, and communications throughout their entire journey, tailored specifically to them as unique individuals.

The deep understanding of customer journeys enabled by AI sets the stage for highly personalized engagement strategies. AI systems can identify critical moments in the customer journey where targeted interventions are most likely to be effective. These moments, often called "micro-moments" or "touchpoints" greatly impact consumer's purchase behavior, representing opportunities for marketing interventions powered by AI to improve customer engagement (Chowdhury et al. 2024). By recognizing patterns in customer behavior across various channels (e.g., website visits, email interactions, social media engagement), AI can pinpoint when and where customers are most receptive to communication. This might involve sending personalized product recommendations based on browsing history, offering timely support when a customer seems stuck in the decision-making process, or providing relevant content to nurture leads at specific stages of their journey. Additionally, AI can optimize the timing and placement of content across channels, ensuring that marketing stimuli are delivered at the most impactful moments. This not only improves the efficiency and efficacy of IMC but also enables seamless cross-channel integration, maintaining a cohesive brand identity and delivering a unified consumer experience (Durmus 2024).

By delivering the right message or offer at the right time, businesses can enhance customer engagement, improve conversion rates, and foster long-term loyalty (Abrokwah-Larbi and Awuku-Larbi 2024). Starbucks' AI-powered loyalty program is an example of this, the program uses big data, analytics, and artificial intelligence to analyze customer data from mobile app usage and in-store purchases to deliver personalized offers and recommendations across various touchpoints (Marr 2021). Moreover, the use of proprietary data to create highly personalized customer experiences drives up customer loyalty and offers a competitive advantage difficult for competitors to replicate (Lindecrantz et al. 2020).

3.3.4 AI-Driven Real-Time Optimization of IMC

The ability of AI to process and analyze vast amounts of data in real-time, coupled with its capacity for continuous learning (eg. from previous campaigns), improves the adaptability in the execution of the marketing communication strategy. AI can identify trends, preferences, and shifts in consumer sentiment almost instantly, adjusting content and recommendations based on real-time data of user behavior and engagement; increasing the potential for marketing communications to be relevant, timely and effective (Kumar et al. 2019). For instance, if a customer interacts with a specific product on a website, AI can immediately trigger personalized content, such as a follow-up email with a discount code for that product or an in-app notification showcasing related items. Amazon's recommendation engine, powered by AI, is an example of this capability in action. The engine continuously analyzes customer behavior, purchase history, and browsing patterns to deliver highly personalized product recommendations. These insights allow for the dynamic adjustment of marketing messages and offers in real-time, ensuring that each customer receives the most relevant content.

Furthermore, AI-powered chatbots and conversational AI systems can engage with customers in real time, providing instant responses and personalized recommendations based on the conversation (Mokhtar and Salimon 2022). These systems can also collect data from each interaction, which can be immediately analyzed to refine communication strategies. For instance, if a chatbot notices that customers frequently ask about a specific product feature, marketing teams can quickly create content or campaigns that address this interest.

3.4 The Role of AI in Performance Evaluation of IMC

According to Luxton et al. (2015), IMC capability enables companies to concentrate their resources on their most valuable customers and prospects by prioritizing customer understanding rather than identifying the audience after creating a marketing message. This approach integrates all marketing and communication elements into a coherent, persuasive, meaningful, and measurable process that can be assessed for its effectiveness and efficiency. Demonstrating the effectiveness of marketing communication has become increasingly important for marketers; however, providing effectiveness has also become increasingly challenging due factors such evolving media media contexts (e.g. new channels) and changes in consumer behavior, technology adoption, among other factors (Krizanova et al. 2019).

Artificial Intelligence has emerged as a transformative tool in the evaluation of IMC programs, offering unprecedented capabilities in data analysis, pattern recognition, and predictive modeling (Campbell et al. 2020). Traditional methods of evaluating IMC performance, such as surveys and focus groups, have limitations in capturing the nuanced and dynamic consumer interactions across multiple channels.

In contrast, AI can process vast amounts of data from various sources to provide a holistic view of an IMC program's effectiveness, thus allowing for improvement of key performance indicators (KPIs) (Schrage et al. 2023). This section explores some of the contributions of AI to the evaluation stage of the IMC process.

3.4.1 AI-Driven Real-Time Customer Feedback Analysis in IMC

AI tools can analyze feedback from surveys, reviews, and social media to assess the effectiveness of marketing campaigns. By processing the diverse data, AI provides insights into how well a campaign resonates with its target audience. Additionally, AI-powered tools enable the identification of subtle trends and correlations that human analysts might miss. Techniques like machine learning and natural language processing, can analyze consumer sentiment, track shifts in public opinion, and detect emerging trends in real time. For instance, sentiment analysis algorithms can parse social media posts to measure public response to a marketing campaign, providing actionable insights that can be used to adjust messaging strategies promptly. This dynamic approach to performance evaluation ensures that IMC programs remain responsive and aligned with consumer preferences, thereby enhancing their overall impact.

In addition to real-time analysis, AI contributes to the evaluation of IMC programs by improving the accuracy and granularity of attribution modeling. Attribution models aim to determine which marketing channels and tactics are most effective in driving consumer actions (Nisar and Yeung 2018), such as making a purchase or signing up for a newsletter. Traditional attribution models often struggle with the complexity of modern, multi-channel marketing environments, which can lead to oversimplified or inaccurate assessments. AI-driven attribution models, however, can incorporate vast datasets and complex variables, allowing for more real-time and precise identification of the customer journey and the specific touchpoints that contribute to conversion using multi-touch attribution models (Pattanayak et al. 2022; Pedowitz 2024).

3.4.2 AI-Driven Real-Time Testing and Resource Allocation in IMC

AI can also improve the evaluation phase of IMC by utilizing both historical and real-time data to diagnose performance issues and predict corrective actions. According to Campbell et al. (2020), AI is being used for AI-driven A/B testing, which is used to evaluate and optimize advertising and online features. Unlike traditional methods, AI assists in testing the efficacy of a range of campaigns, websites, ads, and other online, and other online assets, allowing for self-optimization in real time based on user behavior and reactions to different variations. For instance, AI can automatically adjust ad spend, content, format, or placement depending on how different audience segments are responding. If an ad is underperforming, AI can test and implement variations, such as changing the headline, image, or call-to-action, to improve its effectiveness immediately. This real-time test and optimization improves the effectiveness of marketing campaigns, ensuring that the best-performing elements are consistently used.

Additionally, A/B testing can be used to measure and optimize the effectiveness of personalized recommendations. In the context of cross-selling and upselling, A/B testing helps identify which product recommendations resonate most with customers. For example, Amazon's Recommendation Engine uses sophisticated machine learning algorithms to analyze vast amounts of data and segment customers based on their interactions, including browsing history, search queries, and purchase patterns. These segments are updated in real-time as customers interact with the site, allowing for highly personalized and relevant recommendations. The engine delivers personalized product suggestions on the homepage, in search results, and during the checkout process, tailored to each customer's unique profile. Amazon continuously tests and optimizes its recommendation algorithms using A/B testing to determine which recommendations are most effective (Hardesty 2019).

Tailored, data-driven strategies allow for more personalized and effective campaigns, while also optimizing marketing spend in real time (Brobbey et al. 2021). AI analyzes performance data to recommend optimal allocation of marketing budgets across channels and campaigns (Pedowitz 2024). Furthermore, by providing insights into what is being effective, AI-powered dashboards enable companies to replicate successful strategies across different communication channels and allocate resources more efficiently (Haleem et al. 2022).

3.4.3 AI-Driven Improvements to KPI's in IMC

According to Schrage et al. (2023), a recent research study on artificial intelligence and business strategy revealed that companies across various industries are increasingly leveraging AI to enhance their key performance indicators. Some firms are using AI to gain deeper insights into the factors that drive KPI outcomes, while others prioritize the identification of which KPIs offer the most strategic value. Furthermore, beyond refining existing metrics, AI enables managers to algorithmically discover and establish new KPIs that can predict future performance at earlier stages of corporate activities. This early identification fosters better situational awareness and more responsive decision-making in dynamic market environments. Moreover, executives have noted the need to integrate local KPIs into a more cohesive set of metrics to effectively manage their businesses. As KPIs evolve, the ability to anticipate, model, and coordinate the interactions between various KPIs with AI becomes increasingly vital for optimizing both local and macro-level performance. This approach can also be applied to marketing communication KPIs, where AI can enhance the accuracy, integration, and impact of performance metrics, leading to more effective communication strategies.

4 Ethical Considerations and Challenges in the Use of AI in IMC

The integration of artificial intelligence into IMC offers substantial benefits, including hyper-personalization, predictiveness, real-time evaluation and decision-making, and improvements in performance. However, these advantages come with a range of ethical concerns that require careful consideration by both researchers and practitioners. This section examines some ethical issues associated with the use of AI in IMC, including privacy, consent, transparency, consumer autonomy, broader societal impacts, and accountability of AI systems and AI-driven marketing communication practices. The purpose of this section is not to provide an exhaustive analysis, but to highlight some of the most pressing concerns currently affecting AI in IMC; there are undoubtedly other considerations that also merit attention that will also require attention as the technology continues to advance.

4.1 *Privacy, Consent, and Transparency*

Perhaps one of the most pressing ethical concerns related to the use of AI is data privacy. AI systems in IMC rely heavily on vast amounts of consumer data to function effectively. This data often includes sensitive personal information, such as browsing history, purchase patterns, location data, and even biometric information. The collection, storage, and use of this data raise significant privacy concerns (Morton et al. 2024), particularly when consumers are unaware of how their information is being used or when they have not explicitly consented to its collection. Obtaining informed consent from consumers for the collection and use of their data is necessary for ensuring ethical practices. However, the complexity of AI systems and the often-intricate ways in which data is used can make it difficult for consumers to fully understand what they are consenting to. This raises concerns about whether consent is truly informed or if it is merely a formality.

In addition to privacy and consent, interpretability (or transparency) in AI systems is another important ethical challenge. Some AI algorithms operate as "black boxes," where the decision-making processes are opaque even to their developers (De Bruyn et al. 2020). In the context of IMC, this lack of transparency may result in situations where consumers are targeted with personalized content or advertisements without understanding why or how these decisions were made. The lack of transparency and the potential for misuse or unauthorized access to data disempowers consumers and raises questions regarding the fairness and accountability of AI (Linardatos et al. 2020). Therefore, regulation and innovation for guaranteeing interpretability of AI systems, as well as ensuring that consumers have a clear and accurate understanding of how their data will be used is essential for maintaining ethical standards in AI-driven IMC.

4.2 Consumer Autonomy

Consumer autonomy is also an important issue to consider in the ethical debate surrounding AI in IMC. AI systems are designed to influence consumer behavior by delivering hyper-personalized and persuasive content. While this can enhance user experience, it also raises concerns about the extent to which consumers are being manipulated or coerced by AI-driven marketing tactics. The fine line between persuasion and manipulation becomes blurred when AI can predict and exploit individual vulnerabilities (e.g. compulsive purchasing tendency), potentially leading to decisions that are not fully autonomous or in the best interest of the consumer (Morton and Vázquez-Maguirre 2023). Additionally, as AI-driven IMC becomes more prevalent, there is a risk that consumers may feel a sense of intrusion, of being increasingly surveilled and commodified, especially when consumers feel that their personal information is being exploited for commercial gain. This can potentially damage consumers' trust and trigger privacy protection behaviors (Quach et al. 2022), thereby a delicate balance between leveraging AI for marketing communication purposes and respecting the privacy and dignity of individuals is necessary for maintaining positive relationships with customers.

4.3 Social Issues

4.3.1 Job Displacement

Despite the current availability of free AI-platforms, advancements in this technology and potential future costs could exacerbate among large, medium, and small companies. Access to the benefits that AI offers to IMC depends on investment, this can potentially lead to a wider gap between large corporations and medium and small enterprises, with the most effective marketing communication campaigns being those of companies with the most advanced AI technologies. Additionally, the long-term impact of AI on employment is a significant ethical issue. As AI systems become more capable of automating tasks traditionally performed by human workers, there is a risk of job displacement within the marketing industry and increase in social inequalities (Khogali and Mekid 2023). While AI can create new opportunities for innovation and efficiency, it also raises questions about the future of work and the need to reskill and upskill the workforce.

4.3.2 Bias

Additionally, AI algorithms are designed to deliver content that aligns with a user's preferences and behaviors, which can result in the reinforcement of existing beliefs and the exclusion of diverse perspectives. In the context of IMC, this can lead to the creation of highly personalized digital marketing environments that isolate consumers from alternative viewpoints or products. Also, the widespread use of AI in marketing communications has the potential to shape cultural norms and values, influencing everything from consumer preferences to social behaviors. For example, AI in marketing communications could be used to perpetuate harmful stereotypes or promote unhealthy consumption patterns.

Furthermore, AI systems are trained on historical data, which can contain biases related to gender, race, socioeconomic status, and other factors. Buolamwini (2018) wrote an article in The New York Times highlighting a phenomenon she refers to as the "coded gaze," which describes how AI systems are influenced by the conscious and unconscious priorities and biases of the people who design them. She identified this problem when AI-powered facial detection software failed to detect her dark-skinned face and later she decided to study the biases in AI systems at the M.I.T. Media Lab (Buolamwini 2018). If not carefully managed, these biases can be perpetuated or even amplified by AI algorithms, leading to discriminatory outcomes in marketing campaigns (De Bruyn et al. 2020). For example, biased algorithms might disproportionately target certain demographic groups with specific types of advertisements, reinforcing stereotypes or excluding other groups from certain marketing messages.

4.3.3 Accountability

Establishing clear lines of accountability for AI is crucial (Linardatos et al. 2020), particularly when AI systems make decisions that affect consumers. This includes determining who is responsible when AI-driven marketing campaigns cause harm, whether through privacy breaches, biased targeting, or other negative aspects. Ensuring mechanisms in place to hold organizations accountable for the actions of their AI systems is essential for maintaining trust and upholding ethical standards in IMC. Additionally, the issue of algorithmic governance is becoming increasingly important in the ethical use of AI in IMC; as AI systems become more autonomous and complex, the need for oversight and regulation grows (Linardatos et al. 2020). Ethical IMC practices should include robust governance frameworks that ensure AI algorithms are developed, deployed, and monitored in a way that aligns with ethical principles. This could involve establishing industry standards, ethical guidelines, and regulatory bodies to supervise the use of AI in marketing and communication.

5 Conclusions

The integration of artificial intelligence is transforming the marketing landscape, extending its impact from routine task automation to advanced cognitive processes. The application of the three types of AI (mechanical, analytical, and feeling) enables marketers to emulate and enhance human capabilities through the marketing strategic planning process. The AI MarCom ecosystem, which includes diverse components and stakeholders, presents valuable opportunities for companies to innovate their communication strategies and create value. Marketing communications have evolved to leverage AI's capabilities, this evolution not only increases the relevance of marketing efforts but also fosters more meaningful consumer interactions, thereby improving overall campaign effectiveness.

Artificial intelligence holds transformative potential for integrated marketing communications, offering significant advancements in data acquisition, integration, analysis, and interpretation. AI's ability to rapidly analyze vast datasets and provide actionable insights supports every phase of the IMC process, from planning and execution to performance evaluation.

At the planning stage of IMC, AI empowers organizations to make data-driven strategic decisions. For instance, AI-driven technologies provide a more nuanced and real-time understanding of customer behaviors, preferences, and interactions, enabling organizations to plan their marketing communication strategies with greater precision. By integrating diverse data sources, AI offers a comprehensive view of the customer, uncovering hidden patterns that inform more targeted and effective marketing approaches. Moreover, AI's capability to drive dynamic segmentation has revolutionized traditional marketing practices. Unlike static demographic-based segmentation, AI facilitates real-time updates that reflect changes in consumer behavior, allowing for more precise and actionable micro-segmentation. Additionally, AI's predictive capabilities allow for proactive segmentation that anticipates customer needs and desires. Also, by leveraging AI, companies can also gain critical insights from competitor-related data, further enhancing their strategic planning of integrated marketing communications.

Through automation, personalization, cross-channel integration, and real-time optimization, AI fundamentally transforms the execution phase of IMC. AI-driven automation enables the rapid generation of tailored marketing communication materials. This efficiency not only scales content production but also optimizes resource allocation, allowing marketing teams to focus on strategic and value-creating initiatives.

Personalization, powered by AI, has become central to modern marketing strategies, significantly improving customer engagement and conversion rates. AI technologies enable marketers to craft highly personalized interactions by analyzing comprehensive customer data, including browsing behavior and purchase history. This capability allows for the creation of highly tailored content and offers that resonate with individual preferences, thereby enhancing the relevance and impact of marketing communications.

Moreover, in real-time optimization and cross-channel integration ensures that marketing strategies are both dynamic and cohesive. By leveraging AI tools, organizations can deliver consistent and targeted messaging across various platforms, aligning with consumer expectations and optimizing campaign effectiveness. AI's predictive capabilities and real-time data processing provide immediate insights into consumer needs, desires, and emerging trends, allowing for timely adjustments. This dynamic approach ensures that IMC programs remain responsive to shifting consumer preferences and market conditions, thereby enhancing overall effectiveness and driving customer satisfaction, loyalty, and competitive advantage in an increasingly complex marketplace.

The integration of AI into the evaluation phase of IMC represents a significant advancement in marketing performance assessment. AI's ability to process and analyze vast amounts of data in real time provides a more nuanced and comprehensive understanding of campaign effectiveness compared to traditional evaluation methods. Additionally, AI enhances the accuracy and granularity of attribution modeling. AI-driven attribution models can analyze extensive datasets and complex variables to provide a more precise identification of customer touchpoints and their impact on conversions. This capability enables marketers to better understand which channels and tactics drive desired consumer actions, optimizing resource allocation and improving the overall efficiency of marketing efforts.

AI-driven real-time testing and resource allocation represent a transformative shift in performance evaluation.Through AI-driven A/B testing and continuous optimization, marketers can dynamically adjust their strategies based on real-time data, ensuring that the most effective elements are utilized. This approach not only improves the relevance and impact of marketing campaigns but also allows for more efficient budget allocation and strategy replication across channels. By enhancing the accuracy and integration of key performance indicators (KPIs), AI enables marketers to establish more effective and strategic metrics, ultimately driving better decision-making and performance outcomes.

The ethical considerations surrounding the use of AI in integrated marketing communications reveal the complexity of balancing technological advancements with responsible marketing practices. AI presents important opportunities for marketers to enhance communication strategies. However, these benefits must be carefully weighed against critical ethical issues such as data privacy, informed consent, transparency, and the potential manipulation of consumer autonomy. At a broader level, AI's impact on societal structures, including economic inequality, cultural influence, and the perpetuation of biases, emphasizes the profound implications of its integration into marketing communications.

As AI systems increasingly influence consumer choices, marketers must prioritize ethical guidelines that ensure respect for individual rights while maintaining transparency in how data is collected and used. Ethical responsibility extends beyond individual consumer interactions, requiring marketers to consider how AI-driven strategies may reinforce harmful stereotypes or exacerbate existing disparities between large corporations and smaller enterprises. As AI technology continues to evolve, regulatory frameworks and ethical standards governing its use in IMC must also adapt. This requires a proactive and dynamic approach to ethical marketing that not only addresses current challenges but also anticipates future dilemmas as AI reshapes the marketing landscape.

Artificial intelligence will potentially continue to revolutionize integrated marketing communications by transforming the way businesses engage with their audiences, optimize their marketing efforts, and measure success. As AI evolves, its role in IMC may become increasingly sophisticated, enabling greater personalization, efficiency, and innovation. AI can further drive the automation of marketing processes, allowing for more accurate and efficient management of complex IMC campaigns. Additionally, AI's expanding role in content creation could facilitate the generation of high-quality, contextually relevant content across multiple formats, ensuring consistent messaging and voice across all channels.

AI will potentially lead to more sophistication of performance assessment, enabling marketers to better evaluate the impact of each touchpoint in the customer journey. Predictive capabilities might become integral to IMC strategies, providing valuable insights into future trends and consumer behavior. In the long term, the integration of AI with emerging technologies such as augmented reality (AR), virtual reality (VR), and the Internet of Things (IoT) may further expand IMC capabilities, offering immersive and interactive marketing experiences that are highly personalized and contextually relevant.

The future of AI in IMC holds vast potential for transformative change, enhancing both the effectiveness and efficiency of marketing efforts while redefining brand-consumer interactions. However, this evolution requires ongoing ethical reflection. As AI technology advances, so will the ethical challenges it presents. Continuous dialogue among marketers, researchers, policymakers, consumers, and other stakeholders is crucial to ensure that AI is used in a manner that upholds fairness, transparency, and respect for consumer rights.

References

Abrokwah-Larbi K, Awuku-Larbi Y (2024) The impact of artificial intelligence in marketing on the performance of business organizations: evidence from SMEs in an emerging economy. J Entrep Emerg Econ 16(4):1090–1117

Adeola O, Evans O, Ndubuisi Edeh J, Adisa I (2022) The future of marketing: artificial intelligence, virtual reality, and neuromarketing. In Adeola O, Hinson RE, Sakkthivel AM (eds) Marketing communications and brand development in emerging economies volume I: contemporary and future perspectives. Palgrave Macmillan

Ahmad A, Salleh SM (2019) Brand related capabilities and the process of integrated marketing communications (IMC): a resource based view (RBV). J Contemp Res Soc Sci 1(6):136–150

Anabila P (2020) Integrated marketing communications, brand equity, and business performance in micro-finance institutions: an emerging market perspective. J Mark Commun 26:229–242

Batra R, Keller KL (2016) Integrating marketing communications: new findings, new lessons, and new ideas. J Mark 80(6):122–145

Brobbey EE, Ankrah E, Kankam PK (2021) The role of artificial intelligence in integrated marketing communications: a case study of Jumia Online Ghana. Inkanyiso J HumIties Soc Sci 13(1):120–136

Buolamwini J (2018) When the Robot doesn't see dark skin. The New York Times. https://www.nytimes.com/2018/06/21/opinion/facial-analysis-technology-bias.html

Campbell C, Sands S, Ferraro C, Tsao HYJ, Mavrommatis A (2020) From data to action: how marketers can leverage AI. Bus Horiz 63(2):227–243

Chowdhury S, Thapak A, Choudhury S (2024) Optimising the "I-wants": a micro-moments consumer engagement. Int J Nov Res Mark Manag Econ 11(1):139–146

Chui M, Hazan E, Roberts R, Singla A, Smaje K, Sukharevsky A, Yee L, Zemmel R (2023) The economic potential of generative AI: the next productivity frontier. McKinsey & Company. https://www.mckinsey.com/~/media/mckinsey/business%20functions/mckinsey%20digital/our%20insights/the%20economic%20potential%20of%20generative%20ai%20the%20next%20productivity%20frontier/the-economic-potential-of-generative-ai-the-next-productivity-frontier.pdf

Davenport TH, Guha A, Grewal D (2021) How to design an AI marketing strategy: what the technology can do today—and what's next. Harvard Business Review. https://hbr.org/2021/07/how-to-design-an-ai-marketing-strategy

De Bruyn A, Viswanathan V, Beh YS, Brock JKU, Von Wangenheim F (2020) Artificial intelligence and marketing: pitfalls and opportunities. J Interact Mark 51(1):91–105

Deveau R, Griffin SJ, Reis S (2023) AI-powered marketing and sales reach new heights with generative AI. McKinsey & Company. https://digitalrosh.com/wp-content/uploads/2023/05/ai-powered-marketing-and-sales-reach-new-heights-with-generative-ai.pdf

Dora M, Kumar A, Mangla SK, Pant A, Kamal MM (2022) Critical success factors influencing artificial intelligence adoption in food supply chains. Int J Prod Res 60(14):4621–4640

Durmus HN (2024) Artificial intelligence in marketing communication: a comprehensive exploration of the integration and impact of AI. Tech Soc Sci J 55(1):64–81

Falahat M, Ramayah T, Soto-Acosta P, Lee YY (2020) SMEs internationalization: the role of product innovation, market intelligence, pricing and marketing communication capabilities as drivers of SMEs' international performance. Technol Forecast Soc Chang 152(2020):1–7

Gkikas DC, Theodoridis PK (2022) AI in consumer behavior. In: Virvou M, Tsihrintzis GA, Tsoukalas LH, Jain LC (eds) Advances in artificial intelligence-based technologies. Springer, Cham

Gurau C (2008) Integrated online marketing communication: implementation and management. J Commun Manag 12:169–184

Guo L, Sharma R, Yin L, Lu R, Rong K (2017) Automated competitor analysis using big data analytics: evidence from the fitness mobile app business. Bus Process Manag J 23(3):735–762

Haenlein M, Kaplan A (2019) A brief history of artificial intelligence: on the past, present, and future of artificial intelligence. Calif Manage Rev 61(4):5–14

Haleem A, Javaid M, Qadri MA, Singh RP, Suman R (2022) Artificial intelligence (AI) applications for marketing: a literature-based study. Int J Intell Netw 3(2022):119–132

Hardesty L (2019) The history of Amazon's recommendation algorithm. Amazon Science. https://www.amazon.science/the-history-of-amazons-recommendation-algorithm

Haris A, Samosir HE, Lubis SH (2023) Marketing communications as strategy expanding market share in era 4.0. Int J Soc Sci Bus 7(1):188–198

Heavin C, Power DJ (2018) Challenges for digital transformation—towards a conceptual decision support guide for managers. J Decis Syst 27(1):1–8

Huang MH, Rust RT (2021) A strategic framework for artificial intelligence in marketing. J Acad Mark Sci 49(2021):30–50

Hunt SD (2000) The competence-based, resource-advantage, and neoclassical theories of competition: toward a synthesis. In: Sanchez R, Heene A (eds) Competence-based strategic management: Theory and Research JAI Press, pp 177–208

Hyken S (2024) The personalized customer experience: consumers want you to know them. Forbes. https://www.forbes.com/sites/shephyken/2024/04/14/the-personalized-customer-experience-customers-want-you-to-know-them/

Jin J, Ji P, Gu R (2016) Identifying comparative customer requirements from product online reviews for competitor analysis. Eng Appl Artif Intell 49:61–73

Kar S, Kar AK, Gupta MP (2021) Modeling drivers and barriers of artificial intelligence adoption: insights from a strategic management perspective. Intell Syst Account Financ Manag 28(4):217–238

Katragadda V (2022) Dynamic customer segmentation: using machine learning to identify and address diverse customer needs in real-time. IRE J 5(10):278–279

Keller KL (2001) Mastering the marketing communications mix: micro and macro perspectives on integrated marketing communication programs. J Mark Manag 17(7–8):819–847
Keller KL (2009) Building strong brands in a modern marketing communications environment. J Mark Commun 15(2–3):139–155
Khogali HO, Mekid S (2023) The blended future of automation and AI: examining some long-term societal and ethical impact features. Technol Soc 73(2023):1–12
Kitchen PJ, Brignell J, Li T, Jones GS (2004) The emergence of IMC: a theoretical perspective. J Advert Res 44(1):19–30
Kitchen PJ, Proctor T (2015) Marketing communications in a post-modern world. J Bus Strateg 36(5):34–42
Kliatchko J (2005) Towards a new definition of integrated marketing communications (IMC). Int J Advert 24(1):7–34
Krizanova A, Lăzăroiu G, Gajanova L, Kliestikova J, Nadanyiova M, Moravcikova D (2019) The effectiveness of marketing communication and importance of its evaluation in an online environment. Sustainability 11(24):1–19
Kumar V, Rajan B, Venkatesan R, Lecinski J (2019) Understanding the role of artificial intelligence in personalized engagement marketing. Calif Manage Rev 61(4):135–155
Lee Y (2021) Extraction of competitive factors in a competitor analysis using an explainable neural network. Neural Process Lett 53(3):1979–1994
Linardatos P, Papastefanopoulos V, Kotsiantis S (2020) Explainable AI: a review of machine learning interpretability methods. Entropy 23(1):18
Lindecrantz E, Pian Gi MT, Zerbi S (2020) Personalizing the customer experience: driving differentiation in retail. McKinsey & Company. https://www.mckinsey.com/industries/retail/our-insights/personalizing-the-customer-experience-driving-differentiation-in-retail
Luxton S, Reid M, Mavondo F (2015) Integrated marketing communication capability and brand performance. J Advert 44(1):37–46
Madhavaram S, Badrinarayanan V, McDonald RE (2005) Integrated marketing communication (IMC) and brand identity as critical components of brand equity strategy: a conceptual framework and research propositions. J Advert 34(4):69–80
Malthouse E, Copulsky J (2023) Artificial intelligence ecosystems for marketing communications. Int J Advert 42(1):128–140
Manis KT, Madhavaram S (2023) AI-enabled marketing capabilities and the hierarchy of capabilities: conceptualization, proposition development, and research avenues. J Bus Res 157:113485
Mansour H, Aminudin E, Mansour T, Abidin N, Lou E (2022) Resource-based view in construction project management research: a meta-analysis. IOP Conf Ser Earth Environ Sci 1067(1):012057
Marr B (2021) Starbucks: using big data, analytics, and artificial intelligence to boost performance. Forbes. https://www.forbes.com/sites/bernardmarr/2018/05/28/starbucks-using-big-data-analytics-and-artificial-intelligence-to-boost-performance/
Mikalef P, Islam N, Parida V, Singh H, Altwaijry N (2023) Artificial intelligence (AI) competencies for organizational performance: a B2B marketing capabilities perspective. J Bus Res 164:113998
Mishra AN, Pani AK (2021) Business value appropriation roadmap for artificial intelligence. VINE J Inf Knowl Manag Syst 51(3):353–368
Mokhtar SSM, Salimon MG (2022) SMEs' adoption of artificial intelligence-chatbots for marketing communication: a conceptual framework for an emerging economy. In: Adeola O, Hinson RE, Sakkthivel AM (eds) Marketing communications and brand development in emerging markets volume II. Springer, Cham
Morton F, Treviño T, González-Treviño E (2024) Taking customer-centricity to new heights: exploring the intersection of AI, hyper-personalization, and customer-centricity in organizations. In: Machado C, Davim JP (eds) Smart engineering management. Springer, Cham
Morton F, Vázquez-Maguirre M (2023) Consumer's vulnerabilities and potential dignity risks in the context of digital transformation processes. In: Machado C, Davim JP (eds) Management for digital transformation. Springer, Cham

Nisar TM, Yeung M (2018) Attribution modeling in digital advertising: an empirical investigation of the impact of digital sales channels. J Advert Res 58(4):399–413

Ortakci Y, Seker H (2024) Optimising customer retention: An AI-driven personalised pricing approach. Comput Ind Eng 188(2024):1–12

Pattanayak S, Pati PB, Singh T (2022) Performance analysis of machine learning algorithms on multi-touch attribution model. In: 2022 3rd international conference for emerging technology (INCET). IEEE, pp 1–7

Pedowitz J (2024) How marketing teams can move beyond traditional attribution models. Forbes. https://www.forbes.com/councils/forbesbusinesscouncil/2024/05/29/how-marketing-teams-can-move-beyond-traditional-attribution-models/

Press G (2016) Artificial intelligence defined as a new research discipline: this week in tech history. Forbes. https://www.forbes.com/sites/gilpress/2016/08/28/artificial-intelligence-defined-as-a-new-research-discipline-this-week-in-tech-history/

Porcu L, del Barrio-García S, Kitchen PJ (2012) How integrated marketing communications (IMC) works? A theoretical review and an analysis of its main drivers and effects. Commun Soc 25(1):313–348

Proliferation of AI across industries: The driving force behind next-gen industrial and economic revolution (2024) Silicon Valley Innovation Center. https://siliconvalley.center/blog/proliferation-of-ai-across-industries

PWc (2017) Sizing the prize what's the real value of AI for your business and how can you capitalise? PWc. https://www.pwc.com/gx/en/issues/analytics/assets/pwc-ai-analysis-sizing-the-prize-report.pdf

Qin X, Jiang Z (2019) The impact of AI on the advertising process: the Chinese experience. J Advert 48(4):338–346

Quach S, Thaichon P, Martin KD, Weaven S, Palmatier RW (2022) Digital technologies: tensions in privacy and data. J Acad Mark Sci 50(6):1299–1323

Rachmawati MA, Afifi S (2022) The integrated marketing communication in digital environment: a case study of local radio in Yogyakarta. Indones J Commun Stud 14(2):105–119

Ratnatunga J, Ewing MT (2005) The brand capability value of integrated marketing communication (IMC). J Advert 34(4):25–40

Toosi A, Bottino AG, Saboury B, Siegel E, Rahmim A (2021) A brief history of AI: how to prevent another winter (a critical review). PET Clinics 16(4):449–469

Yau KLA, Saad NM, Chong YW (2021) Artificial intelligence marketing (AIM) for enhancing customer relationships. Appl Sci 11(18):8562

Schrage M, Kiron D, Candelon F, Khodabandeh S, Chu M (2023) Improve key performance with AI. MIT Sloan Management Review. https://sloanreview.mit.edu/article/improve-key-performance-indicators-with-ai/

Soleimani F (2024) Dynamic competitor analysis and pricing strategy development using machine learning models. Int J Ind Eng Constr Manag (IJIECM) 2(1):1–10

Sun Y, Liu H, Gao Y (2023) Research on customer lifetime value based on machine learning algorithms and customer relationship management analysis model. Heliyon 9(2):13384

Wankhade M, Rao ACS, Kulkarni C (2022) A survey on sentiment analysis methods, applications, and challenges. Artif Intell Rev 55(7):5731–5780

Wang W, Siau K (2019) Artificial intelligence, machine learning, automation, robotics, future of work and future of humanity: a review and research agenda. J Database Manag 30(1):61–79

Wang Y, Pan Y, Yan M, Su Z, Luan TH (2023) A survey on ChatGPT: AI-generated contents, challenges, and solutions. IEEE Open J Comput Soc 4:280–302

Yang Z, Kankanhalli A, Ng BY, Lim JTY (2013) Analyzing the enabling factors for the organizational decision to adopt healthcare information systems. Decis Support Syst 55(3):764–776

Unlocking Potential: How the Digital Age Is Shaping Tomorrow's Human Resource Management

Catarina da Silva Nogueira and Carolina Feliciana Machado

Abstract Technologies continue to advance at a rapid pace, and so keeping up with digital developments is a necessity. All these advancements have influenced the labor market, causing many processes to change, and be automated. With this new reality of the digital age, many human resource management (HRM) practices have changed, ranging from how we recruit and select, to training and development and even working methods. As such, one of the biggest challenges for human resources professionals will be to develop modern practices that keep pace with these new advancements. This research seeks to understand the challenges of Human Resource Management (HRM) and the extent to which technologies have or have not impacted on management. Therefore, this chapter aims to analyze some human resource management practices in their relationship with technology, as well as how best to implement them. The interpretivist paradigm characterizes the qualitative methodology used to carry out the study. The data was collected through semi-structured interviews, with subsequent use of content analysis. A total of 25 individuals were interviewed from the human resources departments of 22 organizations in the north of Portugal. After analyzing the interviewees' testimonies, the results suggest that technologies have brought several changes and challenges to Human Resources Management (HRM), confirming that these have been felt in recruitment and selection, training and development, and working methods. It can, therefore, be concluded that there is indeed a future trend for the training and development processes to be based on the use of technology. As for recruitment and selection processes, there is still a need to combine traditional and online methods.

Keywords Human resource management · Digital age · Recruitment and selection · Training and development · Working methods

C. da Silva Nogueira · C. F. Machado (✉)
School of Economics, Management and Political Science, University of Minho, Braga, Portugal
e-mail: carolina@eeg.uminho.pt

C. F. Machado
Interdisciplinary Centre of Social Sciences (CICS.NOVA.UMinho), University of Minho, Braga, Portugal

C. Machado and J. P. Davim (eds.), *Challenges and Opportunities in the Artificial Intelligence Era*, https://doi.org/10.1007/978-3-031-85272-5_11

1 Introduction

Currently, no company can remain indifferent to the use of new technologies and, therefore, debates on how to improve digital transformation have increased. However, this is not an easy task, as one of the biggest problems is how to incorporate them and how to use them (Gray and Rumpe 2017; Hess et al. 2016).

The beginning of the digital era led to a strong development in Information and Communication Technologies (ICT), which led to various changes in the area of human resources, in particular, in terms of information and communication used daily in different business activities (Berber et al. 2018).

Given this, companies assume a leading role in the digitalization of processes, especially concerning the evolution of human resources management (HRM) practices, thus contributing to the streamlining of procedures, development of skills and the introduction of new work formats (Horváth 2019; Kagermann 2015).

Currently, the world is within reach of a call or a click, so keeping up with digital developments is necessary. Technologies have enabled many processes to be automated, from recruitment to training or even work. With this new reality, it is crucial to understand the digital era and the challenges caused in HRM.

Therefore, the present study seeks to understand the challenges of human resource management and to what extent technologies have or do not have an implication in its management. Thus, more specifically, we intend to analyze some human resources management practices in their relationship with technologies, as well as the best way to implement them in the digital era.

From the above, there are four specific objectives to be achieved, more specifically to understand the changes and challenges caused by technologies in human resource management practices, analyze the effects of digitalization on different work models, allow for a greater understanding of some practices of human resource management in its relationship with technologies and, finally, understand how to manage new human resource management practices in the digital era.

In order to facilitate the understanding and framing of this study, it was carried out in phases, following a three-section structure.

The first section focuses on the literature review, which focuses on the evolution of HRM and the challenges posed by technological changes, giving special emphasis to recruitment and selection, work methods, and, finally, training and development. Finally, it was also addressed whether or not the digital transformation in the organization affected its performance.

Next, the methodology to be used in the research is presented in the second section. Thus, the chosen data collection technique, characterized by the qualitative interpretative study paradigm, was the semi-structured interview with 25 individuals from 22 organizations belonging to the respective human resource departments. In this same chapter, the characterization of the interviewees and the interview analysis model are also presented. The last section focuses on analyzing and discussing the content collected during the interviews, presenting the results, and final reflections.

2 Literature Review

2.1 From the Conventional Past to the Electronic Future of Human Resources Management

Human resource management is an essential activity for managing individuals and work, in order to achieve an organizational objective (Boxall et al. 2008).

Between the 60s and 70s the first human resources consultants emerged, whose functions included complex and time-consuming tasks, as all records were done manually on paper (Stone and Dulebohn 2013). In the late 1970s, some of these administrative tasks, such as payroll recording, began to be performed automatically. This practice was only possible with the introduction of the first computer systems (Stone and Dulebohn 2013).

In 1980, computer systems evolved, meaning that human resources functions were now able to carry out "(…) applicant tracking, performance appraisal, and training and development (…)" carried out through automated management systems. These new systems were called Human Resources Information Systems (HRIS) (Stone and Dulebohn 2013, p. 2).

The human resources information system (HRIS) encompasses a computer system that makes it simpler to save, retrieve, catalog and analyze the organization's data. The main objective of HRIS is to make decision-making easier, through the efficient provision of information (Armstrong and Baron 2002; Sadri and Chatterjee 2003).

One of the most significant changes for human resources professionals occurred in the late 1980s, with the introduction of the microcomputer and the client-server model, which allowed the existence of human resources databases, which can be accessed by professionals or, by others, in the organization at their workplace (Stone and Dulebohn 2013).

In the 90s, the emergence of the World Wide Web (Web) allowed automated human resources management systems to begin their transition to the internet. In 2000, this new system made it possible to concentrate all the organization's and human resources information, making it accessible via the web, at any time or place, both for workers and potential job candidates. Over the last few years, the systems have come to be called electronic human resources management (e-HRM) (Stone and Dulebohn 2013), a reality that has been accentuated with the increasingly accentuated use of artificial intelligence.

Electronic human resources management (e-HRM) consists of the use of human resources strategies, policies and practices, with the partial or total assistance of technologies (Ruël et al. 2004).

e-HRM has numerous advantages, namely, improving productivity, reducing costs, effectively managing working time, reducing the administrative burden on the human resources department, making information faster and with better quality, in order to support the business planning and produce human resource metrics (Al Shobaki et al. 2017). More and more organizations are adopting e-HRM and with this in mind, the literature already considers it to be a common practice (Strohmeier 2007; Wahyudi and Park 2014).

2.2 Changes and Challenges in Human Resources Management in the Digital Age

All organizations need "(…) agility, speed, flexibility, and the ability to pivot rapidly (…)", in order to keep up with a world of constant change (Johansson et al. 2018, p. 23).

Schwartz, in 2001, already emphasized that digital would be the future, which is why organizations should start developing their digital transformation strategy. In this context, it is anticipated that organizations that are not capable of adapting to digital transformation will suffer from "Digital Darwinism" (Schwartz 2001, p. 7), that is, if they resist and do not follow market trends towards digital, these will be forgotten and surpassed by the competition, even ending up culminating in their disappearance. In contrast, the most capable companies that embrace transformation will prosper, becoming able to differentiate themselves in a competitive market.

Digital transformation can be grouped into three categories: firstly, substitution, in which technologies are used as a substitute for a task or procedure, then as a complement, in the sense that technologies improve the existing product and process and, secondly, lastly, transformation in which technologies are applied to reorient the product and process (Mcafee et al. 2014).

New technologies have caused drastic changes, both in the market and in work processes (Kizilhan and Bal Kizilhan 2016; Kuusisto 2015). Given this, the study by Eurofound et al. (2015) defined four implications of digitalization at work, these being, firstly, changes in functions that are now being adapted to new technologies, therefore emerging new practices. Then, transformations in the work environment, in which there are new physical, psychological and environmental challenges. Third, changes in work contexts, in which contractual benefits are valued and, finally, new approaches to dealing with conflicts in the organization.

At work, digital transformation is a procedure that promises to change the future in several ways, as it restructures necessary functions and skills (Erfurth 2019). Now, physical strength in the past represented one of the essential characteristics in a worker. However, over the years, strength is less and less important. Currently, more importance has been given to the fact that workers have basic knowledge of technology, as well as a good sense of creativity (Gekara and Thanh Nguyen 2018; Prainsack and Buyx 2018).

Literature also proves that human beings have a great capacity for adaptability. As a result, they have always been able to minimize and mitigate the changes caused by technologies over the centuries. Therefore, it is expected that workers in the digital era will be increasingly qualified and have good skills to acquire skills, as now their work will not only be with humans, but also collaborative with a machine

(Manyika et al. 2017). The authors even state that "History shows that the adoption of technological innovation can act as a powerful stimulus on the economy and jobs (…)" (Manyika et al. 2017, p. 37).

It is known that the changes caused by technology are felt not only at work and in the organization but also by all individuals who make up the organization, whether workers or managers. Therefore, everyone could be affected by this change (Balakrishnan and Das 2020; Bresciani et al. 2021; Gurbaxani and Dunkle 2019).

Recognizing the manager as one of the main drivers of change, the responsibility for the successful implementation of a digital transformation falls upon him/her, taking into account that success depends on the speed and flexibility with which organizations rethink their digital transformation strategies and how they absorb technological changes (Bresciani et al. 2021; Rachinger et al. 2019; v. Alberti-Alhtaybat et al. 2019; Vaska et al. 2021; Verhoef et al. 2021).

As a manager, he/she must demonstrate firm leadership, knowledge, and intelligence for the position he/she occupies. Based on research developed by Wrede et al. (2020) on manager involvement in the digital era, they concluded that managers are responsible for three essential factors, namely, "(…) understanding digitalization, setting the formal context for digitalization, and leading change (…)" (p. 1549).

Previously, organizational changes resulting from technological development were analyzed, and it was proven that these existed in terms of the evolution of work, organization, and the role of the manager. However, changes in terms of human resources management must still be included (Fenech 2022).

As mentioned by Hecklau et al. (2016), "An organization's performance and competitiveness greatly depend on how its employees are managed. (…)" (p. 2), in other words, a good HRM allows to obtain "(…) extraordinary results from ordinary people (…)" (Nasir 2017, p. 217).

Digitization has brought simplicity and speed to HRM processes, which has made it easier to monitor and create performance reports, recruitment has become faster, with fewer phases and selection has seen many of its steps automated (Abolhassan 2017; Betchoo 2016; DiRomualdo et al. 2018; Hassan and Javed 2021; Palas 2019).

Since digitalization brings a set of changes, it also brings challenges for HRM, some of which are: how to recruit and select talent in a competitive environment; how to work in an environment with work diversity; how to deal with a multigenerational workforce; how to train and develop the existing workforce; how to motivate and retain talent; how to approach new working methods and, finally, how to manage co-work between humans and robots (Barišić et al. 2021; Bloom et al. 2015; Das and Divakaran 2020; Duvvuri 2021; Nasir 2017; Rajapaksha 2013).

According to Nasir (2017), the existence of challenges in human resources management is due to: the increase in globalization, the emergence of new forms of production, significant changes in the structure of the organization and, finally, because there are changes in the consumer behavior, as well as that of workers.

Given the above, it is clear that HRM faces several challenges, of which particular focus is placed on just three, namely: recruitment and selection, training and development and new working methods.

2.2.1 Digital Transformation in Human Resources Processes: Recruitment, Selection, Training and Development

The organization must recognize people as its best asset. Therefore, one of the biggest challenges is recruiting and selecting motivated, dedicated and capable human resources (Adeola and Adebiyi 2017; Ungerman et al. 2018).

It is imperative that organizations adapt their recruitment and selection techniques in order to attract and subsequently retain the best candidates. However, for this to happen it is necessary that they become visible and attractive to the candidate (Tulgan 2009).

According to Karim et al. (2021), recruitment involves a series of steps designed to identify and attract potentially qualified and talented candidates, with the aim of filling a role in the organization. As for selection, this is the procedure for choosing the candidate who has the necessary skills to fill that same role.

In traditional recruitment, there is low dependence on technology, as this usually occurs, above all, through advertisements in newspapers, radio, and television, delivery of leaflets, among others (Chuks Okolie and Irabor 2017; Cober et al. 2004).

According to Kapse et al. (2012), the traditional recruitment and selection process is divided into seven stages: (1) identification of needs; (2) description of the offer and characteristics sought; (3) publication of the job offer; (4) sending CVs by candidates; (5) selection of some candidates; (6) conducting face-to-face interviews and, finally, (7) analyzing the results collected from the interviews, at which point candidates are informed about who will fill the vacancy.

With the previous description of the traditional recruitment process, it appears that it requires a high effort, in addition to being time-consuming, and can result in high costs for the organization (Kapse et al. 2012).

The literature reports that, currently, the workforce has high expectations related to work. Therefore, to retain and attract them, traditional methods are no longer enough. New innovative methods must be used that take advantage of the advancement of new technologies, especially the internet. These methods are recognized as E-recruitment and E-selection (Chuks Okolie and Irabor 2017; Cober et al. 2004; Slavić et al. 2017).

E-recruitment consists of "(…) using web-based resources for tasks involved with searching, attracting, assessing, interviewing and hiring new employees" (Chuks Okolie and Irabor 2017, p. 117). The main objective of E-recruitment is to make the recruitment process more productive, faster, and less expensive (Singh Hada and Gairola 2015).

According to Stone et al. (2013), E-seleção is defined as the "(…) use of various forms of technology (e.g., web-based job applications, web-based tests, videoconference interviews) (…)" (p. 51), being used to collect data, manage application volume, evaluate skills and the success of the selection process.

The entire E-recruitment and E-selection process contains automation and can be summarized in the following steps: placing an online advertisement with the job offer, candidates submitting their CVs online, CVs analyzed electronically, a system intelligently separates and summarizes resumes, all candidates considered for the job are contacted electronically, online interviews are conducted, working conditions are negotiated, and finally, the job offer is made and the candidate decides whether to accept (Koleva 2023).

E-recruitment has established itself as one of the most effective means of recruiting, as it is just a click away from advertising job vacancies, through the organization's website, social networks, or even on recruitment websites (Galanaki 2002).

According to research by Okoronkwo (2021), most job seekers prefer online recruitment, considering it is simpler and because it allows candidates to apply for multiple jobs, thus reducing search time.

From an organizational perspective, according to Chuks Okolie and Irabor (2017), online recruitment is more than a technology, as it is a system capable of recruiting and captivating the right candidate, where the processes used are consistent and reliable enough to meet organizational needs.

In the Digital Era, due to the high competitive environment, organizations are dependent on effective recruitment and selection. But, in addition, it is also essential to invest in the continuous qualification of the existing workforce. For this to occur, it is necessary to create a good system of training and development of human resources, since high quality is dependent on continued training (Atak and Erturgut 2010).

The concepts of training and development are not always clear, as they encompass several learning methods. According to Niazi (2011, p. 43), training and development "(…) refers to the process to obtain or transfer KSA (knowledge, skills and abilities) needed to carry out a specific activity or task (…)".

Before implementing a training program, it is important to identify and assess needs, especially because this diagnosis allows the training process to be in line with the organization's objectives and workers' needs. Thus, with a good assessment of training needs it is possible to identify the best and most appropriate training, also preventing the organization from spending unnecessary monetary resources on training that, in the end, may not be of interest to it (Mozael 2015; Olaniyan and Ojo 2008).

In training and development, there are several methods and techniques that can be used, some of them being on-the-job training, mentoring, and classroom training, among others (Chatzimouratidis et al. 2012).

As a result of globalization and the demands of the job market, training, and professional development must be constant, which is the reason why the organization has sought new methods. These are more flexible methods, which allow to manage the need for training and work (Kapo et al. 2021; Schwab 2019). With the internet, it has become possible to achieve these goals. Organizations now have the possibility of carrying out training not only through traditional methods, that is, in the classroom, but now using online, at a distance, resulting in e-learning (Dalvi-Esfahani et al. 2020; Kapo et al. 2021).

For Waryanto (2014), e-learning refers to "(…) delivery of learning content or learning experience electronically based on multimedia computer (…)" (Waryanto 2014, cited by Widodo et al. 2020, p. 1).

In effect, e-learning allows training to reach the entire organization homogeneously, at a lower cost and, therefore, becomes extremely profitable (Lee et al. 2011).

Regarding the effectiveness of using e-learning, the literature presents contradictory opinions. Benbunan-Fich and Hiltz (2003) and Schweizer (2004) categorically state that e-learning should not be used as the only training method, as it should be complemented with a face-to-face method, that is, with classroom training, so that interpersonal interaction and communication between participants can be increased.

However, according to the study by Bell and Federman (2013), "(…) e-learning is at least as effective as, and in some cases more effective than, classroom instruction (…)" (p. 174). Beinicke and Bipp (2018) share the same opinion. In their comparative study of the face-to-face method and e-learning, Beinicke and Bipp (2018) concluded that each of them has its advantages and disadvantages, but they end up balancing each other, with no significant difference. For these authors, the context of training or the means of transmission does not mean high success. The focus should be determined by the training content, which reveals its degree of success/importance.

2.2.2 The Emergence of New Working Methods

The traditional work environment has changed and, consequently, other work characteristics are valued, particularly work flexibility (Allen et al. 2024). In this sense and to obtain work flexibility, the organization can use one of the distance work methods, which are called remote or hybrid work (Haque 2023).

For Hunton and Norman (2010), remote work, also known as teleworking, consists of a form of work according to which workers "periodically, regularly, or exclusively perform work for their employers from home or another remote location that is equipped with the appropriate computer-based technology to transfer work to the central organization (…)" (Hunton and Norman 2010, cited by Caillier 2012, p. 462).

Hybrid work, according to Iqbal et al. (2021), covers the combination of two work systems, in-person on the organization's premises and remote with the help of the internet. That said, the worker will spend part of their time in person at the organization and the other part remotely, from the website they choose (Bhatia et al. 2021).

In the literature, when analyzing the advantages of hybrid and remote work, it appears that in both methods, there is an increase in worker satisfaction due to the benefits it offers, in particular, the flexibility in carrying out tasks. It is also reported, increased productivity and fewer distractions. The only difference found between the advantages of the two methods would be that hybrid work guarantees better collaboration and working relationships since there is a moment of face-to-face and physical contact, thus allowing better cohesion between the work team (Bloom et al. 2022; Cooper and Kurland 2002; Gajendran and Harrison 2007; Iqbal et al. 2021).

Although hybrid and remote working methods have several advantages, they also have disadvantages, such as technological dependence to carry out their tasks, the lack of routine, and, finally, the imbalance between professional and family life.

This is because it is common for workers to when working from home, they do not control the time they work, which can sometimes mean that they work more than expected hours (Cooper and Kurland 2002; Gajendran and Harrison 2007; Kiwert and Walecka 2022).

According to Greer and Payne (2014) and Martin and MacDonnell (2012), teleworking will certainly only be successful when organizational goals and results are achieved, as well as when the well-being and satisfaction of workers are guaranteed.

As mentioned by Martin and MacDonnell (2012), organizational goals and results are defined by the increase in productivity, the ability to retain workers, and, finally, due to the organization's performance, that is, whether the work was carried out well and without errors, maintaining innovative teamwork.

Regarding the level of well-being and satisfaction of workers, this manifests itself, above all, when the separation between work and family is guaranteed, in which the worker is able to carry out his functions in the organization and despite the flexible environment, also coordinate his personal life (Greer and Payne 2014).

Regarding hybrid work, as there are workers in person in the organization and others remotely, it means that for it to be successful, some elements must be considered, such as offering support so that workers who, even if they are not present in the offices, feel that they belong to the organization, work expectations must also be defined so that each member of the team knows what they have to do and what results are expected from their work and, finally, it is necessary to encourage collaboration and mutual respect without exclusions (Knight 2020).

2.2.3 Understand the Relationship Between Digital Transformation and the Organization's Performance

One of the essential objectives for an organization is to seek solutions that optimize business performance (Nwankpa and Roumani 2016). This is also known as performance and operational efficiency, that is, it refers to the organization's ability to achieve its objectives and expectations, which can be indicated by the organization's "(…) growth, profitability, and market value (…)" (Bag et al. 2020; Cao and Zhang 2011; Cho and Pucik 2005, p. 556).

According to Oduro et al. (2023), the literature shows contradictory opinions about the influence of digital transformation on business performance.

Chae et al. (2018) considered that investing in digital transformation is not immediately profitable, as it has a high implementation cost and it is necessary to fill knowledge gaps before using digital tools. In turn, Benassi et al. (2022) agree and add that they recognize that there are advantages and positive productivity associated with digital transformation, but they also consider that the company's level of profitability has not been affected, justified by the fact that an investment in technologies takes several years to be profitable. Therefore, for Benassi et al. (2022) the two factors balance each other, resulting in the requirements to consider that performance has improved not being met.

According to Oduro et al. (2023), digital transformation substantially affects the organization's performance favorably, despite how Benassi et al. (2022) mentioned "(…) technological developments may be slow to be cashed in (…)" (p. 1). Therefore, even if it takes time to be profitable, by incorporating Information and Communication Technologies (ICT) it is possible to increase the organization's competitiveness and performance (Dubey et al. 2020; Erkmen et al. 2020; Liu et al. 2023; Wamba et al. 2020).

For Oduro et al. (2023) and Teng et al. (2022), digital transformation is identified as one of the main factors that positively affect the organization's financial performance, which differs from the opinion of other authors, particularly Benassi et al. (2022) and Chae et al. (2018), who claim that digital transformation does not have a relevant impact on the organization's performance, and this can have a negative effect, notably financially.

Oduro et al. (2023) contradict what was argued by the authors above, justifying that financial performance results are negative because resources are produced through the use of technologies. In this sense, if only the cost of its implementation is considered, these will obviously be greater than the value gained from the resources, which will, from the outset, translate into negative performance. However, according to these authors, this return must be looked at from a long-term perspective. This is why they conclude that the effects should not be analyzed at the time of implementing the digital transformation but rather over a longer period of time, so that, in this way, the effects, which are believed to be positive, are seen.

In short, after analyzing the contributions made by different authors at different times, it was possible to conclude that the adoption of the appropriate digital transformation strategy can lead not only to an increase in performance but also to greater productivity and competitiveness (Brynjolfsson and Hitt 2000; Chan et al. 2019; Dibrell et al. 2008; Nwankpa and Roumani 2016; Oduro et al. 2023; Teng et al. 2022).

3 Methodology

3.1 Research Paradigm and Strategy

Regarding the philosophical paradigm used in the research, the present study was based on the interpretive paradigm, with the central objective of understanding some human resources management practices in their relationship with technologies. Therefore, it was considered that the most appropriate research strategy would be grounded theory.

Grounded theory explores social phenomena, investigating the experiences and adversities of individuals in order to analyze how they resolve these issues. One of the characteristics of this strategy is the use of comparison to search for variations, similarities, and differences in data (Cutcliffe 2000; Hallberg 2006).

Another important aspect to be considered is that in grounded theory, there is no restriction on participants in data collection, leaving it up to the researcher to define the sampling limit required (Cutcliffe 2000). Regarding the results, they avoided assumptions and impartialities, reflecting only the experiences of individuals (Engward 2013; Simmons 2006).

3.2 *Data Collection Method and Sample Definition*

With regard to methodology, the study used a qualitative methodology, constituted simply, focused on individuals, facts, and particular situations (Gerring 2017).

In qualitative research, several techniques can be used to collect data, among which the interview stands out, which is the method used in this research.

Berg (2007) understands that the interview allows the interviewee to "(…) speak in their own voice and express their own thoughts and feelings (…)" (p. 96). Alshenqeeti (2014) agrees and adds that collecting data through interviews is one of the best qualitative methods to be used, as it allows contact between interviewee and interviewer, enabling more complete and genuine answers.

In the present study, semi-structured interviews were used, in which open questions were covered, with simple and momentary answers (Baumbusch 2010). To this end, an interview guide was carried out. In an organized and categorized way, this interview script contains, through indicators, all the information. It started with questions that sought to characterize the interviewee and the organization he/she represents. Then, the roadmap was directed to the following indicators: implications of using technologies in human resources management, work methods, training and development, recruitment, and selection.

However, although the structure of the questions was defined, it is important to highlight that this does not mean that all topics were covered, as the interview flowed, without a specific order, giving the possibility of asking questions in addition to the identified.

To carry out the interviews, companies were contacted, to interview individuals who are part of the human resources department, whether they are directors, managers, technicians, or who perform other functions in the department and whose tasks, carried out by them, may include management of people, recruitment and selection, as well as training and development and technological development. The target population focused on companies located in the North of Portugal, particularly their human resources departments.

The search for the target population occurred in two ways. Through a browser search, to identify companies located in the North of Portugal and, on the other hand, through direct contacts, based on the researcher's personal knowledge of the existence of organizations. In addition to geographic convenience (resulting from the interest in which the organization would have to have at least one of its facilities in the North of Portugal), other criteria were also established for the selection of companies to be studied, namely, ease of contact through e-mail and the availability demonstrated by them. Following this procedure, a total of 50 organizations were contacted. The sampling method underlying the study was non-random convenience sampling, which consists of selecting a sample, following convenience criteria, such as suitability, ease of contact, and accessibility of the organization (Acharya et al. 2013; Etikan 2016; Panacek and Thompson 2007).

3.3 Sample Characterization

In January 2024, the first contacts began, carried out via email, in order to secure potential interviews with those responsible for the organizations.

A total of 50 organizations were contacted, of which 22 accepted, 6 did not accept, with one appointment still not being finalized. Overall, of the contacts made, no responses were obtained from 21 organizations. It was during the period from January to February that the six negative responses were obtained. Regarding the missed appointment, the interview was accepted by the organization, but after repeated attempts to schedule, there was no response.

The interviews began on January 25th and ended on March 7th, 2024, and the only preferred method for all interviewees to carry out them was video conferencing, through Microsoft Teams.

Before the date set for scheduling the interview, each participant received an email with a document, for them to sign authorization for the interview. This document was the Free and Informed Consent Form.

The Free and Informed Consent Form states that the interviewee accepted the interview of his/her own free will. Further declaring that they were aware of the respect for the anonymity/confidentiality of the interviewee and the organization; granting authorization to process the collected data and record/transcribe the interview. In cases where there was no response to the email with the respective signature of the document, the term was read at the beginning of the interview and consent to the audio recording was given.

One of the first steps prior to data analysis is to characterize the participants and their organizations. In Table 1, the organizations interviewed were characterized in terms of their sector of activity and their size.

As identified in Table 1, 22 companies were studied. To ensure the anonymity and confidentiality of the interviewees and the organization they represent, in Table 1, they were given the abbreviation "EE" for the interviewee's company and a number. In other words, each company was identified as "EE1"; "EE2" and so on continuously.

Regarding the characterization of companies in terms of the industrial sector, it should be noted that no specific selection criteria were followed and, therefore, the selection is varied. The division principles were used, which appear in the book Global Industry Classification Standard (GICSR) Methodology, which classifies industrial sectors in eleven different ways (MSCI Inc. 2023).

According to a recommendation from the Commission of the European Communities (2003), companies can be defined according to their size as Large, Medium,

Table 1 Characterization of organizations (*own elaboration*)

Organization	Activity sector	Dimension
EE1	Material and industrial	Big (1.000–5.000 workers)
EE2	Information technology	Medium (51–200 workers)
EE3	Basic consumer goods	Medium (51–200 workers)
EE4	Industrial	Medium (51–200 workers)
EE5	Discretionary consumer goods	Medium (51–200 workers)
EE6	Information technology	Big (+ than 10.001 workers)
EE7	Discretionary consumer goods	Big (+ than 10.001 workers)
EE8	Industrial and financial	Big (1.000–5.000 workers)
EE9	Discretionary consumer goods	Big (1.000–5.000 workers)
EE10	Material and industrial	Big (5.000–10.000 workers)
EE11	Information technology	Big (+ than 10.001 workers)
EE12	Health care	Big (501–1.000 workers)
EE13	Information technology	Big (501–1.000 workers)
EE14	Information technology	Big (1.000–5.000 workers)
EE15	Material and industrial	Medium (5–200 workers)
EE16	Industrial	Small (11–50 workers)
EE17	Material	Big (1.000–5.000 workers)
EE18	Energy and industrial	Big (+ than 10.001 workers)
EE19	Basic consumer goods	Big (201–500 workers)
EE20	Basic consumer goods	Big (1.000–5.000 workers)
EE21	Industrial and information technology	Medium (51–200 workers)
EE22	Industrial	Big (5.000–10.000 workers)

Small, and Micro-enterprise, with the classification variables being the number of workers and/or turnover. In particular, in this case, only the number of workers taken from each company's official LinkedIn profile was considered. It is therefore concluded that large (15), medium (6), and small (1) companies were interviewed.

Next, there is Table 2, which briefly lists a set of data relating to the interviewees, such as the number of interviewees; gender; age; position held; working method; time in the organization and time in the role.

As identified in Table 2, the sample consists of 25 interviewees; this is because although 22 companies were studied, on three occasions, not one, but two managers were interviewed, thus resulting in a significantly larger sample.

In Table 2, each participant was assigned the letter "E" for interviewee and a number. In other words, the interviewees were marked as "E1";" E2" and so on. In turn, when there was more than one individual participating, they were numbered by a sequence, this being: "E1.1"; "E1. 2", for example.

Respondents were identified according to their gender and age. Regarding gender, we can see that there were more female individuals (21) than male individuals (4).

Table 2 Characteristics of Interviewees (*own elaboration*)

Interviewee		Gender	Age	Working method	Position held	Time in the organization	Time in role
E1		Male	38	In person	Human resources director	9 years 10 months	4 years 8 months
E2		Female	49	Hybrid	Human resources director	5 years 10 months	1 year 1 month
E3		Male	33	In person	CEO and commercial director	16 years	16 years
E4		Female	27	Hybrid	Career specialist and IT recruiter	2 years 8 months	2 years 4 months
E5		Male	45	In person	Corporate manager and corporate social responsibility manager	10 years 8 months	10 years 8 months
E6		Female	36	Hybrid	Senior human resources business partner	4 years 4 months	4 years 4 months
E7		Female	29	Hybrid	HR operations specialist	1 year 7 months	7 months
E8		Female	45	Hybrid	People and culture director	1 year 11 months	1 year 11 months
E9		Male	30	In person	Chief technology officer	7 years 5 months	3 years 2 months
E10		Female	43	Hybrid	Corporate director of human resources	16 years 2 months	7 years 4 months
E11		Female	31	Hybrid	Talent acquisition manager	3 years 6 months	10 months
E12		Female	32	Hybrid	HR operations specialist	4 years 5 months	4 years 5 months
E13	**E13.1**	Female	32	Hybrid	HR business partner	2 years 2 months	2 years 2 months
	E13.2	Female	28	Hybrid	HR business partner	1 year 7 months	1 year 7 months
E14	**E14.1**	Female	34	Hybrid	HR specialist	4 years 8 months	4 years 8 months
	E14.2	Female	29	Hybrid	Talent acquisition specialist	2 years 11 months	2 years 11 months
E15	**E15.1**	Female	42	In person	People and carriers manager	2 years 4 months	2 years 4 months
	E15.2	Female	24	In person	HR generalist	1 year 7 months	9 months

(continued)

Table 2 (continued)

Interviewee	Gender	Age	Working method	Position held	Time in the organization	Time in role
E16	Female	49	Hybrid	Co-CEO Human capital manager	10 years 10 months	10 years 10 months
E17	Female	57	In person	Head of human resources	20 years 10 months	20 years 10 months
E18	Female	28	In person	Human resources director	4 months	2 months
E19	Female	44	In person	Head of human resources	9 months	9 months
E20	Female	45	Hybrid	Compensation and HR analytics manager	22 years 2 months	1 year 3 months
E21	Female	44	Hybrid	Human resources director	4 years 11 months	1 year 4 months
E22	Female	41	Hybrid	Corporate marketing and recruitment director	9 years 4 months	3 years 4 months

As for ages, they range from 24 years old to 57 years old. With regard to work methods, it is worth highlighting that they correspond to the work model used by each interviewee, that is, whether they use the in-person, remote, or hybrid regime. That said, the use of face-to-face (9) and hybrid (16) regimes was verified.

Regarding the position that the interviewees occupy in the organization, they are diverse, however it should be noted that they vary between the roles of Human Resources Director, HR Operations Specialist, Talent Acquisition Manager and HR Business Partner, among others.

In the sample, and in relation to time working in the organization and time in the role, it is observed that almost all of the interviewees contacted have been working for approximately one year both in the role and in the organization, going up to ten or more years, translating into have valid experience and knowledge to be able to report their experience as professionals.

3.4 Data Analysis and Processing Methods

After carrying out the interviews, the collected data was processed to carry out content analysis.

The analysis and interpretation of data was guided by the content of the interview. According to Kondracki et al. (2002), content analysis is based on a set of techniques that aim to develop objective conclusions on a subject, and the content of the interview is organized, analyzed, and classified into categories in order to select only the essential information for the investigation.

4 Analysis and Discussion of Results

After completing all interviews, the results obtained were transcribed and organized into a word document. From this document, only the most relevant transcriptions were selected, which are those used in this section.

4.1 Changes and Challenges Felt in Human Resource Management

Human resource management becomes difficult, since all processes in an organization must be constantly updated (Bilevičienė et al. 2015). For this study, it is important to understand the changes felt in human resources management and the direct influence, or not, of technologies.

When asked about the changes felt in HRM, interviewees did so in two ways. The first, establishing a comparison between what was practiced at a technological level in the past and what was operated in the present; and the second, stating digitally advanced practices. Below you will find Table 3, which contains some of the participants' opinions regarding the changes in HRM. It should be noted that, in order to facilitate the analysis, the key words/phrases mentioned by each interviewee were highlighted.

With Table 3, we can see the existence of a diverse set of changes, evident, above all, in administrative tasks (**E2**; **E10**), but also in the way of communicating (**E14. 1**) and in HRM practices, namely, in training and development (**E14. 1**), recruitment and selection (**E4**; **E7**), the performance evaluation system (**E10**), salary processing (**E19**; **E21**) as well as employee management tools (**E19**; **E21**). Remember that these are some examples of the answers most frequently given by interviewees.

According to Bilevičienė et al. (2015), Hendrickson (2003), Rohilla (2017) and Stone et al. (2015), technologies contributed to changes in the training and development of human resources by facilitating and increasing the development of new and improved skills. They were also important, in terms of shortening distances, for more effective communication between workers, allowing for better management and exchange of information. In the case of recruitment and selection, technologies are necessary as a way to increase the number of candidates, in order to hire a talented and diverse workforce.

Human resource management systems have evolved a lot since sharing information between systems became possible. Some of the examples include, firstly, payroll

Table 3 Changes brought by technologies in HRM (*own elaboration*)

Interviewee	Changes in HRM
E2	"(…) we had huge lockers, where we had employee files, with all the information (…), employment contracts, copies of identification cards (…). Now, in the organization where I work, this does not exist; everything is in digital format; this alone represents a big change in the way administrative tasks are carried out (…)"
E4	"(…) in terms of interviews, we have a platform that allows me to do online interviews, I have never done any with in-person candidates (…)"
E7	"(…) a recruitment platform we use makes it possible to access applications in great detail (…). At the end or during the process it is possible to extract reports (…)"
E10	"(…) when I entered the HR area, there was still a lot of things that had to be done by hand, a lot of paperwork, things in Excel (…). We went from paper-based performance assessment systems in 2007 to being computer-based in 2014 (…)"
E14.1	"(…) the registration of training sessions, which was traditionally done on paper, as well as the registration of people's attendance, we also have an internal system developed by us, which allows us to completely do without paper (…). Another point is communication, which new technologies have made much easier (…)"
E19	"(…) here we had the implementation of a payroll tool (…), which came to allow there to be an integrated system, from the arrival of the employee, through their biometric registration, to their departure and all their day to day, let's say. As regards attendance, it is also handled electronically (…)"
E21	"(…) the employee portals, where the employee can access their personal file and make immediate changes, whether in the emergency contact (…), but also allows the management of vacations (…) they can register absences, provide justification and this is integrated with the payroll program (…). We also internally have a benefits management platform (…), this platform allows employees to choose the benefits that make the most sense for them for that amount. (…)"
E22	"(…) I can say that, although in the form of pilot tests, we have already tried to introduce artificial intelligence to our employees and even in the area of recruitment, for example, we already have some tools that provide some artificial intelligence functionalities., to reduce employees' task time, if this is exponentialized and optimized, it will have a brutal impact (…)"

software, where there are all kinds of information about the worker, from their arrival to their departure. Next, we also have performance evaluation systems, which allow the manager to evaluate and analyze department trends and thus fill potential gaps with training (Bussler et al. 2002).

In short, it appears that what is defended by the interviewees is in line with the literature, and the main changes were considered, such as in the form of communication, distribution and management of information, recruitment and selection, training and development, and in human resource management systems, such as salary processing and performance evaluation (Bilevičienė et al. 2015; Bussler et al. 2002; Hendrickson 2003; Rohilla 2017; Stone and Deadrick 2015).

For Fernández-Martínez and Fernández (2020), the use of artificial intelligence (AI) has grown considerably to support recruitment and selection. Reinforcing what was expressed, for example, by **Interviewee 22**, these authors emphasize that this development is still in its infancy, and has not yet reached its maximum potential. This means that although AI helps to simplify the process, as it synthesizes the candidate's information, the responsibility of carrying out the interview and making the decision about who to hire is still on the human recruiter.

As we have just seen, HRM has undergone multiple changes. However, in parallel to these, the interviewees were also asked about the challenges they considered most pertinent, in the field of HRM, with technological evolution.

From the opinions expressed, it appears that, with regard to the perception of those interviewed in relation to the challenges caused by technologies, they mainly focused on resistance to the use of technology, the difficulty of defining the balance of human work and the use of technologies, the complexity of deal with different forms of work, as well as how to keep workers involved and motivated, using remote work models, and finally how to train, develop, recruit and select workers. The challenges listed are illustrated, for example, in the statements of **E1; E8; E12; E13.2; E16** and **E19**:

E1—"(…) those people who are averse to technology, how do we, here invert the thinking of something that we are fully aware is an opportunity, but that the person can at first interpret as a threat (...)".

E8—"(…) what is the balance point? Where the introduction of technologies is allowed and where the human part of human resources management should not be allowed to fall (…)".

E12—"(…) the way we work in Portugal is one way, (…) in Spain they work another way (…) and having to manage all these forms of work is difficult (…), the cultural distinction will be always present (…)".

E13.2—"(…) how to keep people engaged and motivated, when the work model is not face-to-face and they do not have the opportunity to be in the office on a daily basis and get in touch with colleagues? How do you ensure that there continues to be a sense of belonging and identity with the company's mission, vision, and values (…)".

E16—"(…) reskilling people, (…) adapting people to new technologies and new ways of working, getting rid of many old habits (…)".

E19—"(…) all areas that are directly related to people, the area of development and recruitment, I would say are the most demanding (…)".

The challenges identified by the interviewees are widely validated in the literature. Duvvuri (2021), Nasir (2017), Stone and Deadrick (2015), and Strohmeier and Parry (2014), identify as challenges, arising from technologies in HRM, the difficulty of workers in accepting change easily; globalization that allows organizations to work anywhere in the world, which resulted in different cultures, therefore different ways of working; the constant need for training to improve or develop new skills; and finally, how to recruit and select the right and talented candidate for the job opening.

According to Turnea and Claudia ARUŞTEI (2023) and Walkowiak (2023), the technologies used in HRM practices must contain a human and technological touch, that is, computer systems must be in harmony with human beings, working together. However, this collaborative work can be a real challenge. Turnea and Claudia ARUŞTEI (2023) and Walkowiak (2023) highlighted why collaborative work is important. For example, if only AI were used to select CVs, this would run the risk of being discriminatory, since specific selection parameters are created and AI does not allow exceptions, leaving room for candidates to be eliminated, not because they do not have skills, but because they do not fit the pre-defined profile. Another example given concerns performance evaluation, because if this is carried out only by a human being, there is the possibility of its own judgment interfering in its evaluation, ceasing to be transparent and fair.

Technological evolution has allowed other work models to emerge, notably hybrid and remote. Just like the more traditional method of work, face-to-face, these also give rise to challenges, namely, keeping the worker involved and motivated, so as to feel that their well-being is not at stake and maintain a feeling of belonging in the organization, despite little face-to-face contact with co-workers (Wadhera et al. 2023).

4.2 Hybrid and Remote Work: Changes Felt When Using Different Work Models

Technologies have brought multiple effects to HRM, which can occur in different ways and in different practices and processes. That said, it proved pertinent to understand the implications brought by digitalization to different work models. It is important to highlight that the questions asked to interviewees regarding this issue were limited to organizations that use at least one of the hybrid and/or remote work models, that is, of the 25 interviewees, only the responses of 16 were considered, as only these use these ways of working.

Respondents were asked about the functions to be performed according to the type of work model, that is, whether they consider that the hybrid and/or remote regime can cover all functions in the organizations or whether they are faced with any type of limitation.

Through the analysis of the interviewees' statements, it is clear that they identified the same limitations, that is, all functions are possible to be carried out in a hybrid and/or remote regime, with the exception of those in which greater human contact is necessary or require an inevitable physical presence. Of the responses that were collected in this question, it is important to highlight some:

E6—"(…) in my company it is possible to be 100% remote in all functions, with the exception of back office functions, namely, this HR function, financial function, accounting function, marketing (…), in which closer contact with people is necessary (…)".

E8—"(…) there are functions, by their nature, that do not allow for hybridity, if I think about a reception (…), if I say that each of them can stay at home for 3 days, 2 days at home (..), otherwise I'll have an empty reception if you think about some support areas, we at the company provide breakfast and snacks for everyone, that is, you guys (…) if you stay at home, the snack won't show up alone, that is, everything that has to do with more physical work or service is not enough (…)".

As can be seen from the example transcripts above, **E4** states that, with the exception of functions where there is a need for human contact, all others can use a hybrid and/or remote regime. Interviewee **E8** highlights that there are functions in which physical presence is a necessity since their interactive nature does not allow them to be physically far from their workplace.

Like the interviewees, the literature also makes a distinction about the functions that are or are not suitable for remote work regimes. According to Hansen et al. (2023), the areas in which there is a greater tendency to carry out distance work are those related to technology, education, and management. Those that would be unlikely to use these models are those that require the handling of specific equipment or those that involve greater contact with people.

In this context, it is worth highlighting that the interviewees were asked about the functions affected by the hybrid and/or remote regimes, as it is fundamental to ask about what will have changed in these. The aim will then be to understand whether the digitalization of the work model has brought changes to their role.

It was found that the interviewees consider that there are no considerable differences in the functions they perform, as they use hybrid and/or remote work regimes. They observed that they just had to adapt to new techniques/tools, both for the organization of work and for the way of communicating with each other.

E6—"(…) I don't think there are any changes, but in itself, it allows a different adaptability and a different flexibility due to the fact of having this regime (…)".

E12—"(…) in itself they did not undergo any changes, what suffered was the way of organizing work, this is because I realize that, often, people try to organize their lives so that when they are physically they try to do more physically meetings with the people who are there and not as many meetings as the one we are having now (…)".

Despite this, no interviewee interpreted the recurring changes in the work model as an obstacle, as did, for example, **Interviewee 20**. Others also considered them as something that is part of their development as a worker.

E20—"(…) nothing has changed, in practice I think there was a time when we were all teleworking, at the time of covid (…). People got used to having meetings via Teams and I think it's all very natural. Sometimes we are in the company and it was unthinkable a while ago to have meetings that were not in person, now we are in our place, and we have our meetings (…)".

Unlike the interviewees, Grey (2023), Ng et al. (2022), Vartiainen (2021) and Wadhera et al. (2023) note that the digitalization of the work model led to changes in the preponderantly used technologies, especially those connected to communication, collaboration and information sharing. These tools made it possible to shorten distances, obtain talent, bring flexibility, and increase productivity. That said, in the literature, there is a clear identification of what has changed, although for the interviewees they are not significant.

4.3 *Training and Development*

For organizations, the training and development of workers is considered a long-term investment, as it leads to improvements in the skills necessary for workers to perform fundamental tasks. Therefore, it is essential that training programs are relevant and efficient (Beqiri and Mazreku 2020; Kapo et al. 2021). In this sense, the interviewees were asked about their organization's training programs.

Through the interviews, it was noticed that continuing education is valued by organizations, so much so that, annually, each organization offers training programs that demonstrate concern and interest in the worker's personal and professional development.

E1—"(…) we have a program every year called a training needs survey (…). All managers receive a report that says what training each person on their team had that year and what training the manager believes they should have the following year (…). We put this training and development plan into practice throughout the year, whether it be more technical training or training related to soft skills (…). In addition, we also sponsor (…) doctorates, postgraduate degrees, CTeSP and master's degrees (…)".

E14. 1—"(…) we place a lot of ownership of development issues on the person themselves, but we also have solutions provided at an organizational level (…). The needs identified by the organization (…) whether technical or non-technical, that is, they can be more from the perspective of hard skills or soft skills and we then build a training plan (…). Most of these trainings are open to all interested parties, ok? In other words, we identify needs, but then we do not restrict participation and we give all employees the opportunity to sign up, if it makes sense for them (…). On the other hand, we have individual needs, to which we respond (…), with an individual learning budget (…), the logic is, I will identify what I need, what is my need for training and I will look on the market for what meets this need (…), then we have other internal resources, (…) LinkedIn Learning (…) that they can use as they see fit (…)".

Despite what was mentioned above, not all organizations have training programs. Pay attention to the cases of **Interviewee 3** and **Interviewee 21**:

E3—"(…) it is not a previously defined program, but yes, we certainly provide training for all operators (…), technical training directly linked to the need at the production point, sales training and, last year, we also did training in stress management (…), emotional intelligence, that is, managing feelings (…)".

E21—"(…) we don't have a program as such (…). Every year we approach managers to identify training needs (…) and 2 years ago (…) we did training in the area of communication (…), family budget management. It was not training to develop technical skills for the role, but it was training that our employees showed interest in taking (…)".

Through the interviews, it is clear that the training programs carried out in organizations are made up of pre-defined training, which takes into account criteria resulting from the survey of training needs, both at an organizational, functional, and individual level. The training program is then discussed and developed, which is finally implemented. Regarding individual training needs, it can be seen that, in some cases, the choice of training is the sole responsibility of the worker, since it is he/she who decides what he/she intends to accomplish, thus giving him/her the opportunity to actively participate in the decision of what to do, and that he/she believes is necessary to develop. These trainings can be carried out in a work context or not.

Regarding the content of the training, in all interviews, it was found that not only technical skills are developed, but also soft skills, notably personal development and emotional intelligence, among others. During the interviews, some training tools were also identified, namely courses developed on e-learning platforms, whether developed by themselves or on Linkedin Learning, among others.

Like the interviewees, the literature also considers that training and development are crucial and necessary activities. Therefore, they must be stimulated and maximized (Mozael 2015; Olaniyan and Ojo 2008). Furthermore, it is the organization's responsibility to give meaning and importance to them so that the desired development is achieved (Niazi 2011).

For a training and development program to be successful, it is necessary to fulfill a set of requirements, namely: assessment of training needs, preparation of training, creation of a training plan, implementation, evaluation and monitoring to improve training (Noe et al. 2010). The interviewees fulfilled the first five steps identified by the authors for carrying out a good training and development program. However, in the interviews it was not clear how to use the last stage of evaluation and monitoring.

The worker's perception of training affects its success, therefore, training programs must take into account what the worker likes and finds captivating, so that they feel motivated and absorb the maximum amount of knowledge (Sudhakar et al. 2011; Uma 2013). One (2013) goes so far as to state that it should be up to the worker to choose the training courses to attend, their duration and format. Gogunskii et al. (2016) agrees with Uma (2013), reinforcing that both workers and specialists in the field must be able to identify and define which training to undertake. It can be considered that, like the interviewees, the authors also validate this approach when choosing training.

Given the importance recognized by the interviewees in relation to training and development, it is important to understand which methods are used for learning in their organizations.

The training methods used by the interviewees are diverse, as exemplified by the subsequent transcriptions. Generally, both methods are used simultaneously, face-to-face and e-learning, but there are also exceptions when only one of these is used. In addition to these, another method was also mentioned, b-learning, which combines resources from distance training via e-learning, with resources from face-to-face training.

E4—"(…) e-learning. Yes, essentially! (…)".

E6—"(…) it depends, there is a lot online, a lot of e-learning (…), but there is also in-person training (…). I would say that it is mainly online (…)".

E7—"(…) both and we also have the mixed model, that is, the b-learning model, that is, we have face-to-face, e-learning and b-learning (…)".

E19—"(…) we have both forms (…), so, it depends on the entity we work with (…). Of course, internally we give priority to in-person (…)".

The face-to-face training method has always been the method traditionally used by organizations, however, with technological development, organizations felt the need to keep up with changes and transform their training and development process. This transformation occurred and allowed training to be carried out very quickly in a given period, thus giving rise to e-learning (Al-Hadrawi et al. 2023; Beinicke and Bipp 2018; Cheng et al. 2012; Davis 2000). Currently, training and development methods are varied, however Wahdaniah et al. (2023) emphasize that human contact can never be replaced by technology and, for this reason, most organizations choose to maintain the face-to-face method, combining it with e-learning.

The use of e-learning, instead of the face-to-face training method, has been increasing substantially, mainly due to the ease of transmitting training and the cost/efficiency component (Al-Hadrawi et al. 2023). However, according to Maxwell (2012), to obtain the best results in terms of training, it is expected that the organization uses more than one training method, which may be e-learning, face-to-face and b-learning.

Due to the exponential growth in the use of e-learning as a training method, it was crucial to understand the interviewees' perspective regarding the positioning of e-learning as a strategic tool for training in organizations.

The majority of respondents consider that e-learning is a strategic tool for organizations. Here are some examples where this happens:

E11—"(…) yes, without a doubt! I think it would bring a lot more interest. Okay, in the area of human resources, we obviously have here (…) an annual number of training courses that we have to provide and, as a rule, companies always fall far short, because, effectively, they do not want to dismiss employees during working hours. (…) I think this e-learning part would be much more, much more interesting (…), it would make people much more interested in the area of training and doing more training and specializing (…)".

E18—"(…) yes, because let's say that in this type of training, we can spend much less time having online training, than having face-to-face training and it is much less work, so to speak, in having to organize one online and having to organize a face-to-face meeting (…)".

Although the majority identify e-learning as strategic, there are exceptions, namely, for example, **Interviewee 3** who mentions "(…) for me it is not (…)" and **Interviewee 5** who mentions "(…) context always counts, you know. So, the type of people we have, the context of activity, in our case for our reality, e-learning is not strategic, it will be used case by case, when it makes sense (…)".

An important aspect to be considered, when analyzing the interviewees' perception in relation to e-learning, as a strategic tool, is the fact that, whenever they agree, they do so by identifying advantages of its use, in addition, in some cases, identify how this method prevails over the face-to-face method.

Cheng et al. (2012) and Derouin et al. (2005) consider e-learning an important and strategic tool for training and development in organizations. In the same way as the interviewees, the authors also associate the fact that it is strategic with the advantages of its use. Some of the advantages identified are the convenience compared to in-person, as well as the fact that it offers flexibility and reduces costs, among others.

According to a study developed by IBIS Capital (2013), 41.7% of companies, which belong to the Fortune Global 500, use technology as a means of training and developing workers. Beinicke and Bipp (2018) support the aforementioned, stating that organizations that invest in the use of e-learning are those that stand out as "(…) market leaders (…)" (p. 503). Finally, it is reiterated that e-learning is already the future of learning in organizations, despite not always being recognized. Over time, it is believed that it will increasingly be perceived as a valuable and indispensable tool.

4.4 Recruitment and Selection

As human resources are a valuable asset for the organization, it must recruit and select the right person. In this sense, the first step will be to understand, together with the interviewees, how their organizations carry out the recruitment and selection process.

The recruitment process, in general, was characterized by the interviewees as occurring both internally and externally, following a set of steps that are similar to all interviewees, but with some differences in the mode of operation. The steps that constitute the process were (1) identification of the need, (2) organization and description of what they are looking for for the position, (3) publicizing the offer, (4) selection of some candidates, (5) conducting interviews and, Finally, (6) the job offer is made. Below, to illustrate these steps, we have the answers from **E9, E11, E13.1** and **E13.2**:

E9—"(…) we submit a vacancy, this vacancy is advertised on LinkedIn or advertised on the company website (…). There is the sending of applications and then I do 2 interviews (…), the selection process (…). I don't do any tests, there are no tests, there is simply not an interview, but a conversation (...). A sincere conversation to effectively understand what skills the person has needs to include some practical examples here (...). I focus a lot on other issues, which have to do with loyalty, teamwork, empathetic capacity, I even value this much more than technical skills (...)".

E11—"(...) the process always involves opening a vacancy, whether internal or external (...). Then the person applies, we call the candidate, talk to them a little, understand their motivation for applying, salary expectations, prior notice they have already given, what their professional experience was. Okay, if we think the candidate is a good fit, we present the CV (...), we schedule the first interview, it is always online (...), all interviews (...) take place online (...). Then, if it is justified for more specialized areas, there is also a second interview, more technical (...) and for very high level positions, assessments are also carried out with an external company, like psychotechnical tests (...), if everything goes well an offer is made, we always send an email with an offer (...)".

E13.1—"(...) there is a first interview, which is a phone screening by our talent acquisition team to see if the person performs here with what we want (...)" **E13.2** (...) then there is *devskiller*, which is a technical testing platform. Depending on the result, the person continues with the process or not (...), then an interview takes place with someone from the technical area (...), they will ask questions much more oriented to the knowledge that the person has, the experience they have, a technical perspective and not so much imagine exploring motivation or CV background (...)" **E13.1** "(...) then there is a final interview (...), from there the offer is made (...), the whole process it occurs practically online or over the phone (...)".

During the interviews, the interviewees highlighted another recruitment method in addition to the usual method of advertising job offers, namely, for example, **E6**-"(...) in these technical areas (...), because there are normally no applications (...), we have to recruit people on LinkedIn regularly (...)", that is, a direct search is carried out for candidates who meet the profile of the need and from there the job proposal is made. **E6** also mentioned another: "(...) we have a referral program, employees can refer colleagues/friends they know and who they think have skills (...) for a certain position. They send the CV, and it follows the entire workflow (...) ". This means that any worker in the organization can be an active member in recruiting colleagues.

When carrying out the interviews, it is clear that some of the interviewees carried out online interviews and others face-to-face. Then, the process mainly consisted of two interviews, but there were also cases of three interviews. Subsequently, there were also different perspectives on how interviews should be conducted. On the one hand, technical and psychotechnical tests are carried out. Still, the perspective of a simple and formal interview was also presented, in which the motivations and skills of the individual interviewed were assessed.

The stages of the recruitment and selection process identified above are in accordance with what was mentioned by authors Khan and Abdullah (2019) and Thebe and Van Der Waldt (2014). They argue that the process consists of the emergence of a need, the preparation of the job proposal, the dissemination, the analysis of the CV, the selection of some candidates, the interviews, and the job proposal. Regarding recruitment techniques, the most used is advertising the vacancy. However, there is also referral by workers in the organization. This technique proves to be quite beneficial, as it reduces the time spent on the process, as well as the associated costs for the organization (Abbas et al. 2021; Thebe and Van Der Waldt 2014). The techniques identified by the authors validate the interviewees' responses.

As, for example, **Interviewee 6** identified, Zide et al. (2014) ensure that the usual recruitment methods are not always sufficient for specific recruitment profiles, and because of this, the organization has expanded its horizons, creating more active participation in the search for the ideal profile for the job vacancy. The preferred platform used for this purpose is LinkedIn.

In the same way that it is crucial to recruit candidates, it is also essential to know how to select them correctly. For this to happen, it is important to have knowledge about who the candidate is. That said, the method used to achieve this objective is often the interview, both online and in person (Abbas et al. 2021; Thebe and Van Der Waldt 2014).

During interviews, candidate validation techniques can be used, which go beyond resumes. One of them involves carrying out tests, namely, aptitude, personality, abilities, honesty, and motivation. Carrying out tests helps the recruiter to obtain more detailed information about the candidate, which can be decisive in the hiring decision (Campion et al. 2019; Hamza et al. 2021; Sivabalan et al. 2014).

After identifying the steps that make up the recruitment and selection process, the interviewees were asked about the methods they use in this same process. That is, whether these are based on traditional or online recruitment methods.

Respondents, in general, show a preference for online recruitment methods. Furthermore, some of the tools used for this purpose were also identified, namely the organization's website, job sites, and social networks.

E12—"(…) everything is digital, all announcements are made via LinkedIn. Our website often even has direct contact with LinkedIn, with a profile that has been identified, recruitment companies for some processes (…), traditional methods no longer make sense and are no longer part of our advertising methods (…)".

E18—"(…) it is usually the websites, that is, *Net Emprego*, *Sapo Emprego*, *Custo Justo*, *Indeed*, normally, they always have to do with this. We already tried, at the time of Covid, to make a few more flyers and other types of advertisements on social networks, because we were having a little more difficulty recruiting, but it didn't help much, so we continued only with online methods (…)".

From the perspective of the interviewees, as exemplified above, traditional methods do not adapt to the current organizational reality, as candidates looking for employment, as a rule, are already present on some platform or online tool. That said, for interviewees, online methods are the ones that work and are the ones that have allowed them to find the ideal candidates. Despite the predominance in the use of the online method, there was only one exception, that of **Interviewee 15.1** "(…) Newspaper, yes! But only when they are very specific processes, but it is very rare (…)". This exposes some situations where his organization still uses traditional recruiting methods.

When analyzing this issue, interviewees refer to online recruitment methods, however, without delving into the issue in terms of selection. Previously, when asked about the steps that constituted the recruitment and selection process, the majority identified that in the selection process, at least in the first interview, online methods were used. Furthermore, the methods for sending the proposal were also referenced, which included communication via email or telephone call.

As the selection process is not linear in the use of technological tools compared to recruitment, doubts arose as to whether this would still be considered E-selection. Literature was used to clarify the above and it was found that for Kapse et al. (2012), the recruitment and selection process to be considered E-recruitment and E-selection must use a set of technological tools. This is because in E-recruitment, firstly, technological methods are used to publicize the vacancy, these being social networks or the organization‘s website, among others. In E-selection, the first contact with the candidate must be made through technological means, but at the final moment, the decision-making moment, there may be moments of face-to-face contact. Now, from the authors' perspective, even if there are moments in the process that are not technological if most of them are, then it will be an online recruitment and selection process. Therefore, it can be concluded that there is a preference for both online recruitment and selection.

In online recruitment and selection, technologies are used as a way of attracting potential candidates. This means that, normally, the means of dissemination used go through organizational websites, job websites, CV databases, and social networks, among others (Ayu et al. 2024; Kapse et al. 2012).

E-recruitment and E-selection aim to overcome some of the disadvantages of traditional methods, such as high costs, delays in searching for candidates, and even difficulty in reaching them. Based on the advantages presented, it is expected that the use of online recruitment and selection methods will increase and that more organizations will opt for these methods compared to traditional ones (Al-Hadrawi et al. 2023; Ayu et al. 2024; Chuks Okolie and Irabor 2017). It is therefore confirmed that the literature perceives online recruitment and selection as more advantageous for organizations and admits that it has grown, in line with what the interviewees defended.

As online recruitment was an evolution of traditional recruitment (Al-Hadrawi et al. 2023), it was relevant to ask interviewees whether they consider online recruitment to be a substitute or a complement to traditional recruitment.

It appears that, in this matter, it is difficult to determine what the preference is between traditional and online recruitment, since the opinions are evenly divided. Therefore, there are two perspectives to respond to this: (1) that online recruitment is a substitute for the traditional one and (2) that the two methods complement each other.

First, **E11**'s answer is used to exemplify online recruitment as a substitute for traditional recruitment:

E11—"(…) I think that at this stage, it makes perfect sense for everything to be online (…). Obviously, I think it's important for the person to always have the camera on, it's always important for us to associate at least one voice with the person who is talking to us, a voice or an image, let's put it that way, but I don't think so It makes sense, at this point, for us to force people to go for a face-to-face interview and then go to the office again (…), so I think it's online! Undoubtedly! It should replace traditional methods (…)".

So, to illustrate the perspective of the two methods complementing each other, we have the **E13.2** answer:

E13.2—"(…) I think both complement each other and should be used depending on the context. I think we should be very careful when we say that any new approach is a substitute; I think that eventually, they are evolutions of each other and that they should complement each other (…)".

Also in the literature there are various perceptions about whether traditional recruitment has been replaced by online or whether they still complement each other. On the one hand, Al-Hadrawi et al. (2023) and Sołek-Borowska and Wilczewska (2018) argue that online recruitment is a substitute for traditional recruitment, as it brings speed, less costs, makes it possible to reach several candidates and makes the process more efficient. On the other hand, for Kapse et al. (2012) and Tyers et al. (2003), traditional and online methods should be used complementaryly. Thus, these authors also recognize that online brings benefits in terms of cost and time spent, but they consider it beneficial to use it in conjunction with traditional ones, as it can bring other advantages, since the traditional one is capable of bringing the human touch to the process.

In short, the two methods are a complement, especially because at the moment there is evidence to support that in certain situations, although online recruitment is the future, it still needs the support of traditional recruitment. In other words, even though the majority of the process takes place online, depending on the situation, the job opening and the organization, the methods may vary (Sills 2014). That said, after evaluating the context, what makes sense for the organization and for hiring, the ideal would be to have a balance between the two.

5 Conclusion

As mentioned throughout the chapter, technologies have caused major changes in the job market. All these changes gave rise to new processes and triggered new challenges, especially for human resources management. In the present study, the aim was to increase understanding of the challenges of human resources management and the extent to which technologies have or have not brought implications.

Thus, four specific objectives were established, achieved with the development of the research, namely: (1) Understanding the changes and challenges caused by technologies in human resources management practices; (2) Analyze the effects of digitalization on different work models; (3) Allow a greater understanding of some human resources management practices in their relationship with technologies; and, finally, (4) Understand how to manage new human resources management practices in the digital era.

After analyzing all interviews and discussing the respective results, it was possible to draw conclusions that directly responded to each objective.

Regarding the first objective, its answer was divided into the themes of changes and challenges. Starting by identifying the changes, it was found that from the interviewees' point of view, they occurred at the training and development level with the introduction of new methods that allowed workers to acquire and improve a set of skills. In relation to recruitment and selection, it was found that technologies are necessary as a way of diversifying and increasing the number of candidates. And, finally, in human resources management systems, it was found that the evolution made it possible to share information, which guaranteed greater internal communication for the management of the entire employee process, be it the salary level or evaluation of their performance.

Regarding the challenges brought by technologies to HRM, it was highlighted the resistance to the use of technology, the difficulty of defining the balance between human work and the use of technologies, the complexity in facing the different forms of work, how can we engaging and motivating remote workers, how to train and develop workers in a technologically developed world, and finally, how to recruit and select the right and talented workers.

In the second objective, it was clear that most functions can use remote and/or hybrid work, with the exception of those whose functions require greater contact with people and the handling of specific equipment. It was also confirmed that the interviewees considered that there were no significant differences in the functions they performed, as they used remote work arrangements. They only reported that they had to adapt to new techniques/tools, both in the organization of work and in the way of communicating with each other. However, this adaptation was not considered an obstacle to acceptance of the working models.

For the third objective, some HRM practices were analyzed, these being training and development and recruitment and selection. From the analysis, it is understood that continuous training is valued by organizations and, therefore, they carry out training programs. It is also noted that, effectively, there is a concern for the development of workers' skills. Regarding training methods, face-to-face and e-learning methods are used, both simultaneously and individually.

Regarding recruitment and selection, the process follows a set of steps similar to all interviewees, that is: (1) identification of the need, (2) organization and description of what they are looking for in the position, (3) disclosure of the offer, (4) selection of some candidates, (5) conducting interviews and, finally (6) the job offer is made. To publicize job vacancies, the methods used are the organization's website, job sites and social networks. As for how the recruitment and selection process is triggered, this involves conducting face-to-face and/or online interviews. During interviews, tests may be carried out or they may be simple and formal, in which the motivations and abilities of the individual interviewed are assessed.

Finally, in the fourth objective, it was found that for training and development, the use of e-learning has been growing and is increasingly associated as a strategic method for the organization, so the forecast will be that in the near future this will become indispensable. With regard to recruitment and selection, there was difficulty in defining exact conclusions, however evidence supports that traditional recruitment methods have not yet been completely replaced by online ones and, therefore, these still represent a determining role. Therefore, both traditional and online methods must be used for recruitment and selection.

In short, the results obtained in the research reveal that there was a set of changes and challenges brought by technologies for human resources management, felt in training and development, in recruitment and training and in work methods. According to future perspectives, it is expected that training and development will be based on the use of technologies, however, in recruitment and selection, online still needs development and, therefore, it is necessary to combine it with traditional methods. It is hoped that with this study, knowledge about the effects of technology on HRM and its practices has been increased and deepened.

References

Abbas SI, Shah MH, Othman YH (2021) Critical review of recruitment and selection methods: understanding the current practices. Ann Contemp Dev Manag HR 3(3), 46–52. https://doi.org/10.33166/ACDMHR.2021.03.005

Abolhassan F (2017) Security: the real challenge for digitalization. In: Management for professionals. Springer, Cham, pp 1–11. https://doi.org/10.1007/978-3-319-46529-6_1

Acharya AS, Prakash A, Saxena P, Nigam A (2013) Sampling: why and how of it? Indian J Med Speclties 4(2). https://doi.org/10.7713/ijms.2013.0032

Adeola MM, Adebiyi SO (2017) Employee motivation, recruitment practices and banks performance in Nigeria. Int J Entrep Knowl 4(2):70–94. https://doi.org/10.1515/ijek-2016-0015

Al Shobaki MJ, Abu Naser SS, Abu Amuna YM, El Talla SA (2017) Impact of electronic human resources management on the development of electronic educational services in the universities. Int J Eng Inf Syst 1(1):1–19

Al-Hadrawi RH, Alkaseer NA, Alasady AAA (2023) The role of digitalization of human resources management (HRM) practices in promoting employees' green creativity: an analytical study. J Inf Syst Eng Manag 8(4), 1–8. https://doi.org/10.55267/iadt.07.14010

Allen KS, Grelle D, Lazarus EM, Popp E, Gutierrez SL (2024) Hybrid is here to stay: critical behaviors for success in the new world of work. Personality Individ Differ 217:1–12. https://doi.org/10.1016/j.paid.2023.112459

Alshenqeeti H (2014) Interviewing as a data collection method: a critical review. Engl Linguist Res 3(1). https://doi.org/10.5430/elr.v3n1p39

Armstrong M, Baron A (2002) Strategic HRM: the key to improved business performance. Chartered Institute of Personnel & Development

Atak M, Erturgut R (2010) Importance of educated human resources in the information age and view of information society organizations on human. Procedia Soc Behav Sci 2(2), 1452–1456. https://doi.org/10.1016/j.sbspro.2010.03.217

Ayu R, Universitas PS, Mamuju M (2024) The influence of digital technology on human resource management practice Pengaruh Teknologi Digital Terhadap Praktik Manajemen Sumber Daya

Manusia. Manag Stud Bus J 1(1), 108–115. https://journal.ppipbr.com/index.php/productivity/index
Bag S, Gupta S, Luo Z (2020) Examining the role of logistics 4.0 enabled dynamic capabilities on firm performance. Int J Logist Manag 31(3):607–628. https://doi.org/10.1108/IJLM-11-2019-0311
Balakrishnan R, Das S (2020) How do firms reorganize to implement digital transformation? Strateg Chang 29(5):531–541. https://doi.org/10.1002/jsc.2362
Barišić AF, Rybacka Barišić J, Miloloža I (2021) Digital transformation: challenges for human resources management. ENTRENOVA Enterp Res Innov 7(1), 365–375. https://doi.org/10.54820/GTFN9743
Baumbusch J (2010) Semi-structured interviewing in practice-close research. J Spec Pediatr Nurs 15(3):255–258. https://doi.org/10.1111/j.1744-6155.2010.00243.x
Beinicke A, Bipp T (2018) Evaluating training outcomes in corporate e-learning and classroom training. Vocat Learn 11(3):501–528. https://doi.org/10.1007/s12186-018-9201-7
Bell BS, Federman JE (2013) E-learning in postsecondary education. Future Child 23(1):165–185. https://doi.org/10.1353/foc.2013.0007
Benassi M, Grinza E, Rentocchini F, Rondi L (2022) Patenting in 4IR technologies and firm performance. Ind Corp Chang 31(1):112–136. https://doi.org/10.1093/icc/dtab041
Benbunan-Fich R, Hiltz SR (2003) Mediators of the effectiveness of online courses. IEEE Trans Prof Commun 46(4):298–312. https://doi.org/10.1109/TPC.2003.819639
Beqiri T, Mazreku I (2020) Lifelong learning, training and development employee's perspective. J Educ Soc Res 10(2), 94–102. https://doi.org/10.36941/jesr-2020-0029
Berber N, Đorđević B, Milanović S (2018) Electronic human resource management (e-HRM): a new concept for digital age. Strat Manag 23(2):22–32. https://doi.org/10.5937/straman1802022b
Berg BL (2007) Qualitative research methods for the social sciences, 6th edn. Pearson
Betchoo NK (2016) Digital transformation and its impact on human resource management: a case analysis of two unrelated businesses in the Mauritian public service. IEEE Int Conf Emerg Technol Innov Bus Pract Transform Soc (EmergiTech) 2016:147–152. https://doi.org/10.1109/EmergiTech.2016.7737328
Bhatia R, Upadhyay RK, Sharma CP (2021) Future of work: managing talents in hybrid workplace system. Elementary Educ Online 20(2), 2528–2534. https://doi.org/10.17051/ilkonline.2021.02.269
Bilevičienė T, Bilevičiūtė E, Paražinskaitė G (2015) Innovative trends in human resources management. Econ Sociol 8(4), 94–109. https://doi.org/10.14254/2071-789X.2015/8-4/7
Bloom N, Han R, Liang J (2022) How hybrid working from home works out (w30292). https://ssrn.com/abstract=4173636
Bloom N, Liang J, Roberts J, Ying ZJ (2015) Does Working from home work? Evidence from a Chinese experiment. Q J Econ 130(1):165–218. https://doi.org/10.1093/qje/qju032
Boxall P, Purcell J, Wright PM (eds) (2008) The Oxford handbook of human resource management. Oxford University Press. https://doi.org/10.1093/oxfordhb/9780199547029.001.0001
Bresciani S, Ferraris A, Romano M, Santoro G (2021) Digital transformation management for agile organizations: a compass to sail the digital world. Emerald Publishing Limited. https://doi.org/10.1108/9781800431713
Brynjolfsson E, Hitt LM (2000) Beyond computation: information technology, organizational transformation and business performance. J Econ Perspect 14(4):23–48. https://doi.org/10.1257/jep.14.4.23
Bussler L, Davis E, Good LB, Society S, Minnesota W (2002) Information systems: the quiet revolution in human resource management. J Comput Inf Syst 42(2), 17–20. https://doi.org/10.1080/08874417.2002.11647482
Caillier JG (2012) The impact of teleworking on work motivation in a U.S. Federal Government Agency. Am Rev Public Adm 42(4), 461–480. https://doi.org/10.1177/0275074011409394

Campion MC, Campion ED, Campion MA (2019) Using practice employment tests to improve recruitment and personnel selection outcomes for organizations and job seekers. J Appl Psychol 104(9):1089–1102. https://doi.org/10.1037/apl0000401

Cao M, Zhang Q (2011) Supply chain collaboration: Impact on collaborative advantage and firm performance. J Oper Manag 29(3):163–180. https://doi.org/10.1016/j.jom.2010.12.008

Chae H-C, Koh CE, Park KO (2018) Information technology capability and firm performance: role of industry. Inf Manag 55(5):525–546. https://doi.org/10.1016/j.im.2017.10.001

Chan CML, Teoh SY, Yeow A, Pan G (2019) Agility in responding to disruptive digital innovation: case study of an SME. Inf Syst J 29(2):436–455. https://doi.org/10.1111/isj.12215

Chatzimouratidis A, Theotokas I, Lagoudis IN (2012) Decision support systems for human resource training and development. Int J Hum Resour Manag 23(4):662–693. https://doi.org/10.1080/09585192.2011.561235

Cheng B, Wang M, Moormann J, Olaniran BA, Chen N-S (2012) The effects of organizational learning environment factors on e-learning acceptance. Comput Educ 58(3):885–899. https://doi.org/10.1016/j.compedu.2011.10.014

Cho H-J, Pucik V (2005) Relationship between innovativeness, quality, growth, profitability, and market value. Strateg Manag J 26(6):555–575. https://doi.org/10.1002/smj.461

Chuks Okolie U, Irabor IE (2017) E-Recruitment: practices, opportunities and challenges. Eur J Bus Manag 9(11), 116–122. www.iiste.org

Cober RT, Brown DJ, Keeping LM, Levy PE (2004) Recruitment on the net: how do organizational web site characteristics influence. Int J Sel Assess 30(5):623–646. https://doi.org/10.1016/j.jm.2004.03.001

Comissão das Comunidades Europeias (2003) Recomendação da Comissão de 6 de Maio de 2003 relativa à definição de micro, pequenas e médias empresas. Jornal Oficial Da União Europeia 124(36), 36–41. http://data.europa.eu/eli/reco/2003/361/oj

Cooper CD, Kurland NB (2002) Telecommuting, professional isolation, and employee development in public and private organizations. J Organiz Behav 23:511–532. https://doi.org/10.1002/job

Cutcliffe JR (2000) Methodological issues in grounded theory. J Adv Nurs 31(6):1476–1484. https://doi.org/10.1046/j.1365-2648.2000.01430.x

Dalvi-Esfahani M, Wai Leong L, Ibrahim O, Nilashi M (2020) Explaining students' continuance intention to use mobile web 2.0 learning and their perceived learning: an integrated approach. J Educ Comput Res 57(8):1956–2005. https://doi.org/10.1177/0735633118805211

Das DCS, Divakaran P (2020) Challenges of human resource management and employee administration. J Critical Rev 7(2):1248–1251

Davis JHS (2000) Traditional vs. on-line learning: it's not an either/or proposition. Employ Relat Today 27(1):47–60. https://doi.org/10.1002/ert.3910270105

Derouin RE, Fritzsche BA, Salas E (2005) E-learning in organizations. J Manag 31(6):920–940. https://doi.org/10.1177/0149206305279815

Dibrell C, Davis PS, Craig J (2008) Fueling innovation through information technology in SMEs. J Small Bus Manage 46(2):203–218. https://doi.org/10.1111/j.1540-627X.2008.00240.x

DiRomualdo A, El-Khoury D, Girimonte F (2018) HR in the digital age: how digital technology will change HR's organization structure, processes and roles. Strateg HR Rev 17(5):234–242. https://doi.org/10.1108/SHR-08-2018-0074

Dubey R, Gunasekaran A, Childe SJ, Bryde DJ, Giannakis M, Foropon C, Roubaud D, Hazen BT (2020) Big data analytics and artificial intelligence pathway to operational performance under the effects of entrepreneurial orientation and environmental dynamism: a study of manufacturing organisations. Int J Prod Econ 226:1–12. https://doi.org/10.1016/j.ijpe.2019.107599

Duvvuri A (2021) Recent trends and challenges in human resource management. Int J Innov Res Eng Multidiscip Phys Sci 9:6–11

Engward H (2013) Understanding grounded theory. Nurs Stand (Royal College of Nursing (Great Britain): 1987) 28(7), 37–41. https://doi.org/10.7748/ns2013.10.28.7.37.e7806

Erfurth C (2019) The digital turn: on the quest for holistic approaches. In Fahrnberger G, Gopinathan S, Parida L (eds) Lecture notes in computer science, vol 11319. Springer, Cham, pp 24–30. https://doi.org/10.1007/978-3-030-05366-6_2

Erkmen T, Günsel A, Altındağ E (2020) The role of innovative climate in the relationship between sustainable IT capability and firm performance. Sustainability 12(10):1–26. https://doi.org/10.3390/su12104058

Etikan I (2016) Comparison of convenience sampling and purposive sampling. Am J Theor Appl Stat 5(1), 1. https://doi.org/10.11648/j.ajtas.20160501.11

Eurofound, Fernández-Macías E, Vacas-Soriano C (2015) Recent developments in the distribution of wages in Europe. In: Office of the European Union, pp 1–76. https://doi.org/10.2806/785387

Fenech R (2022) Human resource management in a digital era through the lens of next generation human resource managers. J Manag Inf Decis Sci 25(1):1–10

Fernández-Martínez C, Fernández A (2020) AI and recruiting software: ethical and legal implications. Paladyn J Behav Robot 11(1):199–216. https://doi.org/10.1515/pjbr-2020-0030

Gajendran RS, Harrison DA (2007) The good, the bad, and the unknown about telecommuting: meta-analysis of psychological mediators and individual consequences. J Appl Psychol 92(6):1524–1541. https://doi.org/10.1037/0021-9010.92.6.1524

Galanaki E (2002) The decision to recruit online: a descriptive study. Career Dev Int 7(4):243–251. https://doi.org/10.1108/13620430210431325

Gekara VO, Thanh Nguyen V (2018) New technologies and the transformation of work and skills: a study of computerisation and automation of Australian container terminals. N Technol Work Employ 33(3):219–233. https://doi.org/10.1111/ntwe.12118

Gerring J (2017) Qualitative methods. Annu Rev Polit Sci 20(1):15–36. https://doi.org/10.1146/annurev-polisci-092415-024158

Gogunskii V, Kolesnikov O, Kolesnikova K, Lukianov D (2016) Lifelong learning" is a new paradigm of personnel training in enterprises. East Eur J Enterp Technol 4(2(82)), 4–10. https://doi.org/10.15587/1729-4061.2016.74905

Gray J, Rumpe B (2017) Models for the digital transformation. Softw Syst Model 16(2):307–308. https://doi.org/10.1007/s10270-017-0596-7

Greer TW, Payne SC (2014) Overcoming telework challenges: outcomes of successful telework strategies. Psychol Manag J 17(2):87–111. https://doi.org/10.1037/mgr0000014

Grey S (2023) The future of work: adapting to remote and hybrid work models in a digital age. J Bus Financ Aff 12(1), 1–2. https://doi.org/10.37421/2167-0234.2023.12.443

Gurbaxani V, Dunkle D (2019) Gearing up for successful digital transformation. MIS Q Exec 18(3), 209–220. https://doi.org/10.17705/2msqe.00017

Hallberg LR-M (2006) The "core category" of grounded theory: making constant comparisons. Int J Qual Stud Health Well Being 1(3):141–148. https://doi.org/10.1080/17482620600858399

Hamza PA, Othman BJ, Gardi B, Sorguli S, Aziz HM, Ahmed SA, Sabir BY, Ismael NB, Ali BJ, Anwar G (2021) Recruitment and selection: the relationship between recruitment and selection with organizational performance. Int J Eng Bus Manag 5(3), 1–13. https://doi.org/10.22161/ijebm.5.3.1

Hansen S, Lambert PJ, Bloom N, Davis SJ, Sadun R, Taska B (2023) Remote work across jobs, companies, and space. www.WFHmap.com

Haque SMS (2023) The impact of remote work on HR practices: navigating challenges, embracing opportunities. Eur J Hum Resour Manag Stud 7(1), 56–84. https://doi.org/10.46827/ejhrms.v7i1.1549

Hassan S, Javed Y (2021) Digital transformation and E commerce in construction industry: a prospective assessment. Acad Strat Manag J 20(1), 1–8. https://www.researchgate.net/publication/350006438

Hecklau F, Galeitzke M, Flachs S, Kohl H (2016) Holistic approach for human resource management in industry 4.0. Procedia CIRP 54:1–6. https://doi.org/10.1016/j.procir.2016.05.102

Hendrickson AR (2003) Human resource information systems: backbone technology of contemporary human resources. J Lab Res 24(3):381–394. https://doi.org/10.1007/s12122-003-1002-5

Hess T, Matt C, Benlian A, Wiesböck F (2016) Options for formulating a digital transformation strategy. MIS Q Exec 15(2), 123–139. https://www.researchgate.net/publication/291349362
Horváth DSRZ (2019) Driving forces and barriers of industry 4.0: do multinational and small and medium-sized companies have equal opportunities? Technol Forecast Soc Chang 146:119–132. https://doi.org/10.1016/j.techfore.2019.05.021
IBIS Capital (2013) Global e-learning investment review global e-learning investment review. https://docplayer.net/491667-Global-e-learning-investment-review.html
Iqbal KMJ, Khalid F, Barykin SY (2021) Hybrid workplace. In: Handbook of research on future opportunities for technology management education. IGI Global, pp 28–48. https://doi.org/10.4018/978-1-7998-8327-2.ch003
Johansson J, Söderholm P, Parida V, Kostenius C, Kokkola L, Öqvist A (2018) Digitalization. In: Ericson Å, Frishammar J (eds) Addressing societal challenges, pp 23–38
Kagermann, H. (2015). Change through digitization—value creation in the age of industry 4.0. In Albach H, Meffert H, Pinkwart ARR (eds) Management of permanent change. Springer Fachmedien Wiesbaden, pp 23–45. https://doi.org/10.1007/978-3-658-05014-6_2
Kapo A, Mujkic A, Turulja L, Kovačević J (2021) Continuous e-learning at the workplace: the passport for the future of knowledge. Inf Technol People 34(5):1462–1489. https://doi.org/10.1108/ITP-04-2020-0223
Kapse AS, Patil VS, Patil NV (2012) E-recruitment. Int J Eng Adv Technol 1(4):82–86
Karim MM, Bhuiyan A, Kumer S, Nath D, Latif WB (2021). Conceptual framework of recruitment and selection process. Int J Bus Soc Res 11, 18–25. https://doi.org/10.18533/ijbsr.v11i02.1415
Khan SI, Abdullah NN (2019) The impact of staff training and development on teachers' productivity. Econ Manag Sustain 4(1), 37–45. https://doi.org/10.14254/jems.2019.4-1.4
Kiwert K, Walecka A (2022) Challenges and problems of hybrid work: employees' perspective. J Manag Financ Sci 15(45), 27–48. https://doi.org/10.33119/JMFS.2022.45.2
Kizilhan T, Bal Kizilhan S (2016) The rise of the network society—the information age: economy, society, and culture. Contemp Educ Technol 7(3). https://doi.org/10.30935/cedtech/6177
Knight R (2020) How to manage a hybrid team. Harvard Business Review. https://hbr.org/2020/10/how-to-manage-a-hybrid-team
Koleva V (2023) E-recruitment and generation Z job-seekers. HR Technol 1, 63–75. https://ideas.repec.org/a/arb/journl/y2023i1p63-75.html
Kondracki NL, Wellman NS, Amundson DR (2002) Content analysis: review of methods and their applications in nutrition education. J Nutr Educ Behav 34(4):224–230. https://doi.org/10.1016/S1499-4046(06)60097-3
Kuusisto M (2015) Effects of digitalization on organizations [Tampere University of Technology]. https://urn.fi/URN:NBN:fi:tty-201511231742
Lee YH, Hsieh YC, Ma CY (2011) A model of organizational employees' e-learning systems acceptance. Knowl Based Syst 24(3):355–366. https://doi.org/10.1016/j.knosys.2010.09.005
Liu Y, Dong J, Mei L, Shen R (2023) Digital innovation and performance of manufacturing firms: an affordance perspective. Technovation 119:1–17. https://doi.org/10.1016/j.technovation.2022.102458
Manyika J, Lund S, Chui M, Bughin J, Woetzel J, Batra P, Ko R, Sanghvi S (2017) Jobs lost, jobs gained: what the future of work will mean for jobs, skills, and wages. www.mckinsey.com/mgi
Martin BH, MacDonnell R (2012) Is telework effective for organizations? Manag Res Rev 35(7):602–616. https://doi.org/10.1108/01409171211238820
Maxwell A (2012) Technological advancements in methods of training with reference to online training: impact and issues for organizations introduction. Sci Commer Int Ref Res J 87(3), 1–9. www.researchersworld.com
Mcafee A, Bonnet D, Westerman G (2014) Leading digital: turning technology into business transformation. Harvard Business Review Press. https://books.google.pt/books?hl=en&lr=&id=Fh9eBAAAQBAJ&oi=fnd&pg=PR4&ots=o9UqD__nte&sig=UuJmTvDvlt7hzkGIkbFLbJKXEX4&redir_esc=y#v=onepage&q&f=false

Mozael BM (2015) Impact of training and development programs on employee performance. Int J Sci Res Publ 5(11), 38–42. http://www.ijsrp.org/e-journal.html
MSCI Inc (2023) Global industry classification standard (GICS) methodology
Nasir SZ (2017) Emerging challenges of HRM in 21st century: a theoretical analysis. Int J Acad Res Bus Soc Sci 7(3):216–223. https://doi.org/10.6007/IJARBSS/v7-i3/2727
Ng PML, Lit KK, Cheung CTY (2022) Remote work as a new normal? The technology-organization environment (TOE) context. Technol Soc 70:1–8. https://doi.org/10.1016/j.techsoc.2022.102022
Niazi BAS (2011) Training and development strategy and its role in organizational performance. J Public Adm Gov 1(2):42. https://doi.org/10.5296/jpag.v1i2.862
Noe R, Hollenbeck J, Gerhart B, Wright P (2010) Fundamentals of human resource management, 4th edn. McGraw Hill Higher Education, New York
Nwankpa JK, Roumani Y (2016) IT capability and digital transformation: a firm performance perspective
Oduro S, De Nisco A, Mainolfi G (2023) Do digital technologies pay off? a meta-analytic review of the digital technologies/firm performance nexus. Technovation 128:1–20. https://doi.org/10.1016/j.technovation.2023.102836
Okoronkwo GI (2021) Digitization of human resource practices: the realities in the new normal. Int J Bus Syst Econ 13(4):243–261
Olaniyan DA, Ojo LB (2008) Staff training and development: a vital tool for organisational effectiveness. Eur J Sci Res 24(3), 326–331. http://www.eurojournals.com/ejsr.htm
Palas A (2019) Earning movement prediction using machine learning-support vector machines (SVM). J Manag Inf Decis Sci 22(2):36–53
Panacek EA, Thompson CB (2007) Sampling methods: selecting your subjects. Air Med J 26(2):75–78. https://doi.org/10.1016/j.amj.2007.01.001
Prainsack B, Buyx A (2018) The value of work: addressing the future of work through the lens of solidarity. Bioethics 32(9):585–592. https://doi.org/10.1111/bioe.12507
Rachinger M, Rauter R, Müller C, Vorraber W, Schirgi E (2019) Digitalization and its influence on business model innovation. J Manuf Technol Manag 30(8):1143–1160. https://doi.org/10.1108/JMTM-01-2018-0020
Rajapaksha T (2013) HRM in 21st century: challenges of future. Int J Emerg Res Manag Technol 2(6):46–51
Rohilla MJ (2017) Role of information technology in human resources management. Int J Adv Res 3, 566–569. www.IJARIIT.com
Ruël H, Bondarouk T, Looise JK (2004) E-HRM: innovation or irritation: an explorative empirical study in five large companies on web-based HRM. Manag Rev Int Rev Manag Stud 15(3):364–380. https://doi.org/10.5771/0935-9915-2004-3-364
Sadri J, Chatterjee V (2003) Building organisational character through HRIS. Int J Hum Resour Dev Manag 3(1):84–98. https://doi.org/10.1504/IJHRDM.2003.001048
Schwab K (2019) The global competitiveness report 2019. https://www.weforum.org/publications/global-competitiveness-report-2019/
Schwartz EI (2001) Digital Darwinism: 7 breakthrough business strategies for surviving in the cutthroat web economy, vol 2. Broadway Books. https://books.google.pt/books?id=S4r5INmK6gkC&pg=PT3&hl=pt-PT&source=gbs_selected_pages&cad=1#v=onepage&q&f=false
Schweizer H (2004) E-learning in business. J Manag Educ 28(6):674–692. https://doi.org/10.1177/1052562903252658
Sills M (2014) E-recruitment: a comparison with traditional recruitment and the influences of social media. Helsinki Metropolia University of Applied Sciences
Simmons OE (2006) Some professional and personal notes on research methods, systems theory, and grounded action. World Futur 62(7):481–490. https://doi.org/10.1080/02604020600912772
Singh Hada B, Gairola S (2015) Opportunities & challenges of E-recruitment. J Manag Eng Inf Technol (JMEIT) 2, 2394–8124. www.jmeit.com

Sivabalan L, Yazdanifard R, Ismail NH (2014) How to transform the traditional way of recruitment into online system. Int Bus Res 7(3):178–185. https://doi.org/10.5539/ibr.v7n3p178

Slavić A, Bjekić R, Berber N (2017) The role of the internet and social networks in recruitment and selection process. Strat Manag 22(3):36–43

Sołek-Borowska C, Wilczewska M (2018) New technologies in the recruitment process. Econ Cult 15(2):25–33. https://doi.org/10.2478/jec-2018-0017

Stone DL, Deadrick DL (2015) Challenges and opportunities affecting the future of human resource management. Hum Resour Manag Rev 25(2):139–145. https://doi.org/10.1016/j.hrmr.2015.01.003

Stone DL, Deadrick DL, Lukaszewski KM, Johnson R (2015) The influence of technology on the future of human resource management. Hum Resour Manag Rev 25(2):216–231. https://doi.org/10.1016/j.hrmr.2015.01.002

Stone DL, Dulebohn JH (2013) Emerging issues in theory and research on electronic human resource management (eHRM). Hum Resour Manag Rev 23(1):1–5. https://doi.org/10.1016/j.hrmr.2012.06.001

Stone DL, Lukaszewski KM, Stone-Romero EF, Johnson TL (2013) Factors affecting the effectiveness and acceptance of electronic selection systems. Hum Resour Manag Rev 23(1):50–70. https://doi.org/10.1016/j.hrmr.2012.06.006

Strohmeier S (2007) Research in e-HRM: review and implications. Hum Resour Manag Rev 17(1):19–37. https://doi.org/10.1016/j.hrmr.2006.11.002

Strohmeier S, Parry E (2014) HRM in the digital age—digital changes and challenges of the HR profession. Empl Relat 36(4):1–8. https://doi.org/10.1108/ER-03-2014-0032

Sudhakar KF, Kameshwara Rao MM, Koteswara B, Naik R (2011) Employees perception about the training & development: a qualitative study. Int J Res Econ Soc Sci 1(2), 25–37. http://www.euroasiapub.org

Teng X, Wu Z, Yang F (2022) Research on the relationship between digital transformation and performance of SMEs. Sustainability 14(10):1–17. https://doi.org/10.3390/su14106012

Thebe TP, Van Der Waldt G (2014) A recruitment and selection process model. Administratio Publica 22(3), 6–29. https://doi.org/10.10520/ejc-adminpub-v22-n3-a2

Tulgan B (2009) Not everyone gets a trophy: how to manage generation Y, 1st edn. Jossey-Bass

Turnea E-S, Claudia ARUŞTEI C (2023) Augmenting HRM through enhancing the benefits of digital transformation. Cross Cult Manag J 25(2), 105–111. https://seaopenresearch.eu/Journals/cmj/Article

Tyers C (Claire), Perryman S, Barber L (2003) E-recruitment: is it delivering? vol 402. Institute for Employment Studies. https://www.employment-studies.co.uk/system/files/resources/files/402.pdf

Uma SN (2013) A study on training importance for employees of their successful performance in the organization. Int J Sci Res 2(11):137–140

Ungerman O, Dedkova J, Gurinova K (2018) The impact of marketing innovation on the competitiveness of enterprises in the context of industry 4.0. J Compet 10(2), 132–148. https://doi.org/10.7441/joc.2018.02.09

v. Alberti-Alhtaybat L, Al-Htaybat K, Hutaibat K (2019) A knowledge management and sharing business model for dealing with disruption: the case of Aramex. J Bus Res 94, 400–407. https://doi.org/10.1016/j.jbusres.2017.11.037

Vartiainen M (2021) Telework and remote work. In: Oxford research encyclopedia of psychology. Oxford University Press, pp 1–32. https://doi.org/10.1093/acrefore/9780190236557.013.850

Vaska S, Massaro M, Bagarotto EM, Dal Mas F (2021) The digital transformation of business model innovation: a structured literature review. Front Psychol 11:539363. https://doi.org/10.3389/fpsyg.2020.539363

Verhoef PC, Broekhuizen T, Bart Y, Bhattacharya A, Qi Dong J, Fabian N, Haenlein M (2021) Digital transformation: a multidisciplinary reflection and research agenda. J Bus Res 122:889–901. https://doi.org/10.1016/j.jbusres.2019.09.022

Wadhera R, Raja VKS, Kalahasthi P, Gebrehiwot MT (2023) The future of work: navigating HR challenges in the era of remote and hybrid workforces. Boletin De Literatura Oral Lit J 10(1), 2922–2930. http://www.boletindeliteraturaoral.com/index.php/bdlo/article/view/595
Wahdaniah, Sucianti R, Ambalele E, Tellu AH (2023) Human resource management transformation in the digital age: recent trends and implications. Int J Appl Res Sustain Sci 1(3), 239–258. https://doi.org/10.59890/ijarss.v1i3.902
Wahyudi E, Park SM (2014) Unveiling the value creation process of electronic human resource management. Public Pers Manag 43(1):83–117. https://doi.org/10.1177/0091026013517555
Walkowiak E (2023) Digitalization and inclusiveness of HRM practices: the example of neurodiversity initiatives. Hum Resour Manag J 34(3):1–21. https://doi.org/10.1111/1748-8583.12499
Wamba SF, Dubey R, Gunasekaran A, Akter S (2020) The performance effects of big data analytics and supply chain ambidexterity: the moderating effect of environmental dynamism. Int J Prod Econ 222:1–14. https://doi.org/10.1016/j.ijpe.2019.09.019
Widodo S, Wibowo Y, Wagiran W (2020) Online learning readiness during the Covid-19 pandemic. J Phys Conf Ser 1700(1):1–4. https://doi.org/10.1088/1742-6596/1700/1/012033
Wrede M, Velamuri VK, Dauth T (2020) Top managers in the digital age: exploring the role and practices of top managers in firms' digital transformation. Manag Decis Econ 41(8):1549–1567. https://doi.org/10.1002/mde.3202
Zide J, Elman B, Shahani-Denning C (2014) LinkedIn and recruitment: how profiles differ across occupations. Empl Relat 36(5):583–604. https://doi.org/10.1108/ER-07-2013-0086

Index

C. Machado and J. P. Davim (eds.), *Challenges and Opportunities in the Artificial Intelligence Era*, https://doi.org/10.1007/978-3-031-85272-5

The manufacturer's authorised representative in the EU is Springer Nature Customer Service Centre GmbH, Europaplatz 3, 69115 Heidelberg, Germany. If you have any concerns regarding our products, please contact ProductSafety@springernature.com

Printed and bound by CPI Group (UK) Ltd, Croydon, CR0 4YY
30/09/2026
02225568-0005